SEANAN McGUIRE

ASHES OF HONOR

AN OCTOBER DAYE NOVEL

DAW BOOKS, INC.

DONALD A. WOLLHEIM, FOUNDER

375 Hudson Street, New York, NY 10014

ELIZABETH R. WOLLHEIM
SHEILA E. GILBERT
PUBLISHERS
http://www.dawbooks.com

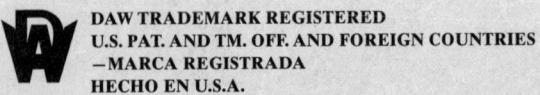

Praise for the *October Daye* Novels

"*Rosemary and Rue* will surely appeal to readers who enjoy my books, or those of Patricia Briggs." —Charlaine Harris

"*One Salt Sea* is the best October Daye book to date; everything that's great about the series comes together in one book. The plot is strong, the characterization is terrific, the tragedies hurt . . . and McGuire's usual beautiful writing and dark humor are present and accounted for. This has become one of my favorite urban fantasy series, and I can't wait to find out what happens next."
—FantasyLiterature.com

". . . urban fantasy that really stands out from the crowd because of the completeness of the world and its characters who could step from the pages and walk down the road in our own world."
—*SFRevu*

"McGuire seems to have fun with *One Salt Sea*, exploring her protagonist's personality and revealing some great origin stories for the world of the fae. Fans of the series will be swept up in this story, hooked to the very end where they get some answers and a sense of satisfaction that few books deliver this well."
—*San Francisco Book Review*

"Second in an urban fantasy detective series featuring a resourceful female detective, this sequel to *Rosemary and Rue* should appeal to fans of Jim Butcher's *Dresden File*s as well as the novels of Charlaine Harris, Patricia Briggs, and similar authors."
—*Library Journal*

"It's fun watching [Toby] stick doggedly to the case as the killer picks off more victims and the tension mounts." —*Locus*

"*An Artificial Night* . . . is wildly and beautifully descriptive, with scenes that will simply take your breath away. If Hollywood doesn't snatch up the rights to this book, they are even crazier than Johnny Depp in *Pirates of the Caribbean III*. That being said, the third installment in the October (Toby) Day series is even better (if that could be believed) than the prior two. Author Seanan McGuire seems to have hit her stride and should enjoy a long career."
—Sacramentobookreview.com

"Wow! is the first thing that comes to mind when reading this fifth installment of the October Daye series. Emotional, action-packed, funny, and just a great story from start to finish, *One Salt Sea* will take readers into a world combining reality and fantasy and have them begging for more even as the story progresses from triumph to loss, fae to mortal, and everything in between! . . . this book was phenomenal!"
—*Nocturne Reads*

DAW Books presents the finest in urban fantasy from Seanan McGuire:

October Daye novels:

ROSEMARY AND RUE

A LOCAL HABITATION

AN ARTIFICIAL NIGHT

LATE ECLIPSES

ONE SALT SEA

ASHES OF HONOR

CHIMES AT MIDNIGHT*

Incryptid novels:

DISCOUNT ARMAGEDDON

MIDNIGHT BLUE-LIGHT SPECIAL*

*Coming in 2013 from DAW Books

*For Deborah,
and all the red-cloaked girls
who ever left the safest path.*

ACKNOWLEDGMENTS:

Book six. Wow. *Ashes of Honor* has been a delight every step along the way, and a lot of that is due to the people who were there to help me with the process of making it the best book it could be. My first and deepest thanks go to the ever-changing membership of the Machete Squad, whose keen eyes and keener pens have forced me to keep improving, whether I wanted to or not. Special thanks to Michelle Dockrey, Amy McNally, Brooke Lunderville, my mom and sister, and Amy's friend Patty, who tolerated Toby's intrusions on our trip to Disney World. I couldn't have done it without you guys.

My solemn gratitude goes to my agent, Diana Fox, my editor, Sheila Gilbert, my cover artist, Chris McGrath, and my website design and maintenance team of Tara O'Shea and Christopher Mangum. Thanks also to Joshua Starr, for administrative awesome on the DAW side, and to Deborah Brannon, for administrative awesome here at home.

Thank you to you, for coming with me this far, for reading, for being a part of this adventure. It has been, and will continue to be, amazing. I'm so glad you're here.

My soundtrack while writing *Ashes of Honor* consisted mostly of *Little Blue Egg*, by Dave and Tracy, *Ceremonials*, by Florence and the Machine, *Queen of*

Spindles, by Talis Kimberley, endless live concert recordings of the Counting Crows, and *Enchant*, by Emilie Autumn. Any errors in this book are entirely my own. The errors that aren't here are the ones that all these people helped me fix.

Thank you for reading. Welcome back to Faerie.

PRONUNCIATION GUIDE
THROUGH ASHES OF HONOR

All pronunciations are given phonetically. This only covers races explicitly named in the first six books, omitting Undersea races not appearing in, or mentioned in, book six.

Afanc: *ah-fank*. Plural is Afanc.
Annwn: *ah-noon*. No plural exists.
Bannick: *ban-nick*. Plural is Bannicks.
Barghest: *bar-guy-st*. Plural is Barghests.
Blodynbryd: *blow-din-brid*. Plural is Blodynbryds.
Cait Sidhe: *kay-th shee*. Plural is Cait Sidhe.
Candela: *can-dee-la*. Plural is Candela.
Coblynau: *cob-lee-now*. Plural is Coblynau.
Daoine Sidhe: *doon-ya shee*. Plural is Daoine Sidhe, diminutive is Daoine.
Djinn: *jin*. Plural is Djinn.
Dóchas Sidhe: *doe-sh-as shee*. Plural is Dóchas Sidhe.
Ellyllon: *el-lee-lawn*. Plural is Ellyllons.
Gean-Cannah: *gee-ann can-na*. Plural is Gean-Cannah.
Glastig: *glass-tig*. Plural is Glastigs.
Gwragen: *guh-war-a-gen*. Plural is Gwragen.
Hamadryad: *ha-ma-dry-add*. Plural is Hamadryads.
Hippocampus: *hip-po-cam-pus*. Plural is Hippocampi.

Kelpie: *kel-pee*. Plural is Kelpies.
Kitsune: *kit-soo-nay*. Plural is Kitsune.
Lamia: *lay-me-a*. Plural is Lamia.
The Luidaeg: *the lou-sha-k*. No plural exists.
Manticore: *man-tee-core*. Plural is Manticores.
Naiad: *nigh-add*. Plural is Naiads.
Nixie: *nix-ee*. Plural is Nixen.
Peri: *pear-ee*. Plural is Peri.
Piskie: *piss-key*. Plural is Piskies.
Pixie: *pix-ee*. Plural is Pixies.
Puca: *puh-ca*. Plural is Pucas.
Roane: *row-n*. Plural is Roane.
Satyr: *say-tur*. Plural is Satyrs.
Selkie: *sell-key*. Plural is Selkies.
Shyi Shuai: *shh-yee shh-why*. Plural is Shyi Shuai.
Silene: *sigh-lean*. Plural is Silene.
Tuatha de Dannan: *tootha day danan*. Plural is Tuatha de
    Dannan, diminutive is Tuatha.
Tylwyth Teg: *till-with teeg*. Plural is Tylwyth Teg, diminu-
    tive is Tylwyth.
Undine: *un-deen*. Plural is Undine.
Urisk: *you-risk*. Plural is Urisk.

ONE

June 3rd, 2012

THE NIGHT SKY OVER SAN FRANCISCO was a patchwork mixture of starry black and cloudy gray, all of it washed out by the ambient light drifting up from the city below. It was a tourist's dream of California summer, perfect as a postcard—and like all postcards, it wasn't telling the full story. I pressed myself in closer to the wall of the alley, one hand on my knife, and waited.

I didn't have to wait for long. Voices drifted down the alley, speaking in the weird mix of whisper and shout that teenagers have used since the dawn of time when trying to be subtle. There was nothing subtle about these kids, but they would never have believed that. They were playing things oh-so-cool, and they thought they were untouchable. In a perfect world, they would have been. In a perfect world, they would have been allowed to have their little rebellions and take their little risks, and nothing would ever have touched them.

We don't live in a perfect world. We never have. And on nights like this one, it seems like we never will.

The kids approaching my hiding spot didn't know it, but I'd been watching them for weeks, ever since I took a trip downtown to investigate reports of a courtier selling pieces of his liege's treasury. The rumors turned out to be true—he got banished, I got paid, and nobody walked away happy—but that wasn't the worst of it.

On the way to a meeting with his fence, the courtier had kicked aside a glass jar that someone had left discarded near the base of a garbage can. It fell on its side and rolled to a stop against a nearby wall. The smell of its contents assaulted my nostrils, and I immediately forgot about my job. I had something far more dangerous to worry about.

I crept toward the jar as cautiously as I would have approached a venomous snake, finally crouching a few feet away. I could see smears of purple clinging to the glass—not that I needed the visual. This close, the smell was unmistakable. No changeling who's ever lived on the wrong side of the tracks could fail to recognize the smell of goblin fruit, even if we'd never smelled it before. And, Oberon help me, I'd smelled it before.

Goblin fruit grows naturally in some realms of Faerie. It's a sweet narcotic for purebloods, intoxicating without being physically addictive—although it's definitely habit-forming. Anything that changes the way you feel is habit-forming, as anyone who's ever dealt with someone who says, "It's not addictive, really," while reaching for their next fix can tell you. A pureblood with a serious goblin-fruit problem may spend a lot of time high, but that's about it. They'll still be able to do their jobs, maintain relationships, and put up a good front.

Changelings and humans have a different reaction. For us, goblin fruit creates a level of addiction that no mortal drug can match. People try to dilute it or cut it with other fruits—hence the ever popular use of jam as a delivery mechanism—but the end result is always the same: dependency leads to craving, craving leads to madness, and madness leads, inexorably, to death.

Devin never allowed goblin fruit at Home. We had kids who were hooked on just about every conceivable chemical, from pot and pills to cocaine, heroin, and things they mixed up in the back room. Some kids got high huffing concentrated pixie-sweat, or smoking Dryad leaves. Devin viewed it all with benevolent indifference — he didn't care what we put into our bodies, as long as we were able to do our jobs. But he had a zero-tolerance policy for goblin fruit. Any kid who showed up with sticky fingers and starry eyes was booted, no second chances, because he knew better than any of us that once the fruit had hold of you, it never let you go.

When Oberon locked the doors to the deeper realms of Faerie, the goblin fruit problems should have gone away, since the berries only grow in the soil of Tirn Aill, Tir Tairngire, and the Blessed Isles, and no one's been to any of those places in centuries. Unfortunately for people who don't like seeing changeling kids waste away on a diet of jam and dreams, clever gardeners from the lands where goblin fruit grew naturally brought plenty of soil and seedlings with them when they left. The stuff's gotten rarer since then — and thank Oberon for that — but there are still people who use it for their own ends, and a little bit goes a long away.

All of which led to me standing in a dark alley, waiting for a bunch of teenage changelings to reach me. It had taken me weeks to figure out who the dealers were, as opposed to the ones who were just feeding their own habits. I still didn't know who was supplying them. If this had been going down in Shadowed Hills, I might have been able to ask my liege for backup, but here, I was in the Queen's territory, and I was on my own.

Purebloods won't regulate goblin fruit because it's not a threat to them. Why should they ban a sweet berry that gives them lovely dreams? The fact that it also blows changeling brains out is irrelevant to them.

A globe of light drifted past my position. One of the dealers was a half-Candela girl in her late teens. If her Merry Dancers were here, so was she, and that meant I was in the right place. I pushed away from the wall, releasing the don't-look-here spell that had been hiding me from view. "You kids lost?" I asked.

There were five of them. They stopped where they were, staring at me with varying levels of hostility and confusion. It was the Candela girl who stepped forward and spoke first. "I remember you. You're the girl who got us all kicked out of Home."

"I remember you, too," I said. She'd grown since the time I saw her at Devin's, getting taller and paler as her Candela heritage asserted itself. She'd also gotten thinner, becoming a walking skeleton draped in the winding shroud of her own skin. That was the goblin fruit at work, eating her alive even as it showed her the most beautiful things she'd ever seen. "Didn't Devin teach you to stay the hell away from this shit?" I gestured toward her backpack, which bulged with small, cylindrical shapes.

Her eyes widened briefly. Then they narrowed, and she spat, "Why do you care what Devin taught us? You got him killed. You got us all tossed out on the street. What Devin taught us keeps us alive."

"And he taught you to peddle drugs to kids?" The other dealer in this group was a gangling teenage boy with hedgehog spikes in place of hair. Another survivor of Home. I swung my glare toward him. "You, too. You both know better than this."

"Says the girl who got out," said the Candela.

Her words stung because they were supposed to. Once, I was just like them, and while I never stooped to peddling drugs, I did a lot of other things that I'm not proud of. That was with Devin to protect me — and while he might have abused me in some very profound ways, he made sure I had a roof over my head, food in my stomach, and backup if I needed it. Without Devin and Home, the kids who'd been in his care were scattered to the streets. I'd tried to keep tabs on them for a little while, but Devin taught us all to be good at disappearing. At the end of the night, maybe I didn't try as hard as I could have.

"Hey, girl who got out," said the spiky boy. "You bring anybody with you?"

I hesitated. The boy smirked. At that point, he'd know if I lied, and so I told the truth: "No." The fact that this was a bad idea was beginning to occur to me. There were five of them, and while I'm pretty good at one-on-one, the bad guys never charge you one at a time in real life. I kept my hand on my knife. "I came here to tell you to stop. Selling goblin fruit to changelings is not okay."

"It's not illegal."

"That doesn't make it right."

"You know what does make us right?" asked one of the other kids, one of the ones I'd never seen before I started this ill-advised stakeout. "Strength of arms."

With that, all the kids except the Candela produced guns and knives from inside their coats or from their belts. I took a step backward, trying to keep my expression neutral.

Oh, shit, I thought. "It doesn't have to go down like this," I said.

"Sure it does," said the spiky boy, and shot me in the shoulder. The bullet went clean through. I screamed, but I didn't fall.

Thanks to the vagaries of fae biology, I heal fast. Pain still hurts. I clapped a hand over my shoulder, rocking backward. The pressure made it hurt worse. I didn't let go. Blood loss won't kill me, but it makes the world fuzzy and unpleasant in a way that I can't say I'm fond of.

"She didn't 'go down,'" said the Candela, putting a mocking spin on the words she was quoting. "Shoot her again. I want to see her—urk." The sentence ended not with a threat but with the small, strangled sound of someone having her trachea forcibly crushed.

"Have we reached the point where my intervention will not get me shouted at for being a meddling tomcat who doesn't respect the boundaries of others?" Tybalt stepped out of the shadows behind the Candela, tightening his hand around her throat. "I ask to be polite, you realize. There's no way I'm walking away."

Relief washed over me. "Hi, Tybalt," I said, hand still clamped over my shoulder. "Good to see you, too."

"Isn't it always?" Tybalt gave the Candela a shake. She made a gurgling noise. "Strange taste in company you have these days."

The kids looked confused as to who they should be aiming their guns at. Some settled on me, some on Tybalt, and others wavered back and forth between us. "I don't like goblin fruit on my streets," I said. "I hoped I could talk them into taking up a safer hobby than drug dealing."

"Always the optimist."

"I try."

Our casual conversation was the last straw for the boy with the hedgehog spines. "You sellout *bitch!*" he screamed, and shot me twice more, this time in the stomach. Then he turned and ran, the other kids pelting after him—all except the Candela, who was still held fast in Tybalt's hand.

I was a little too distracted by the pain in my belly to care where they were going, or what they were going to do when they got there. I looked down at myself and made a small gulping sound very similar to the one the Candela had made, watching blood run in ribbons through the fabric of my jeans. The gunshot wound in my shoulder had already closed over. That was good; it freed both my hands to press against the newer wounds, struggling to stay upright as the world hazed gray and black around me.

"*October!*" There was a horrible crunch as Tybalt flung the Candela girl into the wall. Then he was lunging for me, catching me before I could hit the ground. The smell of blood was everywhere. "Toby. Toby? Toby, don't you do this. Don't die. Please. I can't allow . . . you wouldn't dare . . ."

"I'm fine," I whispered. The bullets had gone clean

through. Maybe I wasn't fine yet, but I would be, if I could just be still. "Go after them."

"If you think I'm going to leave you, you're—"

"Right. I'm right." I gathered my magic around me, and it leaped to obey, already half-summoned by the sheer amount of blood that I was shedding. I'm Dóchas Sidhe. For me, all magic is blood magic. "Go after them. Make them understand that goblin fruit isn't welcome here. I'll meet you at the house."

"Fine." He spat the word at me like a curse and let me go, leaving me sitting on the alley floor while he raced off into the darkness.

I sat for a moment. Then I lay backward on the cold pavement, closing my eyes. The smell of blood was everywhere, and my hands were sticky with the stuff. Somehow, that bothered me more than the fact that my shirt and jeans were ruined. I was still bleeding. That was a problem. How much blood does the body hold, anyway?

Answer: not enough. I took a deep breath, pulling more magic out of the air, and forced it down again, trying to press it into my skin. I wasn't sure exactly what I was doing, but I didn't have any better ideas, and I didn't want Tybalt to come back and find me dead in the alley. It would be cruel of me to do that to him after swearing that I'd be fine.

The magic sank into my skin, and the burning around the bullet holes faded to a dull ache as my body finally started focusing on the twin issues of lead poisoning and physical trauma. The sensation of muscle knitting itself back together wasn't exactly what I'd call pleasant, but I gritted my teeth and didn't move until the pain had faded. I touched my belly with one sticky hand and found only equally sticky skin.

I sat up, using the last of my magic to spin an illusion that made me look both human and uninjured. It wouldn't do for me to go staggering down the street looking like something out of a Saturday night horror movie. The effort left me winded again. I stayed where I was for a few more minutes, waiting for my head to stop spinning. Then I stood and began walking back toward the street. I was done. I was exhausted, I was covered in blood, and I was absolutely, without question, *done*. Nothing was going to keep me from going home. Absolutely—

Sudden light blinded me. I raised a hand to shield my eyes, squinting against the glare.

"Stop where you are. Keep your hands where I can see them." The voice was unfamiliar, but the combination of words and tone was unmistakable: that was a police officer talking into a speaker. Which meant someone had reported the gunshots, and I was about to be taken in for questioning. Oh, lucky, lucky me. At least I was wearing a human disguise. I might get arrested, but I wasn't likely to be dissected.

This is my life.

TWO

"**L**ET'S GO OVER THIS AGAIN," said the policeman.

This is also my life: sitting in the Mission police station for almost two hours after getting picked up for standing in an alleyway where gunshots had been reported. I was waiting for the nice policeman assigned to take my statement to decide that he was done and tell me I could go.

I had better luck with the drug dealers.

"I can do that," I said.

Not fast enough, or maybe not enthusiastically enough. The policeman looked up from his paperwork, eyes narrowing. "Unless you had somewhere else you wanted to be tonight?"

"I'm fine with going over my statement again," I said, and smiled.

He didn't. "Good. Now, you were picked up at approximately ten thirty-seven PM—"

He droned on. I kept smiling and nodding, trying to look like as if I was practicing attentive listening and paying attention to every word he said. Little could have been farther from the truth, but sometimes you have to play by the rules, even if they're the rules of somebody else's game.

My name is October Daye. I'm a knight errant in service to the Court of Shadowed Hills, one of the secret Faerie fiefdoms hidden in the state of California. I'm a sort of supernatural troubleshooter, and what I do is technically outside human jurisdiction . . . but that's not something I can explain to mortal law enforcement, since they don't know that Faerie exists.

The policeman stopped talking, apparently waiting for me to say something. I quickly reviewed the last few things he'd said and ventured, "It was dark."

"You've said." He scowled, picking up another piece of paper. "You told Officer Brannon that you were walking home when gunfire broke out, and you didn't see the shooters."

"Yes. It was dark, I didn't expect people to have guns . . ." Darkness isn't actually an issue for me—I see better at night than most humans do in daylight—but it was an excuse. I needed excuses, since there was no way the truth was going to fly with the SFPD.

"Have you lived in San Francisco long, Ms. Daye?"

"All my life." I've never been fond of dealing with the human police. In addition to being a knight errant, I'm a changeling—part fae, part human—and most of the time I manage to restrict my interaction with authority figures to the fae side of things. I don't like dealing with them either, but at least they're honest about what they want. Sure, "what they want" frequently involves my head on a platter, but nothing's perfect.

"Yet somehow you wound up in a *very* disreputable neighborhood, by yourself, after dark. That doesn't seem like the move of a native."

It was getting harder to keep smiling. I gritted my teeth as I said, "I had a fight with my sister and went out to clear my head. As soon as I realized where I was, I turned around."

"Ms. Daye—"

"Let it go, Carl." The new voice came from behind me, male, and familiar in a "maybe we were in the same Starbucks once" kind of a way. I twisted in my uncomfortable plastic chair. He was in his mid-thirties, Caucasian, brown hair, with a face as vaguely familiar as his voice.

Carl glowered at the newcomer. "I have a few more questions for Ms. Daye."

"We're not charging her with anything, and that means we can stop taking up her valuable time." Translation: I wasn't telling them anything useful, and they had better things to do. That was okay by me.

"Fine," said Carl, with obvious reluctance. His attention flicked back to me. "You're free to go. Officer Thornton will take you to retrieve your things."

"I appreciate it," I said, standing. I hadn't surrendered my most important things—the silver knife at my belt and the Summerlands-compatible phone in my front pocket. Both were hidden by the illusion that made me look human. That was for the best, since San Francisco law frowns on carrying hidden weapons and explicitly forbids loitering while armed. Being in the wrong place at the wrong time and loitering aren't quite the same, but I was willing to bet they'd have at least tried to make the charges stick, and I couldn't afford a lawyer.

Carl grunted, hunching over the paperwork he'd been toying with during my amateur interrogation. Officer Thornton gestured for me to follow him out into the station's dingy hallway.

"Let's get you out of here while you can still get a few hours sleep," he said. Out of habit, I squinted at him sidelong, trying to detect the flicker of an illusion. There was nothing. Officer Thornton might be unusually calm for a grave-shift policeman, but he was human. "Your friend is waiting for you up front."

I blinked. "My friend?"

"Yes."

"Right." That could be any one of a number of people. I gave Officer Thornton another sidelong look, this time focusing on his face. "I'm sorry, but you seem familiar. Do I know you?"

"Golden Gate Park. You were wearing a leather jacket in the middle of summer." Officer Thornton grinned at my obvious surprise. "I don't forget a pretty face, especially when it's refusing help for heatstroke. You're not going to do that again this year, are you?"

"Oh! That was you?" I remembered that day in the park. I hadn't been suffering from heatstroke; I'd been poisoned by an old enemy, Oleander de Merelands, who was trying to drive me out of my mind. She came disturbingly close to succeeding. Sometimes I wish my problems were as simple as heatstroke.

"That was me," he confirmed. He turned to the officer manning the desk, and said, "Ms. Daye is being released. Can we get her things, please?"

"You'll have to sign for them," said the officer, frowning at me.

"I've been signing my name since I was six," I said. "I think I can manage."

The desk officer rolled his eyes as he got up and vanished into the back, leaving me alone with Officer Thornton. We stood in silence for a few seconds before he cleared his throat and said, "You have an interesting file."

That was probably an understatement. "Yeah?" I asked, trying to sound uninterested.

"You were the subject of a missing persons case that remains unsolved, since you never told us where you'd been. Your teenage daughter was abducted last fall—"

"Are you implying something?" I interrupted. I didn't care if that looked suspicious. I didn't want him saying anything else about Gillian.

I disappeared because Simon Torquill turned me into a goldfish for fourteen years. My little girl grew up believing I'd abandoned her. My only comfort had been knowing that Gillian was free of Faerie and its dangers ... a solace shattered by Simon's niece, Rayseline, when she abducted my now-teenage daughter. Raysel wanted to hurt me. She succeeded. I lost both my daughter and my lover thanks to her. Gillian was still alive. Connor wasn't. It had been almost a year, and I hadn't had a good day's sleep since that night. The dreams were too much for me.

"Not at all," said Officer Thornton, clearly sensing my distress. "I just thought it was interesting. That's all."

"Try living with it," I said. Living with the things in my file wasn't that hard. It was living with the things that weren't there that was threatening to kill me.

Officer Thornton was saved from replying by the return of the desk officer with my confiscated belongings. Leather jacket, package of tissues, wallet, belt; it was all there and, thankfully, all still covered by the illusion I had spun. Suddenly appearing bloodstains and bullet holes wouldn't have gone over well with the police. I signed the form and slipped my jacket on, relaxing a little as the weight of it settled on my shoulders.

I looked up once everything was back where it belonged. "Is that all?"

"That's all," confirmed Officer Thornton. "You're free to leave."

"Great." That seemed insufficient, so I added, "It was nice to see you again. Despite, you know. The circumstances."

"I apologize that we had to keep you past midnight," said Officer Thornton.

"It's all right. I'm a bit of a night owl." It being after midnight just meant I was fully awake. Fae are nocturnal, and I'm fae enough to be at my best after the sun goes down.

"Get home safely, all right?"

"I'll try." I forced myself to smile before turning to walk through the door to the public receiving area. The sweet air of freedom hit me as soon as I was out of the working part of the station. My smile turned honest. I started for the nearest exit . . . and stopped, blinking.

When Officer Thornton said "my friend" was waiting for me, I'd been half-hoping he meant May. She's legally my twin sister, thanks to some clever paperwork created by Countess April O'Leary of Tamed Lightning; she would have been the logical person for the police to call, if they were going to call anyone.

It wasn't May.

Tybalt was standing near the center of the room with his hands shoved into the pockets of his jeans and an uneasy expression on his face, as though he wasn't sure what he was doing there, either. He was wearing a human disguise that turned his tabby-striped brown hair solidly black and painted round pupils in his eyes. I caught myself smiling and hastily swallowed the expression. I didn't want to be glad to see him. I couldn't help myself.

"Hi, Tybalt," I said and started for the door. "Did everything get taken care of?"

His anxiety vanished in a flash, replaced by a more customary air of mild hauteur. "Once I realized you intended to spend the evening in the company of the police, I saw to it the job was properly completed. Those children will no longer be peddling poison on these streets." He fell into step beside me. "You may show your gratitude later, in whatever way you deem fit."

"And meeting me at the police station?"

"I thought it might prove entertaining." He sighed. "Sadly, I am again disappointed."

"Sorry I let you down. Maybe if you'd brought popcorn, the cops would have felt the need to step up their game." I reached for the door leading out to the street. Tybalt slipped past me, opening it before I could. I kept walking. "I'm fine, really."

"October . . ."

It was late enough that the stretch of Valencia Street outside the police station was virtually deserted. The lights were on at the local bars—last call was more than an hour away—and a few homeless people huddled in doorways or panhandled around the ATMs, but for the most part, we were alone. I still glanced around to be sure that there were no officers on the sidewalk before I said, "I'm a little dizzy, but it's nothing some orange juice and new jeans won't fix. How did you know I was here?"

"I saw the police take you. I couldn't prevent it. So I dropped by your house to see whether anyone was intending to collect you." Tybalt shrugged. "You know what they say about curiosity and cats. Your lady Fetch said she would appreciate it if I would bring you home. As I try never to argue with death omens, here I am."

"What, May couldn't come herself?" May is my former Fetch and current housemate. Not a normal living arrangement, even in Faerie, but she's willing to do at least one thing I'm not: the dishes. Her girlfriend, Jazz, is a raven in her spare time.

"She was otherwise occupied."

"Doing what?"

Tybalt ignored my question. "I offered. She accepted. I felt we could stand to spend some time actually conversing. We've both been rather occupied of late."

"No, Tybalt, *we* haven't been. *I've* been avoiding you. Which is a change from the way things normally go, but change is good, right?" I buried my hands in my jacket pockets. "I needed some time."

"I know," said Tybalt, tone suddenly sober. "I'm sorry."

"Yeah. So am I."

Our relationship—it was too rocky to call it a friendship, although I didn't have a better word—has always been punctuated by long periods of absence. It's just that usually Tybalt was the absent one, while I was the one trying to find him. This time . . . after Connor died, I didn't want to deal with anyone, especially not anyone complicated. Tybalt can be a lot of things, but if there's one thing he's never been, it's simple.

"About earlier . . ." I began, then stopped, unsure how to finish the sentence. The fae prohibition against something as simple as saying "thank you" can be clumsy sometimes. Like now. The gang of changelings would have stuck around to finish me off if Tybalt hadn't stepped in. It was as if my ability to be careful had died with Connor, and I hadn't figured out a way to resurrect it yet.

"The house seems nice," Tybalt said, tone neutral.

I recognized the conversational save and grabbed it with both hands. "We're almost unpacked. I'm getting used to it. It's nice to have everyone in their own room, so I don't trip over Quentin every time I go to get a cup of coffee."

"I'm glad Sylvester was able to arrange the move."

"Me, too." My liege, Sylvester Torquill, had been trying to get me to move out of my apartment for years. When I gave up Goldengreen—the knowe that was briefly in my possession—Sylvester put his foot down, insisting that if I wasn't willing to move into Shadowed Hills, I was at least going to move into a place where I wasn't sharing walls with humans. I'd responded by saying I wouldn't move out of San Francisco. It was the Queen's territory, and it was a long way from Shadowed Hills, but it was home. After some arguing, he acquiesced, and I took possession of one of the many houses he and his wife owned the title to.

The new house was on 20th Street, overlooking Mission Delores Park. It would probably have cost a million or more on the open market. Sylvester did all his real estate investment in that area over a century ago. All he had to do was hand me the keys, and suddenly we had as much room as we needed.

Moving meant boxing up all the things Connor had accidentally left at my place: shirts and sandals, toothbrushes and half-finished paperbacks. I found them, boxed them, and took them with us. I didn't know how to let him go. I don't believe in ghosts, but there were times when I felt like I was being haunted. Worse yet, there were times when I didn't know whether I minded the haunting.

Tybalt cleared his throat. "Quentin's studies are proceeding well?"

"I think so. They seem to be. I've never done this before." Quentin was my squire, making me responsible for teaching him how to be an effective knight of Faerie without getting himself killed. Mostly, this seemed to mean he was underfoot all the time, and Sylvester sent money to pay for feeding him. At least he had his own room now.

"Raj is quite envious, you know."

I shot Tybalt a glance. "Really?" Raj was his adopted nephew and probable heir to the throne of the Court of Cats.

"Really." He nodded. "We have nothing so organized in the Court of Cats. No one teaches a King to be a King. You claim your position the day the old King no longer holds it."

"Because the new King has just kicked his ass?" I asked.

The amusement faded but didn't disappear. "In most cases, yes," he said.

We kept walking. It's not far from the Mission Police Station to Mission Delores Park, but I wasn't hurrying. It was a beautiful night, and I was too tired to hurry. I risked another glance at Tybalt as we walked. For someone who used to be one of my biggest—not enemies, exactly, but annoyances—he's become very important to me. There have been times I was pretty sure I was important to him, too. Maybe I was right, but we'd silently agreed to let the issue rest after Connor died. We both needed some time.

Tybalt managed to seem feline even wearing a human disguise; it was something in the way he moved, something that had nothing to do with the shape of his ears or the color of his hair. Cats have no stripes in the dark, after all. His jeans and flannel work shirt looked at once too mundane and exactly right for him. He was walking slowly to pace me, despite his longer legs, and was staying carefully outside my personal space.

That's something else that changed when Connor died. Tybalt used to take obvious pleasure in standing too close just to watch me squirm. As soon as I went into mourning, that part of his feline nature faded. He's always been a contradiction that way, part arrogant feline, part genuinely compassionate man. It just took me a while to see the second side of him.

As always, walking with Tybalt was strangely comfortable. This time, it came with a new feeling—guilt, as though I was betraying Connor's memory by being comfortable with another man. Finally, to break the silence, I asked, "How did you know where to find me before?"

"Ah." Tybalt sighed. "It was, in a roundabout way, your squire."

"Quentin?"

"Yes. He told Raj, including a complaint that you were going to get yourself killed. Raj, naturally, assumed this was something I might like to know, and, well ..." Tybalt shrugged. "I am sure you would have been fine without me."

"Oh, yeah. I just let you help so you wouldn't feel useless."

Tybalt spared a small smile. "Quite kind of you."

"Don't mention it," I said. "So what was keeping May too occupied to come and get me herself? Not to sound like I'm whining or anything, but it's not like I get picked up by the police *every* night, and it would have been nice of her to come down to the station."

Tybalt made a face.

I sighed. "I meant on foot, like this. Not in the car." May is possibly the worst driver in the world. If there are worse, I don't want to know. I have enough trouble sleeping as it is.

"You have company."

"Company? Please tell me you mean the pleasant kind of company, like Stacy brought the kids over, or even Danny and the Barghests."

"As opposed to ... ?"

"The unpleasant kind of company. The kind of company that's here to arrest and/or kill me. Or maybe kill me, and then arrest me, and then bring me back to life and kill me again."

"Ah. I don't believe the current company falls into either category. It's Etienne."

"Etienne?" I blinked at him. "Seriously?"

Tybalt nodded. "Seriously."

Etienne is one of the other knights in Sylvester's service. He's a traditionalist, and I'm, well, not. We get along reasonably well—we've only ever attacked each other when we had really good reasons—but we've never been friends. I hadn't even realized he knew where I lived, much less had any desire to visit. "Did he say what he wanted?" I asked. We were almost to the house, and suddenly, it seemed way too far away. "Is Sylvester okay?"

"I knew you would ask that, so I made him reassure me that everything is fine in Shadowed Hills. The Torquills are well, and the court continues to thrive."

"So . . . what's Etienne doing at my house?"

"He wouldn't tell me."

I sighed, turning the corner onto 20th Street. "That's never a good sign."

Tybalt smirked. "So little is, when you're involved."

I laughed and kept walking. The businesses of Valencia fell away, replaced by stately old Victorian brownstones. Most had long since been converted into smaller apartments, divided and subdivided until not even they remembered what they'd once been. A few, like mine, were lucky enough to have been in private hands since they were built, and remained spacious reminders of an earlier era. Most of the houses were dark, the gates separating their small yards from the street closed and locked. Tybalt and I kept walking until the light from my living room window told us that we'd reached our destination.

It looked like any other house on the street from the outside. The tiny yard was a mix of heirloom rosebushes and easy-care groundcover, all of which was tended by the groundskeeper Sylvester paid to "protect his investment." In daylight, the paint was maybe a little too bright, an eye-popping mixture of yellow, green, and electric blue. But at night, with the moonlight softening the colors, it was beautiful. Knowing Sylvester, I had faith that it was intentional. Fae eyes would see the house by night, so night was when the house would look its very best.

I opened the gate and started up the path to the porch, pausing when I realized Tybalt wasn't coming. I turned. He was still standing on the sidewalk, watching me walk away. I blinked, once, and then smiled.

Maybe I'd been avoiding him long enough. Maybe it was time to let my friends come in out of the cold. "Well?" I asked. "Are you coming?"

Tybalt's eyes widened, a smile blooming on his face. "If you insist," he said, and followed me inside.

THREE

THE SOUND OF THE TELEVISION drifted quietly from the direction of the living room as I stepped into the house, moving to the side to let Tybalt follow. I shrugged out of my jacket, hanging it on the hook next to the door. "Want to take your coat off?" I asked.

Tybalt looked amused. "Coats removed in your presence tend to disappear from my possession."

"Suit yourself," I said, unable to keep myself from smiling.

The entryway was narrow enough that having two of us there made it uncomfortably intimate. There was a small table next to the door, covered in junk mail, paperbacks, and less-definable oddities, hinting at the tightly controlled chaos to come. May's a pack rat, and neither Quentin nor I are much for housework.

"Come on," I said, starting for the dining room. That was where the clutter reached its peak, since it had bookshelves and a table to gather on.

May was sitting at the dining room table, across from an uncomfortable-looking Etienne, when we entered. It was hard to say what accounted for his discomfort: the mess, my Fetch, or the simple fact of being in my house to begin with. I could tell that May had made an effort to clear the table before sitting down. To someone accustomed to the housekeeping at Shadowed Hills, it probably looked like the whole place needed to be condemned. They both turned at the sound of our footsteps. May smiled, clearly relieved. Etienne started to stand. I waved him down.

"Don't get up." I kept walking, heading for the stairs. "Hi, Etienne. Nice of you to drop by. This is exactly what I needed tonight." Etienne winced. I tried to dial back the sarcasm as I said, "I'm going to change into something less bloodstained and get some coffee. That should give you time to figure out what you're going to tell me that you weren't willing to tell Tybalt."

"Who you brought home with you," said May. "Hi, Tybalt. Welcome back."

"May," said Tybalt, with a courtly nod. "Etienne."

"Tybalt," said Etienne neutrally. It's not that Etienne dislikes Tybalt. Etienne just dislikes chaos, and Tybalt causes almost as much commotion as I do. Sometimes more, when he really sets his mind to it, although my chaos is a little more destructive, if I do say so myself.

It says something about my life that this is the sort of thing I have to think about—and be proud of. "Be right back," I said.

"October—" began Etienne.

I didn't stop walking. "I just got home from the police station, and prior to that I was shot multiple times in an alley," I said. "That means I get to put on clean clothes and make myself a cup of coffee big enough to give me caffeine poisoning before I have to have whatever serious conversation you're here to have. Does anybody else need anything?"

"I'm good," said May.

"No," said Etienne.

"I'd like some coffee," said Tybalt.

I gave him a sidelong look. "Since when do you drink coffee?"

"Since I had to learn how to make it or risk your endless wrath."

I had to smile a little at that. "You can fix your own."

It only took me a few minutes to climb the stairs to my room, drop the disguise that made me look human, and shuck off my blood-drenched clothes, throwing them into the wastebasket next to the door. One more pair of jeans down the drain. I'd need to get one of the hearth-spirits I knew to do something about the holes in my leather jacket. I was willing to get rid of a lot of things, but not that.

I washed the blood off my hands and face in the master bathroom. My reflection was overly pale, even for me; regenerating that much blood had done a number on my system. There was no blood in my hair, for once. I swapped my bloody jeans and T-shirt for clean ones that weren't full of bullet holes. Then I went jogging back down the stairs and through the dining room to the kitchen, where Tybalt was watching with evident amusement as my half-Siamese cats, Cagney and Lacey, cornered Quentin.

My squire was spooning wet food into cat dishes. He wasn't doing it fast enough for their liking, because both cats were yowling. Cats are like that. Tybalt cleared his throat. Cagney and Lacey went silent. They turned to face their King and sat, wrapping their tails around their legs. Quentin looked up, relief written across his face.

"Good one, Tybalt," he said.

"A cat may look at a King," Tybalt replied, waving away Quentin's almost-thanks without commenting on it.

"Greetings, Squire," I said, and ruffled Quentin's hair. I didn't have to get on my tiptoes, but it was close. After one more growth spurt, he'd be looking down on me. I guess that's what you get when you take a teenage boy as your sworn squire. "Is there coffee?"

He looked at me solemnly, doing an admirable job of concealing his annoyance over my hair ruffling, and said, deadpan, "We didn't want you to kill us all, so May told me to start a fresh pot when Tybalt left to get you."

"I have the smartest Fetch in the whole world." I snagged a coffee mug from the rack. "Do you have any clue what Etienne is doing here?"

"I know as much as you do." Quentin bent to set the cat dishes on the floor. "He just showed up saying he needed to talk to you, and he wouldn't tell us why."

There was an anxious note in Quentin's voice. I paused in the act of filling my mug, glancing back at him. "He can't take you back to Shadowed Hills," I said gently. "It's against the rules, and if there's one thing Etienne would never ever intentionally do, it's break the rules."

"I know," said Quentin miserably. "I just . . ."

"I wouldn't concern myself if I were you." Tybalt plucked the coffeepot from my hand, topping off my mug before half-filling his own. "I've had sufficient dealings with the Divided Courts to know there would be much more pointless discussion before we reached that point. Unless she has been found guilty of some dire crime and has neglected to tell the rest of us, you can no more be removed from her custody than I can sprout wings and fly off to take tea with the Swanmays."

"Don't say that where the Luidaeg can hear you, or she'll take it as a challenge." I got the milk out of the fridge. "Quentin, you have my word: I will be your knight until your fosterage ends or you're ready to graduate to a knighthood of your own. And the only people who get to decide when that is are me, Sylvester, and whoever the hell your parents are."

"Yes, sir," he said, smiling.

I rolled my eyes as I dumped milk and sugar into my coffee. "Do the dishes," I said and turned to leave the kitchen. Tybalt paused long enough to fill his mug the rest of the way with milk before following me, chuckling.

When I met Quentin, he was a fourteen-year-old courtier in service to the Duke of Shadowed Hills. Since then, his association with me has gotten him shot, nearly marooned him in Blind Michael's lands, and made him an accessory to jailbreak from the Queen's prison. Somehow, this all made me the best choice to stand as his knight. He's pureblood Daoine Sidhe — a fact his teen-heartthrob looks, bronze hair, and sharply pointed ears makes difficult to disguise even with magic — and he's been sent to the Bay Area on a blind fosterage. That means I don't know who his parents are, and he doesn't tell me. If a couple of unfamiliar Daoine Sidhe ever show up on my porch and start throwing punches, I think I'll have a pretty good idea why.

May and Etienne were still at the dining room table when Tybalt and I returned with our coffee. "All right, then," I said. "So what's so important?"

This time Etienne *did* stand. "I need to speak with you alone."

"Um, why?" I asked. "May lives with me. She's going to hear whatever you say eventually." Tybalt didn't live with me, but I had cats, and that was almost the same thing, as far as gossip goes. Anything Cagney and Lacey overheard would be carried straight back to their King.

Etienne sighed. For the first time, I really looked at his face. I'd been right when I read his expression as discomfort, but I'd been wrong when I assumed he didn't approve of our housekeeping. There was probably some of that in there, too, but it wasn't everything. "I know you'll tell your allies what we discuss," he said. "Just, please. Let me tell you this alone."

"Sure, Etienne. Sure." I turned to Tybalt. "Can you wait here until we come back down? I'd like to catch up a little."

"It would be my pleasure." Tybalt smiled before taking Etienne's vacated seat across from May. "I will remain as long as I must."

"Cool. I'll shout if we need anything." With a final nod to May, I beckoned for Etienne to follow me as I turned and left the room.

Etienne remained silent as we walked up the stairs and down the hallway to the bedroom that served as my home office. I glanced back at him. "Are you okay?"

"No," he said, without hesitation. "I am a long way from 'okay.'"

"Oh," I said, opening the office door. "Sorry about the mess." I clicked on the light before taking a seat at the card table I was using as a makeshift desk. "I promise the chairs are safe. I mean, they haven't broken yet, and Danny sat in one of them."

"Where did you *find* them?" asked Etienne, amazed disgust actually breaking through his shell of discomfort as he stared at the two rickety wooden camp chairs.

"Girl Scout yard sale," I said. "I'm going to replace them, I just haven't been able to get to Ikea yet."

"Ah."

"Anyway. Take a seat, and tell me what's up." I took a gulp of coffee. "You wouldn't have come all the way out here if it weren't major."

"Yes. Major. Yes, I suppose it is, when you put it that way." Etienne sat on the closer of the camp chairs, running a hand through his brown-black hair. "It's not as if I drove."

"Teleporting counts," I said. Like all Tuatha de Dannan, Etienne could teleport short distances—longer if he was moving between knowes, the hollow hills that conceal the majority of Faerie's incursions into the mortal world. Traveling from Pleasant Hill to San Francisco would have been a drain, even if it wasn't a major one. "Look, if you don't want to talk about whatever this is, that's fine. I can wait until you do. But I'm going to want to go downstairs and make myself a sandwich."

Etienne sighed deeply. "October, please. This is hard for me. I know it's in your nature to needle, but please, just this once, can you try to restrain yourself?"

"I do better when I know what I'm restraining myself *for*, Etienne," I said. "If you want me to help you, you need to talk to me."

"I don't know how." He closed his eyes, tilting his head back until his face was almost pointed at the ceiling. "I've made a terrible mistake."

"That's a start. What kind of mistake?"

Etienne was silent.

I bit back a groan. "Do we have to play hot and cold, here? You came to me, not the other way around. I didn't force you to be here."

Etienne was still silent.

"Look, did you kill somebody? That you didn't intend to kill, I mean. Because I would count that as a mistake."

"What?" His chin snapped down, eyes opening. "No!"

"Now we're getting somewhere. Did you steal something? Piss off a member of the nobility? Break an oath?"

"Perhaps the last." He rubbed his face with his hand. "I may have endangered my oaths, if not broken them entirely. I don't know yet."

I gaped at him. "Root and branch, seriously? When?"

"The spring after you disappeared."

That was more than sixteen years ago. I nearly dropped my coffee, but saved it at the last moment as I demanded, "*What?!*"

"If I broke my oaths, I did so the year after your disappearance, when the Duchess and her daughter were ... lost to us." Etienne spoke slowly. "The Duchy was in chaos. The Queen offered no succor, and the Duke ... the Duke was ..."

"Mad," I said. "He was mad, Etienne. I've heard the stories."

"I *endured* them," he snapped, anger kindling in his voice. "You weren't here during Luna's absence, October. I was. You didn't see Sylvester at his worst. I did. I served as his Seneschal during those dark years, Oberon help me, and I did it out of loyalty, and duty, and love. Do you understand that much?"

"I would have been there if I could," I whispered. The "dark years" of Luna's absence corresponded to my own imprisonment as an enchanted koi in Golden Gate Park's Japanese Tea Gardens. Not a place I ever meant to wind up.

Etienne took a deep breath, composing himself. When he spoke again, his voice was steady. "I know. Please believe me when I say I do not blame you. What happened to you was horrible, and we should have found a way to bring you home long before you escaped on your own. That doesn't change the fact that you weren't here. You never saw Sylvester raving at shadows, all but grieving himself to death, while the rest of us fought to keep Shadowed Hills alive and healthy long enough for him to find his own way home."

I shuddered. Sylvester's more than my liege. He's my friend. Even knowing how bad things were for him when Luna and Raysel were missing, hearing it from Etienne hurt more than I would have guessed possible. "Okay. I get your point. I wasn't there."

"Sometimes . . ." Etienne paused, sighing again, before he pressed on: "Sometimes, when it got to be too much for any of us to take, Jin would brew something to make him sleep. Never for more than a day or two. Just enough to let the rest of us recover our strength and brace against the storms we knew were yet to come."

"You *drugged* him?" I asked, almost before the thought finished forming. "Etienne, that's . . . that's . . ."

"It was necessary for the health of the Duchy and the health of the Duke," he said. "He knows everything. He gave us his forgiveness long ago."

I took a breath, trying not to dwell on the thought of how bad things must have been. For Jin to even consider it . . . it must have been a relief for everyone in the Duchy when their Duke wasn't awake to terrorize them. I loved him too much for that idea not to break my heart. "Fine," I said, pushing the images away. "So Jin would knock him out long enough to let the rest of you get some sleep, is that it?"

"We didn't just sleep. We lived our lives." Etienne rubbed his face. "I never stayed in the Duchy while the Duke slumbered. I ran. Like a coward, I ran. Grianne knew where to find me and could send her Merry Dancers if I was needed home, and I needed . . . I needed to be away from all the madness. If only for a little while."

"Something was rotten in the state of Denmark," I said quietly.

Etienne laughed a little. It wasn't a pleasant sound. "If you like. In order to serve properly, I needed time to refresh myself, and I took that time in neutral territory.

Places where no Duke or Duchess would take my presence as an insult or an invitation to battle."

Neutral spots are rare in the Bay Area. I could only think of two big ones. "I'm going to go out on a limb here and guess that you didn't spend much time in Golden Gate Park."

"No," said Etienne. "I didn't."

That left Berkeley. An idea was nibbling at the edges of my mind, making me uneasy. "What happened?"

"I spent a great deal of time in the coffee houses around the University, where no one seemed to notice, or care, if I didn't match the social norms. I was trying to reeducate myself about modern humanity, so I could travel farther abroad without attracting attention." Etienne's lips twisted in what looked like an involuntary smile. "That's where I met Professor Ames."

"Professor Ames?"

"Bridget. She taught folklore, and she liked to argue with people, about, oh, everything. I think she would have argued about the color of the sky if anyone had been willing to engage her in that particular debate. I don't even remember how our first argument started— something about some ballad or other, or maybe over the last scone in the case—but it was infuriating and elating at the same time. I found myself looking forward to our arguments. Then I found myself simply looking forward to seeing her."

"Oh, Etienne." Playing faerie bride—being fae, and loving a human—is never easy. Doing it while serving as the Seneschal of a madman would be virtually impossible. "What happened?"

"What always happens." His smile turned bitter before fading. "I fell in love with a human woman. I did what I had always looked down on others for doing. I wasn't sorry then, and I'm not sorry now. I'm only sorry it had to end. Sylvester was getting worse. Jin was having more difficulty getting him to take the sleeping draughts, and it got harder to slip away. Bridget was understanding at first, and then she was angry, and finally, she stopped answering her phone. I went to the campus during her office hours once, to apologize—I knew better than to think I could get her back, not at that point—and there was a sign on the bulletin board saying she was on sabbatical and would be back the next year."

"And was she?"

"I don't know." Etienne looked at me, dark eyes full of sorrow. "That was the last time I tried to see her. There wasn't time after that; it wouldn't have been fair to either of us. It was the spring of 1996. You'd been gone less than a year. The darkest days were just beginning."

I shivered. "I had no idea."

"We didn't exactly advertise."

"But . . . I'm confused, Etienne. What does all this have to do with anything? I mean, that was sixteen years ago. Did Professor Ames track you down?"

"In a manner of speaking, yes." Etienne shrugged. The gesture was somehow alien on him, like a coat that didn't fit quite right. "I gave Bridget a number where she could reach me in an emergency. I was in love. It seemed the thing to do."

I stared at him. "You gave her the number for *Shadowed Hills?*"

"One of them, yes. I told her it was the office where I worked. There's a special ring when someone calls from a mortal location; whoever took her call would know to be careful."

"And I can't even change the ringtone on my phone," I muttered. More loudly, I asked, "So she called you?"

"Yes. Three hours ago now." Etienne rubbed his face again. "It seems we were both keeping secrets. I didn't tell her I wasn't human."

There was only one thing he could say next, and it wasn't something I wanted to hear. I still prompted him, asking, "And what did she not tell you?"

"That she was pregnant." Etienne dropped his hand away from his face, looking at me despondently. "I have a changeling daughter, October. Almost sixteen years old and raised outside of Faerie's knowledge."

I stared at him, stunned into silence.

Most changeling children have instinctive illusions that make them seem human for the earliest years of their lives. It's a form of defensive camouflage, like spots on a fawn. But that baby magic shorts out as changelings grow, and a changeling who hasn't learned to weave a human disguise by the age of six or seven is a danger to Faerie. Secrecy is the only thing that's kept us alive for so long. Etienne had always played things by the rules and by the book—and now there was a chance that he'd committed the greatest infraction of them all. There was a chance he'd given Faerie away.

There was just one piece missing. "So . . . if your daughter is sixteen, her baby magic must have failed years ago. Why did Bridget call you now? What changed?" I paused, then asked the big question: "How did you not *know?*"

"I never asked," said Etienne. He smiled—the small, painful smile of a man who suddenly saw what he had been doing wrong for years. "All the people I paid to check on her, all the pixies and sprites I bribed . . . I never asked them to check for a child, and I never went myself. I didn't know the girl existed because I never asked."

"Oak and ash," I breathed. "And . . . why now?"

"Bridget called because our daughter is missing." Etienne sat up a little straighter, looking me in the eyes. "She vanished this afternoon, on her way home from school—and I do mean 'vanished.' Her friends said she was there one moment and gone the next. Bridget assumed, quite reasonably, that the faeries had finally found her. She called me screaming, begging for the return of her little girl. She knew exactly what I was, even down to the name of my race."

"Maybe you shouldn't have dated a folklore professor," I said.

"Maybe not," said Etienne. "Regardless, I did, and we had a child together, and now that child is missing. She may have been taken. She may have finally found the magic she was heir to and not known how to control it. Either way, I am here to hire you. Please, October. I need you to find my daughter."

Oh, oak and ash. This wasn't going to end well.

FOUR

I STARED AT ETIENNE. He must have been expecting that reaction, because he didn't bat an eye. He just looked back at me, waiting for me to get it out of my system.

If I'd been asked to list the ten people most likely to have an affair with a human, Etienne wouldn't have come anywhere near making the cut. And if I'd been asked to make a list of the people I could see fathering an accidental changeling, Etienne wouldn't have made the top fifty. Like most Tuatha, he loved rules, and the rules said that sort of behavior wasn't allowed. But Sylvester had been out of his mind with fear and grief, leaving Etienne to hold things together by himself, and that had changed the rules. Tired men make mistakes when they're looking for a place to rest. Etienne wasn't human, but he was still a man.

May's laughter drifted up the stairs, reminding me that time was passing. Whatever had happened to Etienne's daughter wasn't going to unhappen just because I was busy staring at her father. "Etienne—"

"I've already rehearsed every objection you might make. I have answers to them all. Please. Can't we just skip that part and reach the point where you agree to help me? My daughter is alone out there. Time is of the essence."

He was wrong about one thing: she probably wasn't "alone out there." Teenage girls run away from home sometimes—I was a prime example of that—but they don't usually vanish in broad daylight. If she'd disappeared that abruptly, the odds were good that someone *made* her disappear. I hate missing children cases, and that's probably why the world keeps handing them to me. Reality is nothing if not malicious where I'm concerned.

Instead of arguing or objecting, I asked a simple question: "Why me?"

"Because you were the one who dared to go up against Blind Michael. When the sons of Saltmist were taken, you were the one who brought them home. And because my daughter is . . . she's . . ."

"She's a changeling," I said. "You want me, instead of one of the other knights, because you think I'll be more understanding of the fact that she's not a pureblood."

He didn't say anything. He didn't have to. He just nodded.

"I'm going to regret this, but . . . okay," I said. I picked up my mug and downed its contents in a single long gulp. The coffee was hot enough to burn my throat a little, but I didn't let that worry me; I'm a fast healer. I set the empty mug aside. "What's her name?"

"Chelsea." He said her name like it was some strange, undiscovered country, one that had disappeared from maps a thousand years ago. The wonder in his voice would have been touching if we'd been talking about a baby and not a missing half-human teenager. As it was, it was just a little sad.

"You said she disappeared on her way home from school. Do you know what school she attends?" He wouldn't have a picture, since he hadn't known she existed before she went missing, but every school keeps photos of its student body. Breaking into the office couldn't be that hard. It would be easier than breaking into Bridget and Chelsea's house, since schools tend to be closed at night, and that's when I do the bulk of my petty larceny.

"I . . . no, I'm sorry. I don't." Etienne shook his head. "Bridget didn't tell me much. Mostly, she just swore at me. She said I had no right to steal her daughter, not when I'd been gone since before Chelsea was even born. If there's a pejorative term for faerie that Bess doesn't know, I'd be surprised. I think she used them all on me tonight."

I managed to keep a straight face despite his use of the proper Irish diminutive for Bridget. I wasn't even sure he knew he'd done it. "Right. Do you know where they live?"

"Yes."

"Really?" I pushed a pen and paper across the table to him.

"I may have fallen out of touch, but I have always known where Bridget was," said Etienne, taking the pen and paper and scrawling down a street address. Catching my expression, he added defensively, "I never went there. I watched her on campus from time to time, and I had my spies, but I left her with her privacy. I just wanted to be sure that she continued well."

And somehow you managed to never check closely enough to notice that she had a kid with pointed ears? I thought, before inwardly slapping myself. We don't see the things we don't want to see, and mothers are nothing if not inventive when it comes to hiding the truth about their children. Look at my mother. She managed to hide the truth of my race from practically everyone for more than fifty years, raising me as Daoine Sidhe when nothing could make me anything but Dóchas Sidhe—a direct descendant of Oberon, and a natural magnet for trouble. If Mom could pull off something like that with half of Faerie looking over her shoulder, it wasn't hard to believe that Bridget could find a way to hide a changeling girl no one was looking for to begin with. It was harder to believe we were ever going to see that girl alive again.

"Wait—you said you watched Bridget 'on campus.' Does that mean she's still at UC Berkeley?"

"Well, yes," said Etienne. "I believe she's currently the head of their Folklore Department."

"Why am I not surprised to learn that Berkeley has a Folklore Department?" I picked up the paper where he'd written Bridget and Chelsea's address. I glanced at it to be sure that I could read his handwriting, which was perfect enough to border on calligraphy, before folding it in half and tucking it into the pocket of my jeans. "Do you remember Walther?"

"Your friend the alchemist?" Etienne frowned. "Of course I remember him. He helped save the Duchess Torquill's life. We owe him a debt of gratitude."

Trust Etienne to see things in terms of obligations. "Walther teaches chemistry at UC Berkeley. I bet he'd be willing to check on Bridget if I asked. He might be able to get some pictures of Chelsea from her." Which would neatly avoid the possibility of my getting arrested for breaking and entering on a high school campus. "Plus he can sound out her emotional state. She may have been able to hide a changeling from us for sixteen years, but mothers can be unpredictable when their children are in danger. The last thing we want is for Bridget to go to the media saying that the faeries stole her baby."

Etienne's frown melted into a look of sheer horror. "No one would believe her. They would think grief had driven her mad."

"Do you want to bet your life on that?"

He didn't answer me.

"I didn't think so." I stood, picking up my empty mug. "I'll do this for you, Etienne. I'll find her. But I have a few conditions, and if you're not okay with them, you're going to need to find somebody else." I was bluffing. He'd know it, too, if he stopped to think about it. There are a lot of things that I'm capable of. Leaving children in danger isn't one of them.

"Anything," he said. "Whatever you ask for."

Oak and ash, he really was desperate. In Faerie, that sort of promise can get you killed. "You have to pay my operating costs. I can't take any other cases while I'm working on this."

"Done," he said.

I raised an eyebrow. "I haven't even told you what I charge."

Etienne half-smiled. "I've had a great deal of time to invest in the mortal world, October. Will two thousand dollars a day be sufficient to purchase your full attention?"

Two thousand dollars a day was nearly four times my normal rate. "Very sufficient," I said. I almost felt bad about taking that much of his money, but if he was paying me, I wasn't creating a debt between us. I liked Etienne treating me with respect because we were both in Sylvester's service, not because I had a giant favor to hold over his head. That was how the purebloods did business. That kind of thing wasn't for me.

"Good," he said. "What else?"

"No secrets, no surprises. If Bridget calls again, I need to hear about it. If you remember something that doesn't seem important, you need to tell me about it anyway, and you need to tell me immediately. I don't care if it's the middle of the day—call and wake me if you have to." Privately, I didn't think that was likely; if this case was like most, I wasn't going to be sleeping much until it was over. "Right now, we don't know what is or is not going to matter."

Etienne frowned. "I don't understand."

"We're hoping Chelsea disappeared because she figured out how to do that teleporting trick you're so good at, and maybe she did. That's our best case scenario, since it would just mean we needed to figure out where she teleported to, go there, and get her back."

"And if it's not the case . . . ?" asked Etienne, slowly.

"If that's not the case, then someone saw an unprotected teenage girl and grabbed her. Human kidnappers, we're risking exposure. Fae kidnappers, who knows what they want her for?" A lot of things can be done with young, inexperienced changelings. I managed to find people who would spare me from the worst of them— and that's saying something, considering Devin. That doesn't mean I escaped knowing what they were.

Etienne blanched. "If you're trying to frighten me, you're doing an excellent job."

"That's good. I want you to be frightened, because I want you to understand that this is going to be hard. Maybe we'll find her tonight, maybe she just ditched her friends because she's upset over a boy, and she's camped out at the Denny's on Market Street, too pissed to go home and too scared to go anywhere more interesting. Maybe this will all seem like a bad dream tomorrow."

"Then why—"

"But even if Chelsea is found safe and sound, Oberon willing, you'll have to deal with the fact that she exists, and her mother—her *human* mother—knows about Faerie. You broke cover, Etienne. I mean, that's . . . that's something even *I've* never managed to do."

"You've certainly tried hard enough," he muttered, but the growing horror in his tone told me I was getting through. He'd come to me because he knew I had a track record of dealing with lost kids and because an undocumented changeling was a political hot potato no one higher in the food chain would dare to touch. Sylvester couldn't get involved without punishing Etienne for his carelessness. The Queen would love an excuse to punish a knight in Sylvester's service and, by extension, Sylvester himself. That left me.

What Etienne hadn't done was stop and really think about what was about to happen. Because everything in his life, absolutely everything, was going to change. "When I find Chelsea—*if* I find Chelsea—you know what has to happen." He looked away. I raised my voice, saying, "Etienne, you need to tell me you know what has to happen. This is the last thing you have to agree to."

"She has to be given her Choice," he said, in a voice that was suddenly very soft.

"Yeah." I sighed. "She does."

The Changeling's Choice was established by Oberon as one of the ways for Faerie to protect itself. It's supposed to be the defining moment in a changeling's life. It's the day their fae parent sits down with them and asks them to decide where they belong: Faerie or the mortal world. If they choose Faerie, they're whisked away to the Summerlands. Their human parent will never see them again, and they'll be raised the way I was, always an outsider, always held apart, but still a part of Faerie. If they choose the mortal world . . .

Everything mortal dies. That's the main difference between humans and the fae. If our changeling children choose to live as humans, we have to kill them. That's the price of playing faerie bride. At least, that used to be the price—my own daughter, Gillian, was able to choose humanity and walk away, but only because of what I am.

Dóchas Sidhe can't just read blood: we can *change* it. I turned my own daughter mortal, and the Luidaeg wiped her memory, making her forget she'd ever had anything to do with Faerie. But Gillian was only a quarter-blood, if that. Maybe more importantly, she'd been raised in the human world by her human father, with no influence from me. Making her forget Faerie was easy. Chelsea, on the other hand . . .

Bridget had raised her daughter knowing that she wasn't wholly mortal. Chelsea would have her fae nature woven throughout her memories. It might be too closely tied to her identity for even the Luidaeg to remove, no matter how much I changed her blood. If Chelsea chose human, there was a good chance she'd have to die. And either way, there was the matter of Bridget, who was mortal and aware of Faerie. Something would have to be done.

For a moment, Etienne simply sat there. Then he took a shaky breath and stood. "The Choice has always been given," he said. "I have broken enough rules. It is unfair to expect that this rule, too, would be violated for my pleasure."

"There's a chance—" I began, then stopped, realizing what his expression meant. Sylvester never told him. Etienne wasn't there when Gillian had her Choice; he knew I had a mostly mortal daughter, but that wasn't the same as knowing she'd Chosen, or knowing she'd been changed. He still thought of the Changeling's Choice as an absolute, one that ended with either death or temporary exile from the mortal world.

"A chance?" he asked suspiciously.

"Never mind." I shook my head. Chelsea's situation wasn't like anyone else's that I knew of ... and it was kinder not to tell him. "There's a chance she'll choose Faerie, that's all."

"And lose her mother—assuming Bridget can be allowed to live freely after what I've done to her." Etienne sighed. "I've lived my life by Faerie's laws. I've served even when I wondered whether service was truly the only path open to me. But I've never before questioned this strongly whether those laws were fair."

"Yeah, well. The humans call us 'the Fair Folk' because they're trying to make us act that way. Not because we already do." I raked my hair back with one hand. "Is there anything else I need to know before I start moving on this?"

"You know everything I do." Etienne took a step back. He didn't look away. "I'll have your first payment sent over in the morning, as soon as the banks are open."

I briefly considered explaining the concept of the ATM to him but decided against it. Quentin once spent most of an afternoon trying to explain "online banking" to me, and I walked away with a headache and the sincere urge to send mankind back to the Stone Age. As long as Etienne knew how to make a withdrawal, I was happy. "All right. I'll call if I find anything."

"Yes. I suppose you will." Etienne glanced over his shoulder to the door. "I understand that this is terribly cowardly of me, but would you mind very much if I were to—?"

Understanding dawned. "You can go ahead and teleport out," I said. "I'll explain things to the others. We're *going* to find her, Etienne. You have my word." I wasn't going to promise him we'd find her alive—I try to be optimistic, but that doesn't make me an idiot. He looked relieved, all the same.

"I haven't always been a good friend to you, October, and I regret that," he said, tone grave. "I'll never forget that you were willing to do this for me. Believe that."

"I do," I said.

Etienne bowed. Then he turned away, using one hand to transcribe a wide arch in the air. A glowing circle appeared in front of him as the smell of limes and cedar smoke filled the room. I could see one of the halls at Shadowed Hills through the circle; a faint hint of rose perfume came wafting through, making an odd counterpart to the scent of Etienne's magic. Then he stepped into the portal, and it closed behind him.

"I need more coffee," I said loudly, and walked to the office door. "Now I'm opening the door." I grasped the knob, counted to three, and pulled.

As expected, Tybalt was standing in the hall.

"Feeling subtle tonight, are we?" I asked, brushing past him on my way to the stairs. "How long were you standing there?"

"Long enough," he said, turning to follow me. "Is this going to be an issue?"

"No. I knew one of you would be listening and that it wouldn't be May; she's the loudest. Tactically, keeping her downstairs is the right thing to do." I glanced back at him as I walked down the stairs. "You could have brought me a fresh cup of coffee, you know."

"May thought the smell would betray my presence."

"May was probably right," I said, reaching the bottom of the stairs.

"May usually is." May stepped out of the kitchen, holding out a fresh mug. "Peace offering?"

"Accepted." I exchanged my empty mug for her full one, taking a long drink of scalding coffee before I shouted, "Quentin! Wherever you are, stop being there, and get in here!"

"That bad?" asked May.

"Perhaps worse," said Tybalt. I raised an eyebrow in his direction. He shook his head. "I'm not being flippant, October. As I said before, I heard enough."

"That's good. Can I assume you're still here because you're willing to help with this?"

"You can."

May looked between us. "Is this the part where I start freaking out?"

"If you think it would help," I said. Quentin emerged from the kitchen with Spike—the household's resident rose goblin, a sort of animate cat-shaped rosebush with an unfortunate tendency to jump on my lap without warning—riding on his shoulder. I saluted the pair of them with my coffee mug. "Great, we're all here. Follow me."

I led the way to the living room, where I put my mug down atop the pile of papers that obscured our coffee table and turned to face the others.

"Here's the short form," I said. "Etienne had a relationship with a human woman while Luna and Rayseline were missing. It ended when his duties at Shadowed Hills became too pressing. He hasn't seen her since then. Unfortunately, what he didn't know was that Bridget was pregnant when they broke up."

"*Etienne* has a changeling?" asked Quentin, tone both amazed and horrified.

"Yeah," I said, looking at him levelly. "Is there a problem with that?"

Quentin started to reply. Then he stopped, took a deep breath, and said, "I don't know."

He looked utterly ashamed of himself, which said a lot about how far he'd come since we met. Quentin started out as your average pureblood, convinced that he was innately superior to the changelings and just as convinced that there was nothing wrong with that. I'd started slapping that attitude out of him almost immediately, and it had worked, sometimes surprisingly well—for a little while, he'd even had a human girlfriend. They didn't have a happy ending. People who play faerie bride so rarely do.

"Her name is Chelsea," I said. "There's nothing wrong with the fact that she exists, but there's something very wrong with the fact that up until today, Etienne didn't know about it."

Tybalt nodded; he'd already heard this much. Quentin gaped at me, shame melting into surprise. It was May who spoke, exclaiming, "*WHAT?!*"

"He didn't know she existed. He hasn't been monitoring her. And her mother teaches Folklore at UC Berkeley."

Now it was Tybalt's turn to stare at me. He'd apparently missed that part. "He was fool enough to court a *folklorist*?" he asked. "Did he wish to be the one to betray Faerie's existence to the mortals?"

"I doubt he thought about it. People usually don't when they're in love." I raked a hand through my hair again, this time pressing my fingers against the base of my skull. It wouldn't stop the night I was having from giving me a headache, but it made me feel a little better. "Chelsea's mother knows she's not human. We can't change that, although we'll probably have to deal with it before this is over."

"Wait—you mean that's not the problem?" asked May. "Because call me naïve, but that sure sounds like the problem to me."

"It's *a* problem, but it's not the *main* problem." I pulled my hand out of my hair, picking up my coffee cup. "Chelsea is missing. She disappeared earlier today, in full view of her mortal friends. They said she 'just vanished.'"

"Sounds like she figured out how to teleport," said May.

"Or someone figured out she existed and thought she'd be a great way of getting at Etienne," I said. "Maybe I'm being paranoid, but after the last few years, I figure I've earned a little paranoia."

"What do we do now?" asked Quentin.

It was a simple question. It still made me smile, just a little. The situation was bad, and it was going to get worse before it was over . . . but I was part of a "we" now. Once upon a time, not that long ago, I would have been trying to do this on my own, even if there were people willing to help. I hadn't learned to be part of the "we." I hadn't realized how much I needed it.

"We have to find her, and we have to find her fast. I'm going to call Walther and ask him to talk to Bridget, as a fellow faculty member. Tybalt—"

"If you ask that I leave, you will be sorely disappointed by my answer, and I will be even more disappointed by you," he said, with unexpected sharpness.

I blinked. "I wasn't going to ask you to leave. Can you ask your cats to watch for anything out of the ordinary, like an appearing-disappearing Tuatha teenager bopping around the city? We need to figure out where she's been, so we can get the scent of her magic and start tracking her."

"Of course," said Tybalt, not looking entirely mollified.

"What about me?" asked May.

"I'm going to want you to stay here and coordinate things."

My former Fetch frowned. "There has to be more I can do than just that."

"I'm sure there will be. For the moment, though, I need someone at the house to answer the phone, answer the door, and keep everyone posted."

"Okay." May sighed. "Jazz and I can take shifts. She can take over after the sun rises."

"That works," I said, and took a gulp of coffee. "I'm going to call Walther, and then Quentin and I will head for Chelsea's house and see whether we can find her high school. Maybe we'll get lucky and there will be a nice big sign. 'Chelsea Ames was abducted by ...'"

"Wouldn't that be a pleasant change from the norm?" asked Tybalt dryly.

"I'll get my coat," said Quentin, and trotted out of the room, heading for the stairs.

"Okay." I waited until I heard his footsteps on the stairs before looking from May to Tybalt. "You know how this is going to end."

"I do," said Tybalt softly. Even if Chelsea died, Etienne could be accused of treason for betraying the truth of Faerie's existence. And if she lived ... if she lived, life as she knew it was going to be over, one way or the other.

Nothing is ever simple or easy when Faerie meets the mortal world. There are just times when I find myself wishing it didn't have to be quite so hard.

FIVE

I WENT INTO THE KITCHEN to call Walther. I carry a cell phone these days—May and Quentin's nagging wore me down—but I use landlines when I can. It feels more secure. April O'Leary insists the opposite is true, but April isn't objective, since no one's ever going to listen to one of her calls when she doesn't want them to. Being able to control the phone lines has made her a little cocky.

Tybalt followed me. "As we are once again in a state of emergency, I assume we will not be discussing this evening's events," he said, without preamble. His tone was stiff, a sure sign that he was unhappy.

When did I start caring about his moods? "I don't see what there is to talk about," I said, taking the phone off the hook. "I appreciate you helping us look for Chelsea. I know Etienne isn't a friend of yours, but we really need the help."

"I have no quarrel with him," said Tybalt, stiffness becoming sharpness. "October—"

"I need to call Walther." I focused on the phone, dialing Walther's office. Tybalt sighed, making no effort to conceal his irritation. I ignored him. Not the most mature approach to the problem, but it had been working so far. Why mess with a good thing?

Most members of the UC Berkeley faculty ended their office hours around six or seven, when the bulk of the student body was heading off-campus for dinner or back to their dorm rooms to pretend they remembered how to study. Not Walther. His on-duty hours started when everyone else was ending theirs, and he could usually be found in his lab late into the night, mixing chemicals with names I couldn't pronounce for the pleasure of seeing whether or not the result would explode. Explosions seemed to occur more often than not.

"Professor Davies' lab, Professor Davies' mortally endangered graduate student speaking." Jack sounded harried. That was nothing new. Jack usually sounded harried when Walther was playing with hazardous materials. The rest of the time, Jack sounded like someone had slipped sedatives into his mocha. To be honest, I suspected Walther of doing just that.

"Hi, Jack, it's Toby. Is Walther in? I need to ask him something."

"Toby!" Jack's delight was unfeigned. "Are you calling because you're going to take the Professor away for a little while? Because you would not be inconveniencing me in the least. In fact, I would probably be willing to pay you. Actually, take out the 'probably.' I'm supposed to have these papers graded by tomorrow, and he keeps making the lab smell like rotten eggs."

"So why are you doing the grading in the lab at two o'clock in the morning?" I asked, curious despite my own better judgment.

"I share an apartment with three other grad students," said Jack matter-of-factly. "It smells worse than the lab does. Would you like me to get the Professor for you?"

"Please," I said.

"Just a second." There was a scuffling sound as he put the phone down and moved away. I glanced up to find Tybalt watching me with a mixture of curiosity and irritation.

"Walther's graduate student, Jack," I explained. "He's getting Walther for me."

"How charming. Tell me, is he also in a position to get you a measure of common sense? I would gladly reimburse him."

I glowered and was about to demand to know what his problem was when Walther asked, "Toby?"

"Walther, hey." I turned away from Tybalt. "Are you alone?"

"From any other woman, I would assume that question was connected to my social life. From you . . ." Walther laughed. "Yes, I'm alone. I've sent Jack to get us something to drink."

"What are you going to do when he graduates?"

"Find someone new to get my coffee. What do you need?"

I took a deep breath, unsure how to begin. Finally, I took the chicken's route and asked, "Do you know Bridget Ames in the Folklore Department?"

"Sure," said Walther. "She's a nice lady. Single mother. Her students like her. Never yells at me for accidentally triggering the fire alarm."

"How often does that happen?" I asked.

"Often enough that I may never get tenure."

"Right." I took another deep breath. This wasn't going to get easier. "Have you met Bridget's daughter, Chelsea?"

"I haven't had the pleasure." Walther's tone turned suspicious. "Why are you asking?"

"She disappeared on her way home from school this afternoon. Quentin and I are about to go walk her route, see if we can find something that might tell us where she is."

"I didn't know you knew Bridget."

"I don't. I've never met her."

"Then who hired you?"

"Chelsea's father."

There was a moment of silence as Walther thought about that. Finally, he asked, "What aren't you telling me?"

"Her father is Etienne from Shadowed Hills. She's a

changeling, Walther. Bridget knows, and she's managed to keep her hidden from us. And now she's missing."

Walther swore loudly in Welsh before demanding, "How did this happen? How was this *missed*?"

"Etienne likes smart girls who know how to hide their kids from the faeries, I guess. Walther, she's missing, and we need to find her. Is there any way you can talk to Bridget, one faculty member to another, and see if you can get us a picture of Chelsea?"

"Chelsea's disappearance—you don't think it was a normal kidnapping, do you?"

"When a teenage Tuatha changeling disappears in broad daylight? No, I don't. Her friends told Bridget that's what happened—Chelsea just disappeared. If we're lucky, she finally hit the epiphany that unlocked her magic, and she teleported somewhere without knowing how to get back."

"If we're not lucky?"

"Then Etienne's teenage daughter has been stolen by persons unknown, and I have no idea why. You'll talk to Bridget?"

"I will."

"Good. Call me if you learn anything. Open roads, Walther."

"Open roads," he echoed, sounding far more subdued than he had at the beginning of the call, and hung up.

I replaced the receiver in the cradle and turned to find Tybalt watching me. "What?" I asked.

"Are you sure this isn't a matter better left to your liege?"

The question startled me. I'd been expecting another request to talk about what happened in the alley. We'd have to talk about it eventually, since it was clear that Tybalt wasn't going to let the matter drop until we did, but I wasn't ready. "Etienne asked for my help."

"It's true that retrieval of lost things—children, kittens, trinkets—has become a specialty of yours. But are you sure you're prepared for this particular mission?"

"Tybalt . . ."

He sighed. "I don't want to make you angry. I merely fear for your safety."

"I can do my job."

"Really. You can follow a teenage changeling, stolen from her mortal parent, kept from her fae parent, and feel no personal connection that might cloud your judgment?"

I took a sharp breath, forcing myself to count to ten. Finally, when I was sure I could speak without screaming, I said, "This is nothing like what happened with Gillian."

"Isn't it?" Tybalt asked. I wanted to read his tone as mocking, needling me about what happened when Gillian was taken. I couldn't do it. Maybe I'd have been able to do it once, but now, after all we'd been through — after all the times he'd been there when I needed him — I couldn't see his words as anything but what they were: concerned.

"Maybe a little," I said, relenting. "But I have to do this. You know that. I can't just hand this off to someone else and trust that they'll take care of it. I have to bring her *home*."

"Sometimes I wonder if it's because you spent so long lost that you must insist on bringing every lost thing home." Tybalt pushed away from the counter, covering the distance between us in a single fluid motion. He was still wearing his human disguise. I hadn't noticed it before, not with everything else going on. The smell of pennyroyal radiated from his skin. "You can't save everyone and leave yourself lost, October. It isn't fair. Not to you and not to the people who care about you."

"I'm not lost, Tybalt," I said. It was oddly hard to meet his eyes now that they registered as human. His irises were supposed to be malachite green, not muddy hazel, and his pupils were supposed to be oval, not round. "I know exactly where I am."

A smile crossed his face. "If I believed that, I would walk away and never darken your door again. I can forgive you your foolishness only because I know how lost you are. But one day, you'll have to come back home. When you do, I hope you'll find me waiting."

He stepped back abruptly, turning and walking out of the kitchen before I could answer. I stayed frozen where I was, the scent of hot pennyroyal teasing my nostrils.

"What the hell just happened?" I asked.

The empty kitchen didn't answer.

I scowled, for lack of any more definite reaction, and followed Tybalt's path out of the room. Somehow, it wasn't a surprise when he wasn't in the living room. May and Quentin were, both of them watching me approach. Quentin looked confused. May looked oddly disappointed, as though she'd been hoping for some other outcome.

"Don't start," I told her, before turning to Quentin. "You have everything you need?"

"Coat, cell phone, emergency cab fare, knife," recited Quentin.

"Good. Now make yourself presentable."

Quentin nodded, the scent of steel and heather rising as he gathered the magic to weave himself a human disguise. I did the same, pulling strands of air toward me until all I could taste was copper, and the tingling itch of false humanity lay light across my skin.

May was still watching me with disappointed eyes when I finished. I sighed. "Call me if there's any word, okay? Walther's trying to get us a picture of Chelsea."

"Be careful out there." May paused, disappointment turning rueful as she added, "Not that you will be. I just have to say it, you know?"

"I know. Come on, Quentin." My squire followed me out of the house. I paused only to retrieve my leather jacket from the rack by the door. Chelsea needed us. We needed to move.

Our house was huge compared to the San Francisco norm, since it was never reconstructed to suit modern standards. It also had something that elevated it from "nice" to "people would kill to live here": a covered two-car parking area at the end of a short but private driveway. The neighbor to our right had been parking there for years while the house stood empty. He'd been offering me increasingly large sums of money to use the carport since we moved in. So far, I'd been able to keep rebuffing him—although I had a strong suspicion he was behind the noise complaints someone had phoned in to the local police. As if we'd be making inappropriately loud noises at seven o'clock in the morning? We were all in bed by then. Yes, I needed the money. But I needed not to have a random human in my garage even more.

Quentin waited patiently as I performed my customary check for intruders in the back seat—fool me once, shame on you, fool me twice, not in this lifetime—before unlocking the doors. "Where are we going?" he asked.

"Berkeley," I replied. "We're going to walk to Chelsea's high school."

"Do we know which one it is?"

"No. But we know where she lives. If she's being allowed to walk alone or with friends, she must be going to school within a mile of her house."

"I don't go to school within a mile of my house," Quentin said, getting into the car.

I did the same on the driver's side. "One, you don't go to school at all, unless you count your lessons with Etienne. And if you're counting those, you don't walk to Shadowed Hills. Either I drive you or we put you on BART and make you get there on your own. Two, I don't even know where your house is, beyond 'somewhere in Canada,' so I'm pretty sure you're playing by a different set of rules."

Quentin frowned. "I used to go to school."

I paused. For a while, Quentin had attended College Park High School in Pleasant Hill, playing human and learning about the mortal world at the same time. That stopped when Blind Michael stole Quentin's human girlfriend and brought his masquerade to a forced end. "True," I admitted. "And when you did, you were going to a school within a mile of the knowe."

"It still might not be universal. Some people came

from farther away. They'd transferred from other schools in the district, or their parents moved after they started and didn't want to make them switch schools."

He had a point. "Okay. You're right. It's just ... the rules are different for humans. Human parents like to know where their children are all the time, especially when they're school age. Chelsea's sixteen. That means her mother isn't going to want her walking very far."

"Katie's mom was like that," allowed Quentin. "Humans are weird."

"You have no idea," I said, and started the engine.

Quentin was sent to Shadowed Hills by his parents around four years ago. To be honest, every time something went wrong, I expected his parents to summon him home. The fact that they didn't meant one of two things. Either they were incredibly determined to stick by whatever principles caused them to have him fostered in the first place ... or they didn't care. I honestly hoped it was the first. I couldn't imagine sending my child to live with strangers the way they had, but that's because so much of my upbringing was human. Fostering is common among the fae. It's what keeps us from stagnating—and hell, when you and your children can reasonably expect to live forever, what's wrong with missing a few years of teenage rebellion? Quentin mostly seemed to be doing his rebelling by refusing to be left behind when I charged into danger. That was hazardous to his health but probably easier on his parents' nerves than his constantly slamming doors and shouting about how much he hated them.

My teenage years were spent in my mother's shadow, a half-human wraith haunting the Summerlands and praying for a way out. There are worse things than a blind fosterage. If Chelsea's mother wanted to be protective, let her. More parents should get to have that choice.

I realized my thoughts were trending toward Gillian and tried to pull them back, to no avail. Thinking about my daughter was too easy these days, especially after what had been done to her—what *I* had done to her.

Sometimes when I slept, I still saw her in a meadow that never existed, split into three people, one human, one fae, one the changeling girl I carried inside me for nine months. In my dreams, she said "human," and I ignored her, shoving her into an eternal life she'd never asked for and wouldn't know how to handle. Anything so I wouldn't have to dream giving her up over and over again.

Quentin was silent as we drove, not even fiddling with the radio. I could feel the weight of his gaze, his concern practically becoming a third passenger in the car. He was as worried about me as May and Tybalt were. He just didn't know how to go about expressing it. Maybe that was why, of the three of them, he was the one I had the easiest time dealing with.

Traffic was light this late at night, and we made it from San Francisco to Berkeley without delays. Bridget and Chelsea actually lived in Albany, a small suburb far enough from the university that housing was almost affordable. I navigated the twisting side streets sprouting off Solano Avenue like the roots of a tree. Their house was easy to spot: it was the only one on the block with the lights on. I wondered how nocturnal Chelsea was and how much Bridget had been able to adjust her schedule to accommodate her daughter. Chelsea was attending a human high school, but that didn't mean much; teenagers show an amazing capacity to function while sleep-deprived, whether they're mortal, fae, or somewhere in-between.

I drove about a block farther along the street before finally snagging a parking space. I pulled into it, stopping the engine, and turned to Quentin. "It's going to be a little weird that we're out here, but I don't want to throw a don't-look-here if it means we might miss any traces Chelsea's magic left," I said. "If anyone asks, I'm your aunt or something."

Quentin looked at me, clearly amused. "What, you're not my mother?"

"Thankfully, no." We looked oddly similar with our

human disguises on—we both had blue eyes, although his were dulled down from his true appearance, while mine were oversaturated compared to their natural colorless gray. His dishwater blond hair was lightened from its natural bronze, while mine was barely changed. As long as we looked human, we looked enough alike to pass.

"Okay, big sis."

"Don't push it." I climbed out of the car. The air was warmer than it was in San Francisco, but not by much; the smell of the sea and the eucalyptus trees was replaced by freshly mowed grass and wood-burning fireplaces. Everything was silent. This was suburbia, and it was a whole different world from the one we were used to.

"We passed a high school about a mile back," I said. "Think we should check it out?"

"Are you going to care if I say 'no'?"

"No."

"Then yes."

"Good squire. Come on." We walked down the sidewalk, stepping over cracks and around broken pavement where tree roots had managed to break through. There was something comforting about the silence between us. It was free of subtext and accusations and expectations. Quentin just wanted me to be there for him. So far, I was managing that much, if not much more.

Of course, I wouldn't have been managing anything if Tybalt hadn't interrupted those drug dealers. Maybe Tybalt was right when he said that we needed to have a conversation about the way I'd been acting lately. Maybe—

The lingering scent of magic in front of the Ames house hit me so hard that I stopped, staggering backward as if someone had punched me in the stomach. Quentin stopped in turn, his expression broadcasting confusion and alarm. "Toby?"

"Hang on." I raised a hand to quiet him, taking deep, slow breaths as I tried to figure out what I was standing in the middle of. He stopped talking but didn't move away.

My mother, Amandine, raised me as one of the Daoine Sidhe. I didn't find out until recently that she was lying the whole time. She was Firstborn, the daughter of Oberon and an unnamed woman, and I was the first of a new race of fae—the Dóchas Sidhe. Exactly what we were for was yet to be determined. But if there was one thing we were made to do, it was blood magic, and the unique scents that accompany each person's spellcasting are fundamentally tied to who and what they are—their blood.

Etienne's signature was cedar smoke and lime juice. This scent was similar enough that I would have known the caster was related even if we hadn't been looking for his daughter. Not cedar smoke, though; this was sycamore smoke. It was covered by a delicate veneer of calla lily flowers, softening and sweetening it. The trace was complicated, and got more complicated as I looked deeper. Some of it was fresh, but some of it was old—months, even years of little spells overlaying this one spot. Chelsea had been coming into her powers for a while before she disappeared. That wasn't a good sign.

"Oak and ash," I breathed.

"Toby?"

I shook my head. "We're on the right track. This is the way she walks to school."

"Yes, it is," said a voice behind me—female, with the faintest trace of an Irish accent, as though the speaker had been away from home for so long that her roots were just another story. "Now would you like to tell me what you're doing out here, or shall I be calling the police now?"

There are times when I think the universe is only happy when it has an excuse to make me miserable. "We'd rather you didn't do that, if you don't mind," I said, turning. The woman on the sidewalk about six feet away was wearing a blue bathrobe and holding a cast iron frying pan in one hand. "Is there a problem?"

"Etienne sent you, didn't he?"

I couldn't keep myself from flinching. My reaction

was slight, but it was enough. Her eyes narrowed, and she brandished the frying pan at us like a weapon.

Slowly, enunciating each word with great care to be sure I couldn't misunderstand her, Bridget Ames said, "Give me back my daughter right now, or I swear to God, I'll kill you."

Oh, great. It was going to be one of those nights.

SIX

QUENTIN WAS SMART ENOUGH to stay behind me. I raised my hands in a placating gesture, saying, "I don't know who you think we are, but we don't have your daughter. We're not kidnappers."

"Then hold this." She thrust the frying pan toward us. It was cold—it had to be, or she wouldn't be able to hold the handle—but it might as well have been heated to the point of melting from the way it seemed to twist and warp the air when she got it close to me. I must have looked like I was going to throw up, because a triumphant smile twisted the corners of her lips as she said, "I keep it rubbed down with a mixture of crushed juniper berries and rowan ash. Don't you like the way it makes the metal shine?"

That explained the heat. Normal iron hurts, and it's possible to get iron poisoning from staying close to the stuff for too long. It's not a pleasant experience; I don't recommend it. But rubbing the frying pan with two of the oldest charms against the fae had amped its natural properties to the point where I wouldn't be surprised if touching the metal burned my skin.

"It's lovely," I said, taking an involuntary half step back. "Really, though. I don't like to handle other people's cookware."

"That's the best you can manage? That's your bright, bold lie?"

"Look, lady, I don't know about you, but I've never had somebody corner me on a dark street and try to hand me a frying pan before," I snapped. I could hear Quentin moving. I hoped that meant he was getting farther away, not preparing to do something stupid. Sadly, after spending so much time with me, he was just as likely to be getting ready to charge.

Bridget blinked before barking a single, sharp sound I assumed was a form of pained laughter. "This is what the Fair Folk have come to? This is the great threat of the hollow hills?"

"Um, no. This is a San Francisco native and her—" I struggled to find a word that existed in the modern mortal parlance, and settled for the Batmanesque, "—ward, wishing you'd stop waving that thing at us and back the hell off. We don't want your frying pan."

"Because you can't touch it, is that right?" Bridget's lips firmed into a resolute line. "My shirt's inside-out, there's bread in my pockets, and I've a firm grasp on this pan. Take a step toward me, and you'll regret it."

"But you're between us and the car," said Quentin, with puzzled practicality.

"I'm not sure she's thinking clearly right now." I lowered my hands. Shooting for a soothing tone, I asked, "Is there a reason you're out here threatening us with your frying pan?"

Bridget gave me a withering look. "You can refuse to talk to me. You can lie to me—lord knows, it's what your people are renowned for. But don't you dare talk to me like I'm an idiot. My little girl is missing. You bastards left us alone for sixteen years. Why couldn't you have stayed gone? No one believes in you anymore. Why couldn't you let us be?"

I hesitated. The pain on her face was familiar; it was a pain I'd felt myself, when it seemed that the human world had stolen my daughter from me. No mother should have to feel that way. The secrecy of Faerie is one of our oldest traditions . . . but it had already been broken where Bridget was concerned. Etienne broke it long before I appeared on the scene, while I was still wearing fins and scales and unable to do anything for anyone, not even myself.

I glanced over my shoulder at Quentin. He met my eyes and nodded. He knew what I was about to do. I couldn't say whether he approved, but he knew, and that was enough for me. If I was going to blow his cover as well as my own, I wanted him to know that it was coming.

"We don't have your daughter, and neither does Etienne," I said, turning back to Bridget. She stiffened. "He called me because finding lost children is a specialty of mine. I don't take them. I bring them home. Please, believe me. We're not here to hurt you. We're here to help."

"Then why didn't you come to my doorbell and tell me this without being forced?" she demanded.

"Because we're not used to telling humans 'oh, hey, we exist,'" I said. Quentin stepped up next to me as I continued, "And because you thought—maybe you still think, I don't know—Etienne took Chelsea. He didn't, Bridget, I swear it on my father's grave. Etienne isn't that kind of man. He didn't even know she existed before you called him."

A car roared past on the street, abruptly reminding me that there was more to the world than the three of us standing in the dark and discussing things that were never intended to be discussed at all—not with humans anyway. I sighed.

"My name is October," I said. "This is my squire, Quentin. We want to help. We want to make sure that Chelsea is safe. You don't have to believe me, although it would probably be good if you did. I just want you to ask yourself something."

"What's that?" asked Bridget warily.

"If Etienne had your daughter, would he have sent us here? And if he didn't send us, would we have come at all?" Sometimes I think the real tragedy of the intersection between humanity and the fae is how much both sides get wrong. Bridget thought she knew everything about us, and she'd lived in fear when she didn't have to. She would always have lost Chelsea—that's the unfortunate reality of being a human and having a child with the fae—but she could have been with Etienne all that time. She didn't have to spend those years looking over her shoulder, waiting for the ax to fall.

There was a pause as she considered my words. Finally, she lowered the frying pan. "I don't trust you."

"That's fine."

"I *won't* trust you."

"That's fine, too; we're not asking you to trust us. We're just asking you to let us help. Please. For Chelsea's sake, if not yours." I hesitated, and then added, "I mean, technically, I guess we're family."

Bridget barked another of those short, sharp laughs, lowering the frying pan. "Some family you are. You owe sixteen years of birthday presents."

"I'll be sure to let Etienne know." I breathed out a little, relaxing now that the frying pan wasn't being brandished in my direction. "We were planning to walk Chelsea's route to school. Does she go to Colusa High?"

"Yes," said Bridget, wariness returning. "How did you know?"

"I have a daughter, too. She lives with her human father." Saying the words made the tiny wounded place inside me ache even more. Gillian lived with her human father, because Gillian was human. Thanks to me, she would never be anything else. "I know there's no way she'd be walking to school if she had to go more than a mile. Etienne said Chelsea was walking home from school when she disappeared. Colusa High was the only school that fit the profile."

"You have a daughter? With a human man?" Bridget's tone thawed a little; perhaps she was finally allowing herself to believe we might be here for the right reasons. "What's her name?"

"Gillian. She's a few years older than Chelsea. She

was kidnapped last year, and I would have done anything to get her back. *Anything.* Even if it meant trusting people I wasn't sure about." I shook my head. "If a human kidnapper took Chelsea, you called Etienne for nothing. I don't think you would have done that. Not after sixteen years of being careful. That means you really think it was one of us. If you're right, don't you need our help?"

For a moment, I thought I might have pushed too hard. Then, reluctantly, Bridget nodded. "What can I do?"

"Well, first, can we get off the street? I'm feeling a little exposed, and I'd like to see Chelsea's room." If the smell of smoke and calla lilies was this strong on the open street, I wanted to see how strong it was in an enclosed space.

Bridget hesitated before nodding again. "Follow me," she said, turning to march up the walk to her house.

Quentin and I followed at a more sedate pace, neither of us all that anxious to go where the woman with the anti-fae frying pan led. "Are you sure about this?" he asked.

"Nope," I said calmly. "I just don't have any better ideas, and I really want to get a look at that room."

"Tybalt's going to kill me," he muttered.

"What was that?"

"Nothing."

The door was locked, even though Bridget had gone no farther than the sidewalk. She looked back over her shoulder at us as she unlocked it, saying, "You can't be too careful."

A lock wouldn't stop a truly determined Tuatha de Dannan or Cait Sidhe. For once, I thought before I spoke and didn't say that out loud. "It's a scary world out there," I said.

Bridget nodded and opened the door. The smell of sycamore smoke and calla lilies poured out, a hundred times stronger than it had been on the street. Schooling my expression to keep from giving away just how thick the smell of Chelsea's magic was, I followed Bridget inside. Quentin was right behind me.

It only took one look at the living room walls for me to realize there was no need to ask for a picture of Chelsea. There were pictures of Chelsea everywhere. She was a sweet-faced little girl who grew into a beautiful teenager over the course of dozens of images. Her delicate bone structure might have tipped me off to the presence of some fae blood in her lineage, but I would never have pegged her as a full changeling. I frowned, studying the pictures more closely.

"Oh," I said, finally. "I see."

Bridget looked at me. "Do you?"

In every picture, Chelsea's brown-black hair—something she inherited from her father—was styled to cover her ears. The lenses of her glasses were tinted, making it hard to tell what color her eyes were. "Does she need glasses?" I asked.

"No," said Bridget. Her expression softened as she looked at Chelsea's picture, the hard edges going out of it until she was just a mother, scared for the safety of her child. "She started wearing them when she was six. They're tinted glass."

"Rose-colored glasses. Literally," I said. Etienne's eyes had a copper sheen to them, glittering, metallic, and inhuman. If his daughter had his hair, the odds were good she had his eyes as well. "How long have you known?"

"That my lover wasn't human? I suspected from the first, but I told myself I was making up stories. I was new to the department, I missed Ireland, and here was this mysterious stranger come to argue with me and spin me yarns and be exactly what I needed, exactly when I needed it. I thought he had to be one of the Sidhe, come to save me from myself . . . and then thought I was being a fool, because everyone knows the Sidhe don't exist." The smile she shot my way was bitter. "I suppose that makes me twice a fool, doesn't it?"

"No," said Quentin. "It makes us what you said we were. It makes us really good liars."

I glanced at him, surprised by his quick response. He looked at me and shrugged, looking slightly embarrassed.

"It's true," he said. "We are."

"I just didn't expect you to say it," I said.

"That reminds me." Bridget raised the frying pan again. "I'll thank you to take off whatever masks you're wearing. I like seeing who it is I've allowed into my home."

Quentin and I exchanged a look. It seemed like every time I thought we'd broken all the rules, another one popped up for us to violate. "I'm not sure . . ." I began.

"Please."

That stopped me. I sighed, once, and let my human disguise wisp away into the smell of cut grass and copper. Quentin did the same, and the smell of our mingled magics briefly overwhelmed the smell of smoke and lilies. It was a pleasant change, even if it didn't last.

Bridget's eyes went wide and round. It was one thing to challenge two strangers and declare them to be part of a hidden world existing alongside her own. It was something else to have it proved. It probably didn't help that the similarities in our human disguises were washed away by our true appearances. Quentin is Daoine Sidhe, bright and vibrant as something from a fairy tale. I, on the other hand, look as though half my color was stolen from me by the villain from some children's TV show.

Oh, and there were bullet holes in my jacket. Can't forget those.

"What are you?" she whispered, finally.

"Quentin is Daoine Sidhe," I said. "I'm Dóchas Sidhe. We're . . . cousins, I guess." It was close enough; both races descended from Oberon, although Titania claimed the Daoine Sidhe as her own. "What we are doesn't matter. Finding Chelsea is what matters. Can I see her room?"

"Yes, of course," said Bridget, tossing the frying pan onto the couch before beckoning for us to follow her. Apparently, disorientation made her agreeable. Then again, it might also be the deep conditioning of human history at work, the old lessons that say, "mess with the fae, and you'll regret it." Now that she could really see us, maybe she didn't feel she could fight us anymore. Either way, I was just glad she'd dropped the frying pan.

The smell of smoke and lilies got stronger as we walked down the hall. By the time we stopped in front of a door decorated with the poster from the third *Lord of the Rings* movie, it was all I could do not to breathe through my mouth to avoid choking.

"This is her room," said Bridget needlessly.

"I kind of figured," I said. I sneezed, once, before turning to Quentin. "Wait out here with Bridget, okay?"

"Okay," he said.

Catching Bridget's sudden irritation, I explained, "I can sort of detect magic, but it works best when I'm alone." And better still if someone has bled recently, but since Chelsea was taken from the street, that was probably too much to hope for. "I promise I'm not going to do anything to your daughter's things. You can even keep the door open and watch me."

"Oh, I will," she said . . . but she opened the door, releasing a cloying wave of lily-and-smoke perfume. "Don't you dare take anything."

"I won't," I said, and went in.

Chelsea's room was practically spotless, especially for a teenage girl. There were no dolls or plastic horses; instead, she had rows of neatly shelved secondhand paperbacks, build-it-yourself model kits, and what looked like a working microscope. The walls were covered in *Star Trek* and *Firefly* posters, and she had posters for the first and second *Lord of the Rings* movies taped to her ceiling. A too-small bedspread patterned with spaceships and planets was folded over the foot of her bed, the remnant of a childhood she wasn't willing to let go of yet. I turned slowly in place, a lump in my throat that wasn't caused just by the difficulty of breathing through the miasma of Chelsea's magic. She deserved better than whatever was happening to her . . . and she deserved better than what was going to happen to her when she was finally found.

I closed my eyes, breathing deep as I searched for something—anything—that might help us track Chelsea. What I found was enough to make me stiffen in surprise. "Oh, oak and ash, that's not good," I murmured. Opening my eyes again, I looked around the room, gaze settling on the composition notebook next to the microscope. I reached for it.

"What are you doing?" demanded Bridget.

"I need to check something," I said. "Both of you, stay out in the hall, please."

As I'd hoped, a girl who kept her room as neat as Chelsea did, and who had such an obvious interest in science, also kept very careful notes. The notebook was full of columns showing dates, times, locations, and what she called "relevant factors." Everything was written in heavy block letters, making it easy to read, even if it took me a moment to understand.

"Oak and ash," I repeated, and added a human, "Fuck. Quentin, can you come in here?"

"Sure." He walked over to me, followed by Bridget, who seemed to have decided "stay in the hall" only applied as long as she and Quentin were both doing it. I didn't comment on her presence. I just handed Quentin the notebook.

He frowned at the pages, brow furrowing for a moment before it smoothed out as his expression became one of pure surprise. "Was she *experimenting* with herself?"

"She was," I confirmed. Bridget looked utterly bewildered. Taking pity, I explained, "Etienne said that you knew he was Tuatha de Dannan. What you may not know is that they're teleporters, and so is Chelsea. Based on what's written here she's been opening small portals for the last year or so. She's been testing what she can do."

"That's not possible. I would have known."

"Have you ever encouraged her to use her magic? Or

have you told her to hide it, no matter what?" Bridget's silence was answer enough. I continued: "She wanted to know what she could do. And I think she managed to catch someone's attention."

What I didn't say was that if the locations in Chelsea's book were accurate—and I had no reason to suspect they weren't—she was opening portals that stretched a lot farther than she should have been able to manage. Etienne could go from Pleasant Hill to San Francisco, if he stretched. His little girl had recorded trips from Albany to Vancouver. And that wasn't good. There are always stories about changelings with too much power. None of them end well.

"Where is she?" whispered Bridget.

"I don't know. But we're going to find out." I held up the book. "Can I take this?"

Clearly reluctant, Bridget nodded.

"Okay. We have to go now. We have to go and find your daughter." Assuming she was still alive. And that, unfortunately, was looking like an increasingly big assumption.

SEVEN

WE REWOVE OUR HUMAN DISGUISES before we
left. Bridget didn't argue about our leaving—I think
she was too stunned to try to make us stay. She let me
keep Chelsea's notebook and even gave us a recent picture from the living room wall. I gave her my cell number, asking her to call if she thought of anything that
might help us find Chelsea. She wouldn't call. I could see
it in her face. But maybe having something as concrete
as a phone number would give her a little bit of comfort
in the days ahead. I'm a big believer in giving comfort
whenever possible. Maeve knows, it can be a hard thing
to hold onto.

Besides, there was no way she could use the phone
number to track me. April O'Leary set up my account,
and I wasn't sure it strictly existed from the mortal per-
spective. If Bridget decided not to trust me, all she'd get
from tracing my number was a headache.

Speaking of headaches . . . I waited until Quentin and
I were safely in the car, away from human ears, before I
asked, "You realize what our next step is, right?"

Quentin frowned. "Is this one of those questions
where I'm supposed to work out the answer for myself,
as a training thing, or is it one of the questions where you
give me the answer, so I shouldn't even bother trying?"

"The latter," I said. "We need to talk to the Luidaeg."

Quentin's frown vanished, replaced by a wide grin. "I was hoping you'd say that. Do we need to go see Walther first, while we're already in Berkeley?"

"I'll call him and let him know the situation, but we don't need to go by. I still want to drive past Chelsea's school and see whether we can find the spot she disappeared from—the human authorities may have missed something—but we can head for the Luidaeg's after that. Maybe we can even get there before dawn."

"Can we stop for donuts?"

The question wasn't as crazy as it sounded. Yes, we were in the beginning stages of a kidnapping investigation, and yes, time was *not* on our side . . . but if we were going to the Luidaeg, a little bribery wouldn't hurt.

The Luidaeg is the daughter of Oberon and Maeve, which technically makes her my aunt. Maybe that's why she hasn't killed me yet, although it's just as likely to be the fact that I amuse her. May says we're reenacting *The Princess Bride*, one "I'll most likely kill you in the morning" at a time. Whatever her motives, the Luidaeg is one of my strongest, and strangest, allies. If anyone would know how to handle the issue of a changeling with more power than she was supposed to have, it was the Luidaeg.

She was also the single person most likely to let me explain things without freaking out. The Luidaeg is older than any of the laws of Faerie, and remembers a time when humans and the fae consorted openly, with no lies or illusions between us. She might not approve of Chelsea, but she wouldn't be horrified by her the way some others would be.

And the Luidaeg likes donuts. "Sure, we can stop," I said. "What time is it?"

"Almost four-thirty."

"Let's get back to the right side of the Bay, park long enough for dawn to pass, and then swing by Dynamo for the early morning batch. The Luidaeg likes their salted caramel." Quentin wrinkled his nose. I sighed. "I wouldn't take us onto the bridge if I thought there was any chance we'd be caught out by the dawn. We have nearly an hour until sunrise. Trust me?"

"Yes, ma'am," he said.

"Don't call me ma'am," I said, and started the car.

Quentin smirked.

His concern wasn't unfounded. Dawn is anathema to faerie enchantments. Something about the way the sun hits the land during the first moments of the day tears down small spells and weakens great ones, smashing the magic out of the world. It never lasts more than ten minutes, but that was more than long enough to have a fatal car accident if I was behind the wheel when it hit. Dawn isn't as painful for me as it was before Amandine shifted the balance of my blood, but it's still impossible to breathe in those few minutes when the air pushes down like a blanket made of lead and everything tastes of death and ashes.

We drove down Colusa with the windows open. Patches of the smoke-and-lily scent that meant "Chelsea" appeared along the length of the street, some fresh, some faded. None of them stood out as the place she'd disappeared from, and Quentin didn't seem to notice them at all. I stopped the car next to one of the stronger patches, frowning at him.

"Do you smell *anything?*"

"Not really," he admitted. "Her room smelled like old magic, a little. Out here, there's nothing."

"Great. One more attraction for the freak show that is my life—apparently, Dóchas Sidhe are magic detectors, not just blood detectors. Chelsea was here. She was here a lot. I think she opened some of her doors from this spot."

Quentin opened her notebook, riffling through the pages. "Is this the corner of Portland and Colusa?" he asked.

"Yes."

"This says she opened a door from here to . . . um. To Portland, Oregon. And then back again." He raised his head, staring at me. "Can she do that?"

"You've heard the old stories. What do you think?"

He closed the book. "I think we need to find her."

"Yeah. So do I." I glanced at the sky. Our sweep of the street had taken almost twenty minutes. "I guess we're going to be a little late to the Luidaeg's. I'm not risking the bridge this close to dawn."

Quentin looked relieved. "Good."

I snorted and started the car again, hitting the gas harder as I angled up the hill toward Tilden Park. It's a protected nature preserve, surprisingly wild for being so close to human habitation, and it's full of secluded picnic areas where we could wait out the sunrise without being spotted.

The sky was turning rose and gold around the edges by the time I parked in the shadow of one of the old oak groves. Quentin and I didn't discuss what we were going to do next; we just got out of the car, both of us heading as fast as we could for the shelter of the trees. If any early morning joggers wanted to park in this lot, they'd see the car, but they wouldn't see us. Hopefully, that would give us time to put on human disguises, hide, or both before we got caught. The car was just out of sight when the sun came up, and the world came down.

"Not as bad as it used to be" doesn't mean "pleasant." The light knocked the air out of my lungs. I grabbed the nearest tree, clinging for dear life as I tried to avoid crumpling to the muddy path. Dimly, through my tears, I could see Quentin doing the same thing a few trees away. The ashy smell of broken illusions rose around us.

Dawn is difficult to describe. When I was little, I honestly thought I was dying every time the sun rose. I couldn't imagine what it must have been like for Chelsea, whose mother couldn't truly understand what she was going through or why she stopped breathing, like clockwork, every morning at sunrise. It's the death of magic, the end of faerie time, and it hits us like a hammer.

Dawn passed quickly—dawn always passes—and we were fortunate: no joggers or pre-work dog walkers came down the path before we were able to straighten up, put our human faces back on, and make ourselves look halfway presentable.

"Well," I said, with forced jocularity. "Ready to go and sit in rush hour traffic for the foreseeable future?"

Quentin looked at me mournfully. "Can we stop for food first? I'm starving."

"You're a teenage boy. You're always starving."

"That's a good reason to feed me."

I had to smile at that. "Drive-through okay?"

"After as much time as I've spent with you? Please. I didn't expect anything better."

We were still laughing as we walked out of the trees—as much a stress reaction as anything else. In addition to knocking down any small spells, the pressure of dawn tends to cause a massive fight-or-flight response, which is just cruel, since the *pain* of dawn makes both options impossible. The end result is a lot of extra adrenaline in the bloodstream, frequently followed by a massive collapse. There's a reason most fae go to bed shortly after sunrise.

Our laughter died when the parking lot came into view. Quentin stopped dead. I took one more step forward, reaching back to press my palm against his chest. It was the clearest way I could tell him to stay where he was without actually speaking.

Then again, the creature stretched out on top of the car might have been enough to keep him from moving.

"Toby . . ."

"I see it."

Whatever it was, it was the size of a cow, and looked like what you'd get if you somehow managed to cross a beaver and a crocodile, looked at the results, and decided what your new monster really needed was a bunch of extra teeth. Its eyes were closed, and its head was resting on its webbed forepaws. That was probably the only reason it hadn't spotted us yet.

Keeping my hand against Quentin's chest, I started backing him up. He went willingly. Once we were hidden by the trees, I stopped, dropping my hand. "That's . . . new," I said, slowly.

"What is it?"

"Big. Carnivorous, if the teeth are anything to go by. Big. On top of the car. Big. Possibly dangerous. Oh, and did I mention big?"

"I was starting to get the idea that it might be big, yeah," said Quentin, peering around me. Fear made what might have been a sarcastic comment sound sincere. "What now?"

"I don't know. Even if we wanted to ditch the car, we can't get out of here without going past the thing."

Quentin sounded suddenly hopeful as he asked, "Do you have your sword?"

"Yes." He brightened. "It's in the car." He dimmed again. I continued, "Besides, even if I had my sword with me, I'm not going to attack something I've never seen before. What if it spits acid? Or grows new heads when you cut off the old one? Attacking mystery monsters is never a good idea."

"Well, we can't stay in the woods forever. We have things to do."

"I'm aware." I peeked around the trees, checking to be sure the monster was still on the car. It was. At least that meant we knew where it was. I retreated back to my position next to Quentin. "Keep an eye on the thing. Let me know if it moves."

"What should I do if it tries to eat me?"

"Scream." I pulled my cell phone from my jacket pocket, taking a few more steps into the cover of the trees before dialing the most useful number I could think of: Shadowed Hills. When it comes to getting rid of monsters, there's no one better than my liege lord, Duke Sylvester Torquill.

The phone rang six times—enough that I was starting to worry that everyone had gone to bed—before someone picked up the other end. A bleary female voice said, "Hello?"

"Melly, hey." Melly has been working at Shadowed

Hills almost as long as the Duchy has existed. She's also the mother of one of my childhood friends, a half-Hob changeling named Kerry. Nothing happens at Shadowed Hills without Melly knowing about it. "It's Toby. Look, uh, sorry about calling this late. Is the Duke up?"

"Toby?" Melly's tone sharpened, bleariness falling away. "Darlin', what are you doing out of bed, with the sun full up? Are you feeling all right? Do I need to bring you some soup?"

"I'm fine, really, and so is Quentin. I just need to talk to Sylvester. Is he up?"

"For you, m'dear, he's always up. Just you wait here, and I'll fetch him for you."

"Oh, don't worry," I said, glancing toward Quentin. He was staring at the monster, an expression of intent concentration on his face. "I'm not going anywhere."

It took almost ten minutes for Melly to rouse Sylvester and drag him back to the phone—ten minutes Quentin and I spent waiting for the monster on my car to wake up and come looking for a snack. Finally, there was a scuffling sound as the receiver was picked up, and my liege said, "October? What's wrong?"

Voice tight, I said, "I'm in Tilden Park with Quentin. We're at the picnic area near the big lake. There's something on my car, and I don't know what it is."

"What do you mean by 'something'?" asked Sylvester. The cobwebs were clearing from his voice as he woke up, leaving him sharp and focused. That was good. I needed him focused.

"I mean it's the size of a cow, it's got fur and scales and a really disturbing number of teeth, and since I don't know what it *is*, I don't know if it's going to try to *eat* me if I get near it."

There was a long pause. Finally, Sylvester said, "That seems less than ideal."

"Yeah, it is. Do you have any ideas?"

"Yes. You should stay where you are. Etienne and I will be right there."

"Sylvester—" The line went dead. I clicked my phone

shut, glaring at it for a moment before looking toward Quentin and saying, "He's on his way."

"Maybe he'll bring a sword."

"Maybe he'll bring a *tank*." I shook my head. "I hate being rescued."

"So why aren't we trying to get to the car?"

"Because I hate being eaten even more."

We stayed in the shelter of the trees for another ten minutes, occasionally stealing glances at the monster on my car. Our luck was holding, thus far; no humans had shown up to discover our unwanted hitchhiker and freak out as a natural consequence. Most fae know when an illusion is being cast on them. I didn't dare use a don't-look-here on the monster; that might just wake it up, and I had serious doubts about whether it was going to wake up friendly.

The smell of limes and cedar smoke drifted from the clearing behind us a half-second before I heard footsteps crunching on the blanket of fallen leaves covering the dry ground. I turned, relieved, to see Sylvester and Etienne stepping out of a hole cut into the air.

"Your Grace," I said, dipping a quick curtsy. Etienne's eyes were fixed on my face as I straightened, clearly searching for the answer to a question he wasn't willing to voice aloud. I gave a small shake of my head. He looked disappointed, but nodded.

Sylvester looked between us, one eyebrow raised. "Is there something I should know?"

"Not yet," I said.

"There are times when I wish I didn't trust you quite so thoroughly," said Sylvester, looking faintly amused. "I am glad you called me."

"Who else am I going to call when there's a monster on my car?" Still, I let him pull me into a hug, taking a moment—just a moment, but a precious one—to relax into the dogwood and daffodil smell of his arms. Sylvester has meant safety my whole life, ever since the night he stepped out of the air and asked whether I wanted to be fae or human. It's supposed to be your fae parent who offers you the Changeling's Choice. Amandine wouldn't, so he did. He's been a sort of father to me ever since, even when I wasn't willing to admit that to myself.

Like Quentin, Sylvester is Daoine Sidhe. Also like Quentin, Sylvester is upsettingly attractive, with hair the color of fox fur and eyes like summer honey. Every Torquill I've ever met has had those eyes. He used to be a hero, before he retired to Shadowed Hills and took up full-time regency. He's also the man who taught me how to hold a sword, although he's a hell of a lot better than I'm ever likely to be. I attribute it to a combination of natural talent and centuries of practice.

Sylvester let me go, stepping back. "Now," he said. "About this monster."

I appreciated that he wasn't going to take this as an opportunity to remind me that I was welcome at Shadowed Hills whenever I wanted to come, or to tell me I didn't visit enough. Shadowed Hills had meant Connor for too long, during the years when he was married to Sylvester's daughter, Rayseline. I was already haunted by my own memory. I didn't need to be haunted by the halls where my lover had lived.

Motioning for everyone to be quiet, I waved Sylvester and Etienne to the edge of the trees and pointed to the brown hulk atop my car. Sylvester gasped. And then he did the last thing I expected: he left the cover of the trees and ran, empty-handed, toward the monster.

"Sylvester!" I hissed. I whipped around to stare at Etienne. "Stop him! He's going to get hurt!"

Etienne had an odd look on his face, like he was unsure whether or not he was dreaming. "No," he said, slowly. "I don't believe he is."

"Whoa," said Quentin.

I turned back to the parking lot. Sylvester had reached the creature and was scratching it behind one of its small round ears. The creature was awake, and seemed to be enjoying the attention; it was wagging its spadelike tail, slamming it against my car's rear windshield.

"What the . . . ?"

"It is an Afanc," said Etienne, sounding stunned. "There is an Afanc atop your car."

My own eyes widened. "What? No. That's not possible. Afanc don't exist anymore."

"The evidence would seem to suggest otherwise."

I just stared. Afanc are fae monsters, like Barghests or bogeys. They live in lakes and marshes and are reasonably harmless, as long as you don't startle them and get yourself drowned. At least, that's what the old stories said. No one had seen one in centuries. They weren't indigenous to the Summerlands, and so far as I knew, they'd never managed to establish a population outside of Faerie. Even if they weren't extinct, there was no way an Afanc should have been in the mortal world, crushing the roof of my car.

"This is wonderful!" Sylvester twisted around to beam at us, still scratching the Afanc. "I thought they had all been sealed in Tirn Aill!"

A sudden chill washed over me, bringing with it a host of realizations I really didn't want to have. "Oh, Maeve's tits," I whispered.

"What is it?" asked Quentin.

I looked toward him and shook my head before saying—softly enough that Sylvester hopefully wouldn't hear—"Chelsea."

It's easy to forget, living the way we do, that once, every race of fae had a homeland—a place that they came from. Modern fae make knowes and shallowings, carving their homes out of the membrane between the Summerlands and the human world. Firstborn made worlds. Blind Michael's land, an islet anchored between the Summerlands and one of the lost realms, was the closest I had ever been to those Firstborn-made worlds, and it had been huge and terrible and incredible, all at the same time. Modern fae make homes. Firstborn made homelands.

They didn't do it alone; maybe that's why all Blind Michael had was an islet, and all my mother had was a tower. Tirn Aill was the ancestral homeland of a dozen races, including the Tylwyth Teg, Ellyllon, and Coblynau. Their Firstborn had worked together to open and shape it, making it a perfect place for their descendants to live. None of the deep realms were paradise — paradise gets boring — but they were perfect. And they had been lost for over five hundred years, the doors sealed by Oberon himself before he disappeared.

Once, the Tuatha de Dannan were responsible for guarding the doors between worlds. It was their duty and their joy, at least to hear them talk about it. They kept each world's monsters safely contained and prevented wars from spilling from one world into the next. When Oberon sealed the doors, the Tuatha were left with no purpose. But a Tuatha changeling with more power than she knew what to do with, who didn't know yet what was impossible . . .

Chelsea was in real trouble. So were the rest of us.

Sylvester had managed to coax the Afanc off the car, although it had shattered the rear windshield in the process of getting down. It was flopped on its back in the gravel, letting him scratch its belly. One of its hind legs was waving lazily, like there was also a bit of dog worked into the beaver and crocodile soup of its heritage. "Come meet him!" he called. "He won't bite."

"Says you," I said, stealing a glance at Etienne. He looked stricken. I suppose hearing me imply that his daughter might have started importing monsters from the deeper realms of Faerie was a bit of a shock. I started forward, gesturing for Quentin to follow. "How's my car?"

Sylvester stopped scratching the Afanc as he looked up and grimaced. "I can pay for the repairs."

I winced. "That's not what I wanted to hear." The Afanc was a lot less scary-looking stretched out on the ground with its tongue lolling. I gave it a thoughtful look, putting off checking my car as long as I possibly could. "Why does it have all those teeth if it's friendly?"

"The Afanc is a fish eater, and some of the fish in Tirn Aill are well-equipped to defend themselves," said Sylvester. "October, what *are* you doing out here?"

So Etienne hadn't told him. Swell. "I'm on a case. We needed a place to park while the sun came up, and when we tried to get back on the road, your beastie was crashed out on the roof of my car." That was it; I couldn't put it off any longer. Lifting my head, I looked at the car and cringed.

I could probably have handled the cracks in the front windshield, and the sudden absence of the rear windshield. I've driven worse. But the weight of the Afanc had collapsed the roof of my poor VW bug, pressing it down until the metal actually grazed the tops of the seats. There was no way I could drive the car like that. I've lost cars in the line of duty before. Usually, I'm at least driving them at the time. I raked my hair back with both hands, staring at the damage.

"I'm sorry, October. The Afanc didn't know." Sylvester sounded genuinely apologetic. That wasn't going to fix my car. "I *will* pay for your repairs."

"That's nice," I said faintly. "What are you going to do with the Afanc?"

"Take him back to Shadowed Hills. There's a lake near the rear wall of the ballroom. We can let him stay there until we find out where he came from." I turned to blink at Sylvester. He shrugged. "Whoever has lost him must miss him. To keep a creature this magnificent in such good health for so long ... it's a labor of love. I wouldn't want his owner to worry."

Understanding dawned: Sylvester thought the Afanc had escaped from some sort of menagerie. It wasn't that far outside the realm of possibility. Fae nobles keep all sorts of strange things in their knowes, and exotic pets are popular, even in Faerie. The Afanc would have been the jewel of someone's collection. It would have been nice to think that he was right. But when I breathed in deeply I could smell the faintest trace of sycamore smoke and lilies, along with a sweet, clean scent, like air that had never known human pollution. The Afanc didn't come from a menagerie. It came from Tirn Aill.

I continued turning until I was facing Etienne. When he met my eyes, I raised an eyebrow and waited. He gave a small shake of his head, expression pleading.

Sometimes I hate being a soft touch. "Can I borrow Etienne before you take the Afanc home? I need to get to the Luidaeg's. Quentin and I have business with her, and I'd really like to catch her before she goes to bed for the day." I wasn't lying, not really. I was just leaving certain things out, like where the Afanc had probably come from.

"Certainly. If you leave me the number for your mechanic, I can call and arrange both the collection of your car and payment for service."

I hesitated. Sylvester has more money than he could spend in a dozen lifetimes, but I sometimes still feel bad about letting him spend it on me. A glance at my wounded car killed the hesitation. If he could afford the repairs, let him. "I don't have a mechanic, but Danny does."

"Then we'll call Danny and have him call his mechanic."

"I appreciate it." I read off Danny's number from my cell phone.

Sylvester didn't write it down. He just nodded, continuing to rub the Afanc's belly. I blinked. He smiled. "Come from an era where courtship depends on how much poetry you can memorize, my dear, and you, too, will develop an excellent memory."

Thinking about Sylvester courting Luna was like thinking about my parents having sex. I wrinkled my nose. "I'm going to skip dwelling on that one. We'll have Etienne back to you as soon as we can."

"Keep him with you for as long as you have need of him."

"I will." That was a lie, sort of; with my car out of commission, we could really use a personal teleporter. Keeping Etienne around would still have been more trouble than it was worth, especially since we were going to be dealing with Bridget again before this was over.

Etienne started toward us. He was almost there when Sylvester added, in a mild tone, "I trust you all to tell me what is going on once you feel that it is safe to do so."

"Yes, your Grace," said Etienne, shoulders hunching. He didn't look back. Maybe he didn't trust himself to hold his silence if he saw his liege's face.

I'm less of a stickler for the rules than Etienne is, and I was having trouble looking at Sylvester without spilling the whole story. "Come on, Quentin," I said. "We need to get going."

"Coming." He trotted over, waving to Sylvester as he passed him, and reached me at the same time as Etienne.

"The Luidaeg's, please," I said.

"As you wish," said Etienne. His hand traced a wide circle in the air, trailing the smell of cedar smoke and limes. A hole opened. Through it, I could see the familiar dirty walls of the alley that led to the Luidaeg's apartment.

"Open roads and kind fires," Sylvester said.

"Open roads," I echoed, and stepped through the circle in the air. Quentin and Etienne followed me.

The three of us were standing in the dim San Francisco alley, miles from Tilden Park, when I realized that I'd managed to leave my sword in the car.

Well, crap.

EIGHT

"THIS WAS AS CLOSE AS I could bring you. The Luidaeg's actual domain is shielded against teleportation." Etienne looked around the alley, nose wrinkling. It was an understandable reaction, considering the condition of both the alley and the slice of street visible through the alley's mouth. The Luidaeg could have lived anywhere she wanted, either in this world or in the Summerlands. She chose a place where the cockroaches were reluctant to live, and she seemed entirely content to stay there.

"When are you going to tell him, Etienne?" I asked, before he could open a portal to take himself back to Tilden Park. "He knows something is going on, and I *won't* lie for you. Omit things, maybe, if it's necessary. But not lie."

"Neither will I," added Quentin.

"I wouldn't ask you to." Etienne looked down as he said, "I am simply having trouble deciding how best to tell my liege that when he needed me most, I betrayed his trust."

"You did no such thing," I said. "You made a mistake, and now you're trying to make it right. That's all Sylvester expects from any of us. That when we make mistakes, we do our best to fix them."

"Perhaps that's what he expects from you, October, but I was his representative in those dark days. I must hold myself to a somewhat higher standard."

I sighed. "I'm going to ignore the swipe you just took at my social status, because I know you're stressed. But you need to tell him sooner rather than later, because I'm not keeping your secrets forever."

"I'll tell him. Just give me time."

Time was something we didn't have much of. I shook my head. "I'll give you what I can. I don't know how much that's going to be."

"Hopefully, it will be enough." Etienne waved his hand through the air, opening a portal back to Tilden Park. He stepped through before I had the chance to say anything else.

"Always has to have the last word," I grumbled. "Come on, Quentin. Let's go see the sea witch." We turned, and walked down the alley to the Luidaeg's apartment.

Her front door was warped and water stained, and it looked like it would fall apart if subjected to the slightest pressure. Appearances can be deceiving, especially when the Luidaeg is involved. I raised my hand and knocked briskly, not hammering, but not gently tapping, either. There was no immediate answer. Quentin and I exchanged a look. The Luidaeg normally opened her door almost instantly, sometimes even before we had a chance to knock. Then again, it was more than an hour past sunrise, and even sea witches have to sleep sometime.

"I wish we'd been able to stop for the donuts," said Quentin.

"You and me both," I said and knocked again.

This time, we heard movement on the other side of the door: feet, shuffling down the hall. I lowered my hand, and the door swung open, revealing a sleepy-eyed, apparently human woman with tousled brown hair, tan skin, and freckles warring with the ghosts of teenage acne scars for ownership of her cheeks. She was wearing a blue bathrobe over a floor-length white cotton nightgown. She looked like she couldn't be more than a few days over seventeen.

I knew better. "Hello, Luidaeg," I said. "Can we come in?"

The Luidaeg blinked. "Toby?" She glanced to my companion. "Quentin? What are you two doing here? You didn't call."

"We were going to, but I had car trouble, and it sort of slipped my mind. It's why we didn't bring donuts. Please can we come in? There's something we need to talk about, and I'd rather not do it standing on the porch."

The Luidaeg looked at us again and then looked back over her shoulder at the hallway. The door blocked whatever she was looking at. Finally, she sighed. "All right, you can come in—but don't you *dare* say a word about the condition of my apartment. I didn't have time to get ready for company."

Considering that the Luidaeg's apartment normally looked like a cross between a compost heap and the dumpsters behind a Goodwill, that was a terrifying statement. "Sure," I said. "We won't say anything."

The Luidaeg scowled at me. "Yeah, you will," she said. Then she turned and retreated into the hall, leaving the door open so we could follow her inside.

I stepped over the threshold and stopped. Quentin froze beside me, the two of us staring wide-eyed at something even more unexpected than a monster sleeping on top of my car.

The hall was clean.

The carpet—visible for the first time in the years that I'd been visiting—was the color of fresh kelp. The walls were cream-colored, decorated with a few judiciously placed fishnets. They filled the air with the pleasant scent of fresh seawater, salty without being briny.

"Toby . . ."

"Yeah, kid. I see it, too."

The Luidaeg stopped at the end of the hall, turning back to scowl at us. "Are you going to come inside or not?"

Quentin and I exchanged a look before stepping into the hall. The door swung shut behind us, and we walked down the hall to the pristine living room. The couches—which had always been splotched with patches of muck and mold before—were clearly antique but well cared-for. There were even a few pictures on the walls, all images of oceans. I recognized one of them as having been taken at Half Moon Bay, near the home of Connor's family. The Luidaeg has an ... interesting ... relationship with the Selkie families. They owe her their existence. She's planning to call in that debt soon, and I'm pretty sure it's going to involve me.

"What the hell happened here?" I asked, looking toward the Luidaeg.

"Like I said, the place isn't ready for company. If you'd called first ..."

The Daoine Sidhe are illusionists. Maybe that's why Quentin was the one to say, indignantly, "You mean you've been pretending this place was a pigsty all this time?"

"I never said 'this place is a pigsty,' did I?" asked the Luidaeg. "I never lied to you. I've never lied to either of you. I just let you think what you wanted to think. If you'd ever asked ..."

I shook my head. "But let me guess. If I'd asked, 'Is the apartment always like this?' you would have said, 'No, sometimes it's a mess,' and let me think it just got worse instead of telling me that it was spotless under a glamour."

"Yup," said the Luidaeg. "Or if you'd asked, 'Don't you ever clean?' I would have said I cleaned all the time. Lies and truth are all in how you're looking at them. That's something you, out of everyone, should have figured out by now." She yawned, covering her mouth with the back of her hand. "Now what the fuck do you people want? This is 'rip your heads off and leave your bodies as a warning to others' early."

Quentin grinned. Apparently, threats of dire physical harm from the Luidaeg made him happy. Weird kid. At least I could take some small pleasure in knowing that I was part of what made him that way. "It's good to see you, too."

"Uh-huh." She went stomping toward the kitchen. "I'm making some fucking tea."

Sometimes I think the Luidaeg uses human profanity as much as she does just because she's trying to shock me. I ignored it and followed her, with Quentin close behind me.

The kitchen was as clean as the rest of the apartment. None of the appliances were newer than the early 1970s, but they were all spotless, with no dents or signs of rust. "You want some?" the Luidaeg asked, picking up a kettle and moving to fill it with water from the tap.

"Depends. Is that freshwater or saltwater?"

She cast a wry smile in my direction. "You're catching on to the way things work. No tea for you. Now what in Dad's name are you two doing here? Shit's got to be pretty bad if you're showing up on my doorstep before I've had my beauty sleep."

I couldn't think of a way to ease her into the situation, so I didn't bother: "Etienne has a changeling daughter that nobody knew about, including him. And now she's missing."

"So?" The Luidaeg put the kettle on the stove. "Sounds like that saves him the trouble of giving her the Choice."

"Etienne's Tuatha."

"So?"

"So the 'car trouble' I mentioned? Was the roof of my car getting smashed in by an Afanc looking for a place to sleep."

The Luidaeg turned to stare at me. I kept on talking.

"Sylvester assumed it escaped from someone's menagerie. He's taken it back to Shadowed Hills until they can track down whoever owns it. But they're not going to find an owner, are they? That thing came straight from Tirn Aill. Chelsea—Etienne's daughter—her magic smells like sycamore smoke and calla lilies. I smelled it on the Afanc."

The Luidaeg paled. That, in and of itself, was terrifying. "It's happening again," she said, almost in a whisper. "Oh, sweet Mother, it's happening again."

"What's happening again? Luidaeg, talk to me. I need to know what's going on. I need to find Chelsea."

"Oh, you need to find her, all right," said the Luidaeg. She shook her head. Somewhere in the middle of the gesture, the humanity left her face, acne scars and tan fading away. She was left with a faint mother-of-pearl undertone to her skin . . . and the freckles. They seemed to be permanent, no matter what shape she took. The Luidaeg can be distressingly protean, and I may never know what she really looks like. I'm not certain I want to. "You need to find her *now*."

"How?" asked Quentin. We both turned to look at him. He was frowning. "I know we need to find her. That's why we're here. We can't teleport. How are we supposed to find her?"

I looked back to the Luidaeg. "How bad can this get?"

"Bad," she said. "I'm assuming you've both heard about the changelings who go wrong when their magic comes in."

"Instead of getting all the limits and none of the power, they get all the power and none of the limits," I said. "I think everyone's heard those stories."

"Yeah, well. Have you ever met one of those changelings?"

"No." Every changeling I'd ever known, myself included, was magically weaker than their fae parent. The horror stories about uncontrollable changeling magic destroying knowes and burning human cities had always seemed to be just that: horror stories, usually trotted out by pureblood kids who wanted to remind us that we weren't just less than they were, we were potentially going to go bad.

"So if they're that rare, why do the stories endure?" asked the Luidaeg. "Faerie is usually happy to forget the bad things. Hell, we practically race to see who can forget them first. Maybe some people don't like changelings, but shouldn't they still be happy to forget about the disasters that happened years ago, to somebody else?"

I didn't say anything. Neither did Quentin. We just waited.

The Luidaeg shook her head. "We remember because when it *does* happen, when this sort of thing *does* go wrong, it's so fucking bad that no one can pretend it didn't happen. The last time there was a Tuatha de Dannan changeling with the strength to smash his way through the walls Oberon erected between us and everywhere else, it was . . . bad."

"Bad 'well, that sucks' or bad 'end of the world'?" I asked, cautiously.

"Bad 'he punched a hole all the way through to the central lands of Faerie, and some people were never heard from again,'" said the Luidaeg. "I'd tell you to go ask your mother, if I thought she'd be willing to talk to you about it. She was there. She was one of the people who had to seal the door he'd created before it could destroy all the worlds."

Amandine had been rattling at doors no one could see since she went mad. Maybe she really could see something that the rest of us couldn't. I frowned. "What happened to the changeling?"

"He died." The Luidaeg's tone made it clear that there would be no further discussion of the dead. Her kettle began to whistle. She took it off the stove and opened the nearest cabinet, taking down a mug. "If your Chelsea is that kind of changeling, you've got two choices."

"What are those?" I already half-knew what she was going to say. I was hoping she'd come up with another option.

"You shift her blood all the way in either direction—make her human, or make her fae so that her blood will give her the power blocks she's missing—or you kill her. She doesn't walk away from this the way that she is now. Do you understand me? No one who can open a door to Tirn Aill without my father's permission can be allowed to go free."

"Why is that so bad?" asked Quentin. "I mean, when Oberon locked the doors, did he know he was going to be gone this long? Maybe people would fight less if they could go home."

Faerie wars used to be bloody and unpleasant, but they always ended, because eventually the warring parties just went home. When your annoying neighbors live in a different pocket universe, it's a lot easier to ignore the fact that they never mow the lawn. Locking all the inhabitants of Faerie in two worlds—Earth and the Summerlands—might have made out-and-out conflict rarer, but with nowhere else to go, the warring parties just kept at it until one side was all but annihilated. Just ask the Kingdom of Silences.

"It's not my place to question my father's decisions," said the Luidaeg frostily. Then she sighed, thawing a little as she said, "Without him, Mom, and Aunt Titania to keep the Heart of Faerie under control, the deeper lands are unstable. They're open to influence, and they're going to be looking for it anywhere they can find it. If we went back to the deeper lands without them, we'd all wind up dead, trapped, or worse."

I didn't ask what "or worse" could be. Faerie is nothing if not creative when it comes to that sort of thing. Instead, I asked, "The Heart of Faerie?"

The Luidaeg didn't answer. She just looked at me and waited.

Right. "So how are we supposed to find Chelsea?" I asked, dropping the subject. "She can teleport, and we don't even have a car anymore, thanks to the Afanc."

"What did you say her magic smelled like?"

"Sycamore smoke and calla lilies."

"And she's Etienne's kid. What does his magic smell like?"

"Um . . . it smells like cedar smoke and limes."

"Okay. Okay. Her line . . . she must be descended through Amorica." Catching our blank expressions, the Luidaeg sighed. "You know, there was a time when everyone in Faerie knew the descendant lines of the Firstborn. It helped people not get turned inside out when they *pissed us off*. Amorica and Elton are the Tuatha de Dannan Firstborn. Twins. Amorica's magic smelled like burning heather—like all the fields in the world were on fire at once. Elton smelled like that same field at dawn, when the dew was heavy and fire seemed impossible. If your missing kid were from Elton's line, she'd smell like, I don't know, wet concrete and whatever."

Quentin and I kept looking at her blankly. The Luidaeg scowled before picking up the kettle and pouring a stream of dark liquid into her mug.

"Did you never consider that maybe—just maybe—your magic said things about you?"

"I knew it usually reflected one or both of your parents somehow and that it could change as you got older, but I didn't realize it identified your Firstborn," I said. "Or that the Tuatha had two Firstborn."

"Yeah, well, 'had' is the right word there. Amorica died the first time we went to war against each other—and don't," she held up a hand, "ask me why we went to war, or who was on which side. It doesn't matter now, and it's one of the questions I'm not allowed to answer."

"Okay," I said slowly. "So she's one of Amorica's descendants. What does that mean from a practical standpoint?"

"It means I can mix you a tracking potion." The Luidaeg sipped her tea, grimaced, and set the cup aside before opening her refrigerator and starting to rummage around inside. "You won't be able to follow her if she gates out of the Summerlands, but at least you'll be able to tell where she enters and exits."

"What's the catch?" asked Quentin.

The Luidaeg's magic always comes with a price. Both Quentin and I have learned that lesson firsthand. There are people who would say we got off easy—we're both still breathing, after all—and maybe they're right. That doesn't make the Luidaeg's bills easy ones to pay.

"Well, for one thing, you won't be able to stop looking until you find her." The Luidaeg straightened, a jar of unidentified green sludge in each hand. She closed the refrigerator door with a bump of her hip before moving to the counter. "For another thing, if she dies before you manage to catch up to her, you're going to get it dropped on your head."

"Like riding the blood all the way to a death?" I asked.

The Luidaeg looked up, meeting my eyes, and nodded. "It would be a lot like that. The nature of the connection is similar. Quentin would probably bounce back. You, on the other hand . . . there are downsides to being what you are."

I shuddered. I couldn't help it. Blood magic is always dangerous; maybe that's why there are so few races in Faerie that specialize in it. Water magic, sure. Flower magic, why not? But blood magic? That's the sort of thing that can get you killed. I should know. It's come close to killing me, more than once.

"I'm not going to get her memories, am I? Because that would be a little bit distracting. Puberty was annoying enough the first time."

"No. We'd need an actual sample of her blood for that." The Luidaeg opened both jars of sludge. One, she poured into her teacup. The other, she dumped into a large ceramic mixing bowl that looked like it was made sometime in the 1970s. "This is the best I can do without having her on hand."

"Which would make this whole thing unnecessary," muttered Quentin. I glanced toward him. He winced a little, looking apologetic. "Sorry."

"Don't worry about it," said the Luidaeg. She reached into a second cabinet and pulled out several jars of spices, all of which she uncapped and began dumping into the bowl. "You don't have to drink this shit."

"We don't?" asked Quentin and I, in relieved unison.

The Luidaeg snorted. "Not this time. Once in a while, I make things you don't need to ingest." She pulled a wooden spoon from the jar next to the stove, beginning to stir the increasingly vile-looking paste. "Besides, it would probably kill you if you put it in your mouth."

"You never lose sight of how important it is to be reassuring, do you?" I raked my hair back with one hand, eyeing the gunk. "If we don't drink it, what do we do with it?"

"You carry it." The Luidaeg gave the paste one last stir before holding her hand out toward me and saying, imperiously, "Give me your arm."

Long experience has taught me that when the Luidaeg demands part of my anatomy, I'm going to be bleeding soon after. Still. It's not like I wasn't going to wind up bleeding anyway, given the way my life usually goes, and Chelsea was in trouble. If the Luidaeg needed some of my blood before we could find her, she could have it. I stuck out my right arm.

The Luidaeg grasped my wrist, gently turning my arm until my palm was facing toward the ceiling. Still gentle, she pushed up the sleeve of my leather jacket, revealing the skin. I grimaced. She glanced up at me.

"Still don't like the sight of blood, do you?"

"Not really."

"You know, there are times when I could slap Amy for what she did to your head." The comment was made without malice. For the Luidaeg, slapping my mother just made sense. Then she bent her head, pressed her lips against my wrist, and bit down. Hard. Her teeth had looked entirely human when she was talking, but now, feeling them break my skin, I would have been willing to swear that she had a mouthful of shark's teeth. I grimaced, fighting the urge to start swearing.

"Toby?" Quentin sounded concerned. "You okay?"

"I'm good, I'm cool, I love it when people chew holes in me." I glared at the top of the Luidaeg's head. "Haven't you drawn blood *yet*? It feels like you're about to start leaving tooth marks on the bone."

The Luidaeg chuckled—an unnerving noise in and of itself—before lifting her head, smiling at me with bloody lips, and turning to spit a mouthful of blood into her bowl. I slapped my left hand over the wound before I could accidentally catch a glimpse of the damage. It would heal. These days, all my wounds heal. That didn't mean I wanted to see it.

"This should just about do it," she said, seemingly unconcerned by the fact that my blood was dripping down her chin. She stirred the paste again. The herbs-and-slime mixture changed from green to a deep, almost-black shade of red. "Quentin, go to my room and look in the top drawer of my bedside table. There should be a purple velvet box. Bring it here."

"Okay," said Quentin. Turning, he left the kitchen.

The Luidaeg tensed, waiting to hear his footsteps fade. Then she turned to me, speaking quickly and quietly as she said, "This is bad, Toby. You got that, right? This is very, very bad."

"I thought you made that pretty clear."

"No. Not clear enough." She shook her head. "If you don't find her soon, she's going to start opening doors, and she's not going to be able to stop. Those doors *want* to be open, and they'll force her to keep on going. Killing her won't undo the damage she has the potential to cause. If she opens a door all the way to the Heart of Faerie, it won't close. The Heart wants people. It's lonely. And that means it's going to try to pull her toward it."

I frowned. "I'm guessing that would be bad?"

She gave me an indulgent look, the kind adults give to children who think they're smarter than they are. "Purebloods make knowes, Firstborn make worlds . . . what did you think my parents made?"

"They made Faerie," I said.

"They did. And Faerie misses us." She shook her head. "If Chelsea's powers get all the way out of her control, she'll punch a hole straight through to where Faerie was born, and then Dad help us all. You have to stop her."

"And if I can't?"

"Only blood will close a hole that deep—more blood than a body has to spare. Even yours, October. Someone will have to die. Stop her before things go that far."

"I'll do my best." This wasn't my first kidnapping case, not by a long shot. It was the first one where I'd been told that I would have to kill the kid if I couldn't retrieve her safely.

"Good." The Luidaeg straightened a little, smiling toward the kitchen door. "That's the box I meant! Bring it over here, kiddo, and we'll see about getting you two back on the road."

Quentin looked quizzically at us as he walked over to put the velvet box down on the counter next to the bowl of gunk. "What were you two talking about?"

"*How* we were going to get back on the road," I said quickly. The Luidaeg can't lie. Thankfully, I don't share her limits. "The car's been crushed, and Etienne's with Sylvester."

"We can call Danny," Quentin suggested.

"We may have to."

The Luidaeg opened the box, pulling out two small glass spheres. They looked solid until she tapped them with the tip of her index finger. Then they opened like four-petaled flowers, becoming unusually shaped bowls. The Luidaeg spoke as she worked, saying, "I know stupidity comes naturally to you, but this isn't the time for it. You can take my car."

I blinked. "You have a car?"

"Yes, I have a car. I don't drive much, but how did you think I got out to Half Moon Bay before I met you? I sure as shit didn't fly. I don't have the figure for it." She scooped about a half-teaspoon of gunk into each of the glass bowls, checking to be sure the amounts matched. Then she tapped the "petals" again, and they closed seamlessly. "The car's parked at the back of the alley, under a don't-look-here. Keys are next to the front door. *Don't* scratch the paint."

Considering what the Luidaeg did when she liked us, I didn't want to think about what she'd do if we managed to damage her property. "If you're sure . . ." I said.

"I don't make offers when I'm not sure." She lifted the glass spheres to eye level and blew on each one, just once, gently. The gunk inside dissolved, replaced by tiny piles of gleaming red sand, flecked with flakes of gold and black. "Here."

She held the spheres out toward us. I let go of my wrist to reach for mine. My skin was still bloody—no surprise there—but the wound made by the Luidaeg's teeth was gone. That was never going to stop being creepy.

Quentin squinted at his sphere and asked, "What does it do?"

"It finds Chelsea. You need to take it somewhere she's been. That will let it attune to the scent of her magic—just don't get it near any other recent Tuatha portals. After that, it will start pulling you in the direction of her most recent door. If you're lucky, she'll still be there when you arrive."

"So it's like the candle?" The Luidaeg made me a magic candle when I went into Blind Michael's lands for the first time. It helped me find the children he'd stolen. It also got wax *everywhere*, but that was a necessary evil.

"Same principle, different execution," said the Luidaeg. "If you find Chelsea—when you find Chelsea—hand her the spheres. That'll break the connection and keep you from getting hit with any backlash. If she dies before you can get her to take them . . ."

"It'll hurt. Gotcha." I tucked the sphere into my pocket. Quentin did the same with his. "If that's all, then we should probably—"

My phone rang.

The Luidaeg's expression went blank. "You should answer that," she said.

"Why?"

"Just do it."

Frowning a little, I pulled out my phone and flipped it open. "Hello?" My eyes widened. "Bridget, calm down. What did you say?"

Chelsea's mother took a shaky breath, and repeated, "Chelsea just called me. She said she was at a pay phone in *Seattle*."

Oh, oak and ash. "Is she still there? I can go pick her up." Etienne would be able to take me. Even if that was normally farther than he could jump, he'd find a way to take me, for her.

"No. She said she couldn't control where she was going anymore. People *took* her!"

"From the phone in Seattle?"

"No! On her way home! Are you *listening* to me?!"

I took a breath, counting to five before I said, "Yes, Bridget, I'm listening. I just need to know exactly what's going on. Did she say anything about the people who took her?"

"That they want to open a door! A door where? What's going on?" Her voice, never calm, was beginning to take on an edge of genuine hysteria. "*Where is my daughter?!*"

"I don't know. But we're going to find her. We—"

"Why aren't you *finding her?!*"

"We're doing the best that we can. Bridget, I just need you to stay calm, and—" I was talking to the air. Bridget had hung up.

I snapped the phone closed, looking toward Quentin. "We have to go."

"Yes, you do," said the Luidaeg. "And Toby?"

"Yeah?"

She looked at me grimly, her pupils expanding until her eyes were black from side to side. "Hurry."

NINE

THE LUIDAEG'S DON'T-LOOK-HERE POPPED as we approached the car, leaving the scent of brackish water hanging in the air. We were short on time. I knew that; Quentin knew that; we still took a moment to stand there and look at the car, trying to wrap our minds around it.

I wasn't sure what I'd expected the Luidaeg to drive; it was a toss-up between something battered and semi-destroyed or something utterly classic, *Christine* as driven by a badass water demon from the dawn of human history. I was sure of one thing: I wasn't expecting a green Honda Civic. It looked like something a soccer mom would drive. It looked like something *I* would have been driving, if I'd stayed part of Gillian's life long enough to wind up taking her to dance recitals and school plays.

"Do you know how to drive this?" Quentin asked. "It looks, you know. Antique."

"Quentin, you didn't own a pair of pants with a zipper until you were fifteen. You didn't have reliable access to cable television until you moved in with me. Your wardrobe consists mostly of tunics." I unlocked the car as I spoke. Giving Quentin a hard time might be good for both of us, emotionally, but it wasn't going to get us to

Berkeley any faster. That was where we were most likely to find the doors we needed to attune the Luidaeg's charms.

"So you're saying I shouldn't call other people's cars antique?"

"I'm saying that no one who grew up in a live-action Tolkien novel gets to call cars from 1998 antiques."

Quentin smirked and got into the car. "Yes, sir."

"Damn straight."

Some of the influence of the Luidaeg's don't-look-here spell must have been clinging to the car; there was plenty of traffic, but it got out of our way with an ease that was frankly eerie. Quentin played with the radio while I drove. For some reason, it didn't get anything but a Canadian folk music channel and three stations playing hits from the 1940s and 1950s. I expected him to complain. Instead, he announced, "I love this song!" as the band on the Canadian station started singing enthusiastically about boats, and proceeded to sing along.

"Weirdo," I said.

"Canadian," he replied. His stomach growled. "*Hungry* Canadian. We still haven't eaten."

"Believe me, I noticed. I'm the one who had to bleed for the Luidaeg's latest special project, remember? As soon as we get these things attuned to Chelsea, we'll hit the nearest drive-through and buy a sack of breakfast sandwiches. Okay?" Breakfast sandwiches and *coffee*. I wasn't going to do anyone any good if I fell asleep at the wheel and drove into a tree.

"Okay," said Quentin.

I tossed him my cell phone. "Here. Call Walther. Let him know we're coming back to Berkeley. We don't need a picture anymore, but if he can mix anything that would work as a temporary, nonharmful magic suppressant, I'd love to hear about it." If we could shut down Chelsea's ability to open doors for a little while, maybe we'd be able to catch her before she gated herself away. And if whoever took her was on her trail, well . . .

I felt sorry for them. I was cranky, I was tired, I needed

caffeine, and people who kidnap teenage girls piss me off. Call it my way of working through residual anger issues from when Raysel grabbed my daughter, but if I got my hands on Chelsea's kidnappers, they were going to learn that I don't play nicely with people who mess with kids.

Quentin dialed Walther's number and must have reached him, because a few seconds later, he identified himself and started explaining the situation. I tuned him out, focusing on the road instead of my squire. I knew I didn't need to monitor him. If you'd asked me three years ago whether I would trust my status updates to a teenage boy, I would have looked at you as if you were insane. These days, I couldn't imagine doing anything else.

Besides, we were crossing the Bay Bridge, and I've always been a little paranoid about that particular stretch of road. Something about being on a giant iron structure suspended over the water rubs me the wrong way.

"Toby?" Quentin lowered the phone. "Walther wants to know how long the power damper needs to work."

"I don't know. Long enough for us to keep Chelsea from turning the fabric of the universe into pudding. An hour? A day?"

"Got it." He relayed this to Walther. There was a pause before he lowered the phone again, and said, "He can do a year if you don't want it to hurt her. That's sort of the minimum. Anything that doesn't last as long will probably mess her up pretty bad at the same time."

A year was a long time to strip someone of her magic. On the other hand . . . if Chelsea decided to become human, she wasn't going to have magic anymore, no matter what. If she chose to become fae, a year wouldn't matter one way or the other. "Tell him a year should be fine. Anything that lets us get close enough to her to make this stop."

"Okay." He raised the phone again, and I returned my attention to the road. My cell phone landed in my lap less than a minute later. It bounced once before wedging itself between my knees. "He's on it," said Quentin.

"Good. Did he say when we could pick it up?"

"No. He just laughed and hung up on me."

I nodded. "Even better." Working with me has had the unexpected side effect of teaching Walther that sometimes you not only don't get sufficient time to prepare, you don't get any time at all. I liked to tell myself it was good for him. It's too easy for purebloods to get complacent about time management—when you have forever, what's the point of worrying about whether or not you'll get your library books back on time?

"You're terribly hard on your allies," commented Tybalt's voice from the backseat. "It's a wonder any of us remain willing to stand by you for more than a season of abuses."

I yelped, involuntarily jerking the wheel to the side. We swerved across two lanes of traffic, causing the cars around me to hit their brakes and horns practically in unison. Quentin shouted something I couldn't make out over the mingled cacophony of the horns and my own steady swearing. I risked a glance in his direction. He was hanging onto the car's "oh shit" handle so hard that his knuckles were white.

"Really, October, am I worth this much fuss and bother?" asked Tybalt.

"I am going to *murder you!*" I shouted. The car was mostly back under my control, but we were still straddling two lanes, and the drivers around us were still leaning on their horns so hard that it was hard to hear myself think.

"Now that's definitely overreacting," said Tybalt. The scent of pennyroyal and musk filled the cab. I felt the weight of an illusion settle over us. Most of the horns stopped, possibly because the other drivers could no longer see our car.

I got us back into one lane, hit the gas hard enough to send the car lurching forward, and risked looking away from the road long enough to glare at Tybalt in the rearview mirror. "What in the name of Oberon's ass do you think you're *doing?*" I demanded. Something else occurred to me, and I added, "And how did you do that? We're in a moving car. How did you *get* here?"

"Cars cast shadows," said Tybalt. Then he sighed. It was a deep, exhausted sound, and it told me how much effort he had expended in shifting himself into his current position. "The Luidaeg may have provided some small measure of assistance," he admitted. "I arrived at her domicile only a few minutes after your departure, and once I was able to impress the urgency of my errand upon her, she agreed to help me."

"I realize I'm the last person in the world who should be saying this, but have you heard of this amazing new invention called 'the telephone'?" I asked.

"As I have used them to contact you in the past, yes, I am familiar with the concept. This was too important to explain over a telephone line." He paused. "It concerns my nephew."

"Raj?" Quentin let go of the handle, twisting to stare into the back. Much as I wanted to do the same, I kept my eyes on the road. Tybalt only needed to be stared down by one of us at a time. "Is he okay?"

"That is yet to be seen." Tybalt reached forward, placing a hand on my upper arm. "Can you pull over?"

The end of the bridge was in sight up ahead. "In a few minutes," I agreed. "Tybalt—"

"I wouldn't be here if this weren't important enough to be worth the risk," he said.

"I know," I said, and I meant it. Now that my first mingled spike of surprise and anger was fading, it was being replaced by a deeper, slower emotion: fear. Tybalt was born before cars existed. He doesn't like them under the best of circumstances. If he was willing to use the Shadow Roads to get *into* a car ...

This couldn't be good.

I pulled off the freeway in Emeryville and parked next to a polluted stretch of brackish swamp. A heron raised its head, looking at us without interest before it went back to poking among the cattails with its long orange beak, looking for something to eat. Shoving my phone into a pocket, I got out of the car, slamming the door to make my lingering displeasure clear as I turned to wait for Tybalt to emerge. Quentin did much the same.

Tybalt got out slowly, leaning on the car door as he got his feet under him. The last of my anger fled in an instant.

"Tybalt?" I whispered.

He managed a smile. "Now you see my urgency, little fish. Or at least, you see the shape of it."

His clothes were torn and ash-blackened, and a bruise discolored the left side of his face. He couldn't have been beaten that badly without being seriously injured, but—I breathed in deep, testing the air for traces of blood—he wasn't hurt. I would have known in an instant if he'd appeared in the car while he was bleeding, but it was still a relief to taste the air and find nothing. I started to step forward and stopped myself.

"What happened?" I asked.

"A fair question." He looked down at himself, then back up at me. "A fair answer is owed. And as to the question you're so thoughtfully not asking, yes. I was hurt, and hurt dearly. A King of Cats can, and will, recover from a great deal more than one who is not a King of Cats, and I simply did not feel it would be appropriate for me to lie down and die with things in their current state. If you would come with me?"

"I can't leave Quentin," I said. I had to fight not to run around the car and fling my arms around Tybalt. That bruise . . . "Can you take us both?"

Tybalt hesitated, clearly trying to decide what his answer was going to be. "I can get myself to campus," said Quentin. "If the Court of Cats needs you, you should go."

"I'm your knight. I shouldn't leave you on random street corners."

"I'm your squire. That means sometimes I'm the one who gets to stable the horse." Quentin smiled, the concern not leaving his eyes. "Or, you know, the Civic. I'm not a great driver, but I'll stick to side streets, and I know where the faculty parking lot is. Walther can get me a pass."

Or he could make the car vanish altogether. Either way, he had things covered. "The keys are in the ignition. Do you have cash for the cafeteria?" I asked. "You need to get some breakfast in you."

"I have my emergency twenty," said Quentin.

"I hereby decree this an official emergency," I said, teasing a slightly bigger smile from him. "I'll call you as soon as I get back to a place where I can use my phone." I was already walking toward Tybalt, my feet seeming to operate without direct instruction from my brain. "Leave me a message if anything comes up. I'll check them as soon as I get back."

"Got it," said Quentin. He turned his attention to Tybalt. "Don't break my knight."

"I haven't done so yet," said Tybalt, with odd solemnity. He cast a pained smile in my direction. "This is the point at which I ask you to take a deep breath."

"I think I know the drill by now," I said, and offered him my hands. He took them, and pulled me backward, into shadow.

The first time I used the Shadow Roads, I was terrified, cold, and confused. Since then, I've been dragged along them for miles, hauled onto them without my consent—and without enough warning to catch my breath—and even stranded alone in the dark, once, when it was throw me into the shadows or let me get shot with a potentially poisoned arrow. You'd think a place of absolute blackness where I got hypothermia would never manage to seem comforting. You'd be wrong.

Every time I was on the Shadow Roads, Tybalt had me, or Tybalt was coming to get me out of the dark. No matter how cold it was, no matter how dark it was, I always knew someone was going to come and bring me home. There's power in that.

We fell through the dark for what felt like less than a

minute—not even enough time for my lungs to really start aching—before we stepped back into the light. I took a breath, instinctively seeking oxygen after the airless passage along the Shadow Roads, and promptly started to cough as I got a lungful of smoke. Tybalt put a hand on my shoulder to steady me, producing a damp cloth from somewhere inside the tatters of his jacket with the same motion.

"Here," he said. "Cover your nose and mouth."

I took the cloth with a quick nod of gratitude, not even bothering to wonder how he'd been able to carry something wet through the Shadow Roads without it freezing solid. The ways of the Cait Sidhe are strange. Tybalt produced another cloth from his pocket and mirrored my motion. His eyes were watering. I chose to believe that this was due to the smoke, and not due to the damage around us. If I thought he was crying, I'd probably start doing the same thing.

Putting the cloth over my face helped with the smoke, and my coughing stopped almost immediately. What it didn't help with was the smell of blood. It had been masked before, since it's hard to pay attention to subtleties when you're trying not to choke to death, but now . . . I am my mother's daughter, whether I want to be or not, and blood is not a subtlety for me. Blood is a reality. As soon as the smoke was removed, the blood made itself known.

"Oak and ash," I whispered.

All the blood was Cait Sidhe. It spoke to me in whispers and almost-words, identifying the wounded and the slain in a language that was no less valid because it didn't exist. Some of the Cait Sidhe who bled in this room were familiar to me. Others weren't. And at least one . . .

At least one had magic that tasted like pennyroyal and musk, and eyes the color of malachite, and a wonderful, annoying tendency to show up where he was least wanted but most needed. My heart dropped, suddenly aching like a coal in my chest. I turned to face Tybalt, lowering the cloth as I stared at him. "Tybalt?"

"Keep your nose covered." He grasped my wrist with his free hand, pulling my hand back up. Most of his face was covered, but I could still see his eyes, bloodshot from the smoke, worried, and so very, very tired. "I told you I'd been hurt."

"You didn't tell me you *died*."

"I got better."

I glared at him. It was the only thing I could think of to do.

This wasn't the first time Tybalt had died—or come close enough that there was practically no difference—and miraculously recovered. Taking the "cats have nine lives" folktale literally was a perk of being a King of Cats. But I didn't know how many lives he got, or how many he'd used up before he met me. I didn't know when he was going to run out.

Tybalt sighed, letting go of my wrist and putting his hand against the small of my back instead. "You can shout at me for dying later. For now, we have larger things to worry about. Come." With that, he pushed, guiding me into the worst of the smoke.

The first time I visited the Court of Cats, it was a confusing maze of mismatched hallways, rooms that should never have been connected, and completely unrelated architectures. None of that had changed. Still, it was somehow comfortable now; I was in a place where I knew no one would hurt me, not without going through Tybalt first.

Although at the moment, given how recently he had returned from the dead, I wasn't sure I'd let Tybalt stand between me and danger. The reverse seemed to be a lot more likely.

As we walked, I saw scorch marks and signs of burning on the walls and ceilings, but no actual fire. The Cait Sidhe had managed to stop the Court from burning down entirely. It made me feel a little better to realize Tybalt had stayed with his people long enough to put out the fire before coming to fetch me.

We didn't see anyone as we walked. The lingering

smoke had driven them to someplace safer, even if fire was no longer a danger.

Tybalt stopped in front of a closed oak door, taking his hand away from my hip in order to knock three times. There was a long pause before someone on the other side of the door echoed his knock. He knocked again, twice this time, and the door was pulled open by a tiger-striped changeling with hair dyed in streaks of charcoal gray and cherry red. No; not entirely dyed. The red was artificial, but the gray was all ash.

I lowered the cloth from my face and offered the woman on the other side of the door a wan smile. "Hi, Julie," I said. "Mind if we come in?"

Julie looked at me tiredly. There was a time when she would have launched herself for my throat, smoke or no smoke, and tried to kill me before Tybalt could stop her. These days, she restrains herself to a low-level disdain. Hatred takes too much energy. "Yes, but I'm not the one in charge here," she said, and held the door open wider, so that we could come inside. "Hurry up. We don't want too much smoke to get in."

"After you," said Tybalt.

I stepped through the door.

Every room in the Court of Cats used to belong to some other place. Knowe or mortal dwelling, it doesn't make any difference; all that matters is that the place existed and was lost. The cats get the lost places. The Court of Cats is a patchwork maze of those lost places. The room Julie allowed us to enter was probably a barn once, in one of those small towns in the middle of America that wound up abandoned during the Great Depression. The walls had that sort of old-fashioned look, not historical, but aged. There was even a hayloft, and bales of hay were stacked against the walls.

Then there were the Cait Sidhe. The barn wasn't crowded—it was big enough that it could have been used to host a wedding, and it would have taken more than that to make it seem really full—but it was definitely oc-cupied. Most were in their human forms, only oddly colored skin and the occasional tail giving away their feline natures. A few were in full-on cat form, lounging on hay bales or draped across the rafters.

And one of them was striding toward us, mouth twisted into a thin, furious line. He was tall and dark-skinned, with eyes the color of green glass bottles and short gray-and-white hair striped like a tabby's coat. Raj's father, Samson.

Tybalt lowered his cloth, stepping forward so that he was between me and the oncoming Cait Sidhe. "Samson," he said. "Has there been any—"

Samson's fist slammed into his chin while he was still speaking, cutting off his sentence. Tybalt's jaw snapped shut, eyes widening in surprise. Then they narrowed, his expression turning dangerous. I had to fight the urge to step out of the splatter zone.

Samson raised his fist to hit Tybalt again. Tybalt raised his hand, intercepting the blow before it could land.

"Samson," he said again. This time, the other man's name sounded less like an acknowledgment, and more like a threat. "You forget your place."

"I forget *my* place?" Samson spat. He pulled once, trying to free his hand from Tybalt's grasp. He failed, and so he stopped trying, choosing to stand and glare instead. "*I* am the one who remained here, while *you* went rushing off to fetch your changeling whore."

"See, he shouldn't have said that," commented Julie. I risked looking away from the tableau in front of me long enough to glance back at her. She shook her head. "I may not like you, but I know better than to say something like that. Uncle Tybalt is going to beat him down hard for that."

Tybalt's eyes remained narrowed, and his expression hardened into something cold and predatory. "Yes, Samson, *you* forget your place. I went for October because she has a vested interest in the welfare of this Court, and because she may be able to track the girl who did this. I act in the best interests of the Court of Cats."

"We do not need help from the Divided Courts,"

snarled Samson. He pulled away again. This time, Tybalt let him go. Samson staggered several feet backward before catching his balance. Staying where he was, he glared at the three of us. "The Court of Cats has stood alone since Oberon granted us our sovereignty. Would you endanger it for *her?*"

To my surprise, Tybalt smiled, although his expression didn't warm. "I am the King here, Samson. Unless you wish to challenge me—oh, but I forgot, you can't, can you? You cannot stand as King here, or in any other Court. Now, will you allow me to save your son, or will you continue to posture at the edges of a challenge you are far too weak to force? The decision is yours."

Samson hesitated. It didn't take a genius to know that Tybalt was lying about the decision being his. The only question was which way the falsehood would go. If Samson chose to press his objections to me, would Tybalt send me away, or would he leave Raj stranded in whatever undisclosed situation was causing the problem? I knew there was no way Tybalt would abandon Raj. Even if he wanted to, I wasn't going to let him. But I wasn't sure Samson knew that.

Apparently, he didn't. "Perhaps I forget my place, but so do you, *Sire,*" he spat. "A cat may look at a King. A cat may even *be* a King. That does not mean a cat may not also be a fool." He glared at me. Then he stalked away, vanishing into the shadows at the edge of the barn.

Tybalt sighed. "My father, Maeve rest his bones, had the right of it," he muttered. "Take them as your own, and let the parents hang."

"Does someone want to tell me what in the name of oak and ash is going on here?" I asked. "I didn't leave my squire in Oakland to come here and mess with a Cait Sidhe civil war." I paused. "Also, I have no idea what you just said."

"I said I made a mistake when I took Raj as a nephew, and not as a son." Tybalt turned to face me. "Chelsea was here."

I raked my hair back with one hand. "I thought that

was what was going on. Couldn't you have led with that, maybe? Since you know I'm looking for her?" *Or maybe you could have led with the fact that, somehow, she managed to get you killed ...*

"I'm sorry," he said, with apparent sincerity. "I didn't think."

Julie made a theatrical gagging noise before flouncing away, getting out of arm's reach before either of us could decide to smack her.

"I liked it better when she was trying to kill me all the time," I muttered, and took another look around the barn. Some of the Cait Sidhe in the hayloft were bleeding, but only a little; there was nothing as bad as the injuries I'd tasted in the room where we arrived. "So what happened?"

"Chelsea opened a door." Tybalt's expression turned grim. "I doubt she meant to do so; I doubt she even knows what she's doing. I knew it was her only because I can't imagine two terrified, half-human girls are presently ripping holes in the fabric of Faerie. If they were as common as all that, this wouldn't be the first time I'd seen one."

"Opened a door to *where*?" I asked.

"One of the Fire Kingdoms."

I blinked at him. He nodded, and said nothing more.

Faerie is divided into four realms. The Land Kingdoms, where most of the fae I know live. The Undersea, home of Merrow and Selkies and stranger things, accessible only to those who can breathe water or are willing to learn how. The Oversky, anchored in the clouds and even more alien than the Undersea; most people can learn how to swim, and scuba gear is reasonably easy to acquire. Flying suits are a little bit harder.

And then there are the Fire Kingdoms, domain of salamanders and Kesali, Teine Sith and Djinn. No one goes there unless they can survive in a river of lava, and even some of the fae races that *can* live in the Fire Kingdoms choose not to, since no one's been able to figure out how to get cable in the middle of a volcano.

"Oh," I said, slowly. "Crap."

"As always, my dear, you have quite the way with words." He shook his head. "She came through one door and threw herself into another. I doubt she even realized we were here, or knew that she had entered a place that already had people in it. The fire that followed her was an unintended side effect of her flight, not an attack upon my people."

I turned to look again at the Cait Sidhe gathered around the edges of the barn. "Is everyone going to see it that way?"

"I don't know," he said, with weary calm. "Perhaps, if it weren't for the rest of what happened when she appeared here."

My heart was still hanging too low in my chest. Now it felt like my stomach dropped all the way down to my feet. Tybalt had managed to separate me from Quentin by telling me that it was about Raj, and while he might treat me like a cat toy from time to time, he had never, so far as I knew, intentionally lied to me. I shifted slowly to face him and asked the question I was most afraid of:

"Tybalt, where's Raj?"

He shook his head, and answered, "I don't know."

Oh, oak and ash. We were in trouble.

TEN

THE SILENCE OF THE CAIT SIDHE around us suddenly felt a lot more dangerous. I had allies here, people here who owed me their lives, but this wasn't my place, and I was the second intruder in the course of a day. I took a half step toward Tybalt. "Why did you bring me here?"

A smile touched his lips. "Whatever the treaties between your Courts and mine say, you and I both know my nephew is your squire in all but name. You would never have forgiven me if I hadn't told you of his disappearance. Despite appearances, your forgiveness is important to me." The smile faded. "Not that this was the whole of my motivation. I dislike being injured, and while none of my subjects were as hurt as I was, it was luck, not skill, that saved them. I would prefer this not happen again, and I would like my nephew returned."

Luck, and a monarch who was willing to push his weaker subjects out of the way of the onrushing disaster. My imagination has always been vivid. The image of Tybalt wreathed in flames rose in my mind's eye. I shoved it stalwartly down and asked, "Did Chelsea *take* him?"

"Not precisely. He was standing between her and her second door when it opened. She ran for what she viewed as safety—as fast as she came and was gone, I doubt she even realized she'd found a possible sanctuary. He was insufficiently swift in getting out of the way, and he was knocked through the opening. It closed before he could pass back through."

That confirmed what Chelsea had told her mother: she was losing control. I worried my lower lip between my teeth. "Can Raj use the Shadow Roads to get back?"

It was a stupid question. I knew that as soon as I asked it, but Tybalt answered as if it were meaningful, saying, "If he has access to them wherever he is, he hasn't used them to return."

"Right." I took a deep breath, touching the pocket holding the Luidaeg's charm with one hand. "Where did she open the doors?"

"Cover your mouth again, and I'll show you," said Tybalt.

I did as I was told. He led me out of the barn, back into the smoky halls of the Court of Cats. He took my elbow once we were outside, guiding me down the charred hall to a huge solarium. That was where the fire had started; that was where Chelsea first arrived.

Like everything in the Court of Cats, the solarium looked as if it had been on the verge of collapsing when the Cait Sidhe claimed and rebuilt it into a patchwork version of itself. Half the windows were broken and boarded over; the other half were glassless frames that looked out on a seemingly endless succession of rafters and hanging ropes. A room inside a room, which was doubtless somehow inside another room in turn. Faerie has never had much respect for spatial geometry, and the Court of Cats seemed to take a special glee in flaunting that disrespect.

Tybalt led me halfway across the solarium before he stopped, saying needlessly, "This is where the fire began."

"Yeah," I said, biting back the urge to start swearing. "I got that."

There was no trace of Chelsea's magic, but I didn't need her magic to tell me that this was where the door had opened. A large section of wall was burnt black. In some places, it was gone, revealing the empty, echoing room that surrounded us. The silver window frames above the hole had been melted by the heat; some of them were splattered on the floor in oracular swirls, while others had maintained their cohesiveness but lost their form, twisting and curving into something that looked like modern art, assuming your definition of "modern art" involved a preschooler and a blowtorch.

The air smelled like fire, molten metal . . . and blood. Once I started paying attention to it, it became impossible to ignore. I stepped away from Tybalt, moving to a blackened patch on the green marble floor. I knelt there, laying my fingertips against the stone, hearing the blood sing to me through the layers of ash that separated us.

"You died here," I said, very quietly.

"October—"

"I wasn't here, and the girl *I'm* supposed to be finding was, and you *died*." I looked up at him, glaring through the tears in my eyes. I left my fingers balanced on the floor, letting his blood sing its song of pain and longing. Longing to live; refusal to let go of the world. Maybe that's what differentiates the Kings and Queens of Cats from the rest of Faerie. They have a cat's stubbornness and the power to back it up. So when death says, "Go," they just refuse.

My heart hurt. My heart hurt so badly, and I was still trying to recover from Connor, and oh, Titania, I couldn't do this again. The thought startled me. I froze where I was, still glaring.

Tybalt sighed. "I know." He hesitated before adding, "This is not the time, and this is not the place, and my nephew needs us. But I ask you to consider this. I got better. I will always get better." He hesitated again— possibly the first time I'd ever seen him pause more than once after he'd decided he was going to say something.

Finally, he said, "Some of us, October, will not leave you."

I stared at him. Then I pushed myself to my feet, shaking the chill of his words from my skin, and dipped a hand into my pocket to pull out the Luidaeg's charm. As I half-expected, it was glowing a brilliant foxfire green, like a Candela's Merry Dancer, boiled down and concentrated. I held it toward the darkest part of the char. The glow dimmed.

"She didn't open this door," I said, and turned, relieved when the motion put Tybalt out of my sight. He was right; this wasn't the time for that conversation. And he was also right that it was a conversation we needed to have sooner rather than later. Just not now.

The glow didn't brighten again until I was facing an undamaged patch of wall. Even the cobwebs and ancient, tattered curtains were intact, marking this as one of the few places not touched by fire. I moved in that direction, careful to step around the spots on the floor where blood sang to me of injuries and anger. I didn't want to get overwhelmed.

The curtains eddied in a half-felt wind as I approached, and I smelled a faint trace of calla lilies under the veneer of smoke. The rest of her magic was buried, blending into the background smell of the fire. That didn't matter. I had what I needed.

I held the sphere out toward the source of the lily scent. There was a soft sound, somewhere between a sigh and the chiming of a bell, and the sphere changed from foxfire green to lambent white, dimming at the same time, until it seemed as if I had a hand filled with frozen starlight. Emphasis on the "frozen": as soon as the light changed colors, a chill raced up my arm, wrapping itself around my heart. It squeezed once, long enough to make me gasp, and then it was gone . . . but the memory remained. Chelsea and I were tied now. No matter what else happened, I had to find her.

"October?" Tybalt's voice was no closer than it had been a few moments before. He hadn't moved. Smart kitty.

"Hold on." I raked my hair back with my free hand, using the movement to cover my shudder, and stepped closer to the wall. The smell of lilies was stronger here.

The smell of smoke ... wasn't. I frowned, twisting back around to face him. "I don't think she opened a door to the Fire Kingdoms."

"Much as I hate to argue with you, I believe the amount of lava that made an unexpected—and unrequested—appearance proves that the Fire Kingdoms were involved." His mouth twisted into a shape that was half-grimace, half-smile. "Mortal lava doesn't dissolve as it cools."

"I'm not saying they weren't involved, I'm saying *she* didn't open a door to them. She wouldn't have survived in the Fire Kingdoms for more than a few seconds. And I don't smell her blood at all. Wouldn't she have been hurt?" I looked at the dimly glowing sphere in my hand before tucking it back into my pocket. "The Court of Cats is where the lost things go, right? Is there some mechanism that determines what is and isn't lost?"

Tybalt shook his head. "No. When something becomes ours, it finds its way here."

"Well, in that case, I'd call a teenage changeling who can't control her powers pretty damn lost. What if she opened a door looking for a safe place to hide and wound up here? Would anyone have noticed?"

"No members of the Divided Court have ever found the Court of Cats on their own before," he said, hesitantly.

"Chelsea's a special case. Maybe when she got lost, she saw the way. That's all she'd need. Just one signpost telling her which way to go."

"It's ... possible," said Tybalt, still hesitantly—although it was the hesitance of a man facing an unfamiliar concept, not the hesitance of someone who was getting ready to disagree with me. "The doors are supposed to be sealed to all but the Cait Sidhe."

"You brought me here."

A smile ghosted across his face. "Like Chelsea, you're a special case. Before today's excitement, you were the only member of the Divided Courts to walk these halls in centuries."

"That's me—defying expectations wherever I go." I

took a breath. "What was this room used for? Why were you in here?"

"It was one of our dining halls. Many of us used it for napping, or for teaching kits to hunt." Tybalt's tone became tinged with fond remembrance. If it hadn't been for the bruise on his face and the smoke in the air, it would have been almost sweet. "There is little more amusing than watching adult Cait Sidhe play rat-catcher in the mortal alleys for the sake of having live things to bring back here."

That explained why there had been so many Cait Sidhe here to be hurt, if not why Chelsea would have suddenly decided to fill the room with lava. I walked to the worst of the burn, trying not to wince at the way the floor crackled under my heels. Tybalt watched me go, a curious expression on his face, but he didn't stop me.

When I reached the point I judged to be the origin of the blaze, I closed my eyes, breathing in deeply. All I smelled was smoke. I sighed, hand going to the knife at my belt.

It always comes back to blood.

My mother's line, the Dóchas Sidhe, draws power from blood in a way that no one else in Faerie does. Unfortunately for me, that means there's no one to teach me what it is I can do and how I'm supposed to go about doing it. Oh, some of the lessons the Daoine Sidhe use for their children apply to me—that's how I was able to pass for Daoine Sidhe for so damn long—but it's like trying to eat soup with a fork. Just because a few things work out, that doesn't mean you're going about them the right way.

My mother knew how to use her magic. She could have shown me the way to use mine. She didn't. So that's one more thing for the long list of things my mother didn't do, one more thing for me to figure out by guesswork and luck.

Goody.

I keep my knife sharp for situations just like this one. I ran the blade across the knuckles of my left hand, cutting barely deep enough to draw blood. The wounds were already starting to scab over as I brought my fingers up to my mouth. I didn't open my eyes.

The taste of blood chased everything else away—the smoke, the scent of Chelsea's magic, everything. Then every other trace of blood in the room rose, threatening to knock me on my ass. I forced myself to keep breathing. My magic rose around me, cut grass and copper barely sharp enough to distinguish itself from blood. The taste of blood receded, seeming to know what it needed to do, and a dozen more magical signatures announced themselves, ghostly memories of spells long since cast and illusions long since dispelled.

"Chelsea used her magic there and there." I pointed blindly, eyes staying closed as I fought to focus through the overlapping traces left by the Cait Sidhe. Tybalt would see what I was pointing at. "She didn't use it here. She didn't come anywhere *near* here."

"What are you saying?" Tybalt's voice drew closer. His footsteps weren't even whispers in my self-imposed darkness. If he hadn't been speaking, I would never have heard him coming.

"Chelsea didn't open this door." I ducked my head, breathing in deep. There was the faintest distant trace of apples and snowdrops—but then it was gone again. "I . . . she didn't. I'm sure she didn't. There's a ghost of her magic here, but it's too thin. She didn't do this."

"Then who did?" The question was softly asked, and all the more dangerous for its seeming gentleness. Tybalt was merciless in the defense of his people. If Chelsea hadn't opened the door that burned his Court . . .

"I don't know." I opened my eyes, meeting his frown without shying away. "Believe me, if I knew, I would tell you. Nobody gets to kill you but me."

"I should not find that so comforting. Tell me, if you can't tell who *did*, how do you know it wasn't the girl?"

"Because I can follow her magic across the room, and she never came near this wall." I swallowed, clearing the taste of blood from my mouth. The spell burst, and the scent of old magic faded, mercifully taking the memory of all the blood that had been spilled here along for the ride. For just a moment, it was as if my senses had been set back to where they used to be, when blood magic was the tool of last resort and not the one thing I had to truly depend on. "Whoever opened the door onto the fire used a blood charm, which is how I know anyone opened a door here at all—but Chelsea didn't do this."

Blood charms are almost exclusively the domain of the Daoine Sidhe, which didn't explain how someone had been able to replicate the Tuatha door-opening power with one—unless they'd used Chelsea's blood in the mix, which would also explain why her magic seemed to be spread unevenly around the room. Whoever had her wasn't above bleeding her.

Tybalt breathed out slowly. Then he nodded. "For her sake, I am glad. Cait Sidhe justice can be cruel," he said. "For mine . . . I am troubled."

"Yeah," I said quietly. "If it wasn't her, who was it?"

We stood in that flame-blackened room, looking at each other. Someone had snatched Chelsea. Someone was pursuing her, for reasons we still didn't know. And whoever it was, they were able to follow her into the Court of Cats, and they didn't care who got hurt.

ELEVEN

WE STEPPED FROM THE SHADOWS onto the hard-packed earth edging the creek that runs through the heart of the UC Berkeley campus. The creek's small footbridge shielded us from mortal eyes; between that and the hanging ivy threatening to block the sun, we could practically have pitched a tent and had a cookout down there.

"I should go."

"I wish you didn't have to." I turned to Tybalt. He was standing in the deepest part of the shadow. I could still see the bruise on his cheek and the exhaustion in his slumping shoulders. "Are you sure you don't want a cup of coffee or something?"

"Your love of artificial stimulants will be the death of you one day," he said, a smile turning up the corners of his lips. "I must attend to my Court, and you must attend to matters here. I will find you when I have the freedom to do so."

"Okay," I said reluctantly. The smell of pennyroyal and musk rose as he opened the door onto the Shadow Roads, and he was gone, leaving me alone.

If any of the students who saw me emerge from beneath the bridge thought it was strange, they kept their thoughts to themselves. This was UC Berkeley. Strange women in leather jackets with ash-stained hands probably crawled out from under their bridges all the time. The student body continued about its business, and I continued on mine.

Even if Walther didn't have anything useful for me yet, he had my squire, and I wanted him back. Quentin was a smart kid, and that extended to going where I told him to go, as long as he didn't think I was trying to be heroic and self-sacrificing. "Walther had *better* have coffee on," I muttered, and kept walking.

As a junior faculty member, Walther barely rated an office. He didn't rate one that was easy to find. It was located in a maze of twisting hallways that seemed to have been designed by an architect who dreamed of one day having a real Minotaur lurking to devour the unwary. No legendary Greek monsters leaped out to grab me as I walked, finally stopping in the open doorway of a small, cluttered room that held two legendary monsters of its own. I rapped my knuckles against the doorframe.

"If one of you doesn't have coffee for me, I'm going to be cranky," I announced.

Walther and Quentin had been bent over something on the counter. They straightened and turned at the sound of my voice. Walther smiled. Quentin didn't bother with the preliminaries. He grabbed a paper cup and trotted over to me, holding it at arm's length.

"Here," he said. "Coffee."

"And thus am I reminded why I allow you to live," I said. The coffee was cold and the "creamer" had never seen the inside of a cow, but I didn't care. The caffeine was all I needed. I lowered the cup after chugging a third of its contents, asking, "What's our status?"

"Come in, come in," said Walther, beckoning me forward. "And close the door." His glasses were askew, and his hair was mussed. Not enough that anyone who didn't know him would notice, but Walther worked very hard to maintain his superficial "I am the perfect professor" appearance. Mussed hair didn't go with that ideal.

"Long night?" I asked, doing as I was bid. The office was considerably dimmer once the light from the hall was blocked. All the overheads were off, leaving us in a room that would have been substantially too gloomy for mortal eyes.

Good thing none of us had mortal eyes. I sipped my coffee as I walked across the room, drinking more slowly now that the first rush of caffeine was in my system. With the ambient light blocked by the door, it was apparent that whatever Walther was working on was glowing faintly, like a light stick the morning after Halloween. It was a steady glow, at least, and not a candlelight flicker. I hate candles.

"I was already here when you called, tinkering with some personal projects. You just focused me," said Walther. He turned back to the counter. "I'm not technically supposed to be here today, but I knew no one else was using my office, so I just kept going."

"He took a break for breakfast," said Quentin helpfully.

"I bet he did." By the time Quentin got to campus, he was probably so focused on food that he could have convinced an invading army to stop long enough to get some oatmeal and bacon. Teenage boys are good that way. "Is it safe to assume we're all standing here in the dark because you managed to make something we could use?"

"I wouldn't use the word 'safe' when talking about this stuff, but yes." Walther picked up a beaker with excruciating care. He was wearing heavy gloves, and he still looked uncomfortable holding the thing. It was half-full of a viscous liquid glowing a soft, somehow menacing shade of orange. I looked at it and had absolutely no desire to get any closer.

Too bad I was going to have to get closer—a lot closer—if I wanted the stuff to be of any use. "Is this the power dampener?" He nodded. "Tell me about it."

"For a start, do not ingest. The only way this could be more toxic is if I milked a rattlesnake into it to add a little extra zing." Walther put the beaker down, looking relieved when it was safely on the counter. "It's meant for topical application. Skin contact triggers its effects."

"Which are . . . ?" I prompted

"It blocks all access to higher magic for a year and a day. No illusions, transformations, blood workings, anything. I'm not sure what would happen if you spilled it on a shapeshifter, so let's try not to find out." Walther grimaced. "If there's a counter for the stuff, I haven't been able to find it. It takes about twenty minutes for the effects to stabilize, but they'll kick in almost immediately." He picked up another beaker. This one was filled with pale green liquid that didn't glow at all. "Scrub off all traces of the potion with this and you should be fine — stress on *should*. I wouldn't want to wait until minute nineteen before I started looking for a place to rinse my hands."

"Got it. At least there's a window." I eyed the open beakers. "Is there any way you can decant those into something we can carry without worrying about spilling things on ourselves every time we hit a pothole?"

"I was working on that when you showed up." Walther traded beakers again, waving me and Quentin back. He didn't have to tell us twice. We stepped clear before he began pouring the glowing liquid into a set of thin-lipped glass jars. "This isn't the most stable thing in the world."

"Is it going to explode?"

"No, but it may modify its own properties if you wait too long to use it."

That didn't sound good. "Modify how?"

"Maybe it'll stop working. Maybe it'll turn permanent. I have no way of telling. Alchemy is half science, half magic — and when it's something like this, *all* guesswork." Walther's shoulders sagged as the last of the glowing liquid trickled into the final jar. He turned to place the beaker gingerly in a waiting basin. Catching my curious expression, he said, "Milk. That should neutralize the potion on the glass, and if I leave it overnight, it'll be safe to handle."

"This becomes a more and more exciting adventure." I finished my coffee, setting the empty cup down on the nearest desk before saying, offhandedly, "Someone tried to flood the Court of Cats with lava. Chelsea was there, but I don't think she did it."

"Was anyone hurt?" asked Walther.

"Tybalt was killed, but he got better. Kings of Cats are annoying like that." The words felt odd. It was odder still to realize that they made total sense to me. "There weren't any other serious injuries that I saw. I was a little distracted trying to figure out where Chelsea had been."

"Did you?" asked Quentin.

In answer, I dug out the charm the Luidaeg had provided and held it up, letting him see the way that it was glowing. Then I paused. "Hey. Get yours out. I want to see something."

Quentin frowned, looking puzzled, but did as he was told. His charm was still dark. I leaned over and tapped it with my own charm. There was a chiming sound, and the charm in Quentin's hand flared into sudden light. He yelped, nearly dropping it. I made a grab with my free hand, closing my fingers around his before he could let the charm go.

"Careful," I cautioned.

"What did you do?"

"My charm was already tuned to Chelsea. Touching it to yours passed the tuning along."

"You could've warned me," he grumbled, giving the glowing charm a mistrustful look before sliding it back into his pocket. "Now what?"

"Now we take what we came for, and we go." I turned back to Walther. "I swear I'm not trying to be rude, but I have two missing teenagers, and—"

"Two?" interrupted Quentin. "What do you mean, two?"

"Quentin—"

"Why was it so important that Tybalt had to come and see you? The Court of Cats does just fine without our help all the time. Who's the other missing kid, Toby?"

The cold edge on Quentin's questions told me he already knew the answer; he just wanted to hear me say it. I sighed. "Raj disappeared when Chelsea tore through the Court of Cats," I said. "Tybalt thinks he was knocked through the portal she used to leave. He obviously can't access the Shadow Roads wherever he is, or he'd be back by now. That's why Tybalt thought I needed to be involved. Because I'm already looking for Chelsea, and Raj is . . ."

If he weren't Cait Sidhe, I'd have claimed him as my squire a long damn time ago.

". . . my responsibility as much as he is Tybalt's," I finished, with barely a pause. "We all know that. This is just making it a little closer to formal." And when we got Raj back, we were going to make it all the way formal if we possibly could. I was already training both of them. I might as well be allowed to send them both to pick up Chinese food.

Quentin scowled. "We have to get him back."

"I know."

"This will help." Walther stepped between us, holding a disposable Styrofoam cooler. "You have four jars of the dampening solution and four jars of the counter solution. *Do not drop this.* I don't think I could handle mixing that stuff again."

"Noted." I tucked the Luidaeg's charm into my pocket and took the cooler. "You do good work," I said, avoiding the forbidden "thank you."

"I like a challenge," he replied, with a small smile. He knew what I wasn't saying, and he appreciated it.

"Good, because I think we're going to have plenty of challenges ahead of us. Quentin?" But he was already halfway to the door, not looking back as he made his way out of the room. I cast Walther an apologetic look and followed him. Not only was time something we couldn't afford to waste, Quentin was the only one who knew where the car was.

Walther walked me as far as his office door and stopped there, waving tiredly as Quentin stalked down the length of the hall and I followed. Soon Walther was out of sight, and soon after that, we were outside and Quentin was charging down a gravel path toward the faculty parking lot.

I didn't dare run with the cooler full of jars, so I settled for walking as fast as I could. When it became clear that I wasn't going to catch up with him like that, I stopped, tucking the cooler under one arm as I placed the first two fingers of my now-free hand in my mouth and whistled shrilly. Every visible head—human, canine, and squirrel—turned toward me. Every head but one. Quentin just stopped where he was, hands fisted at his sides, head down.

He stayed there as I walked the rest of the short distance between us. Once I pulled up alongside him, he started to walk again, pacing me.

"We're going to find him."

Silence.

"Tybalt wouldn't have told me Raj was missing if he didn't think we could help."

Silence.

"If this is going to interfere with your ability to help me look for Chelsea, I swear by the root and the tree, I will send you back to the house right now."

Now his head came up, eyes narrowing. The sunlight cast bronze glimmers off the metallic halo of his hair. I remember when he was a cornsilk blond, wide-eyed and innocent, and would never have dreamed of looking at his sworn knight like that. Good times. And I wouldn't trade a single glare to have them back again.

"You wouldn't," he said.

"I would," I replied calmly. "What's more, I would make sure May and Jazz were under strict instructions to keep you in the house, no matter how much you argued. So how about you keep on working with me, and we bring them both home?"

Quentin sighed, seeming to deflate. "He's my best friend," he said, like he was admitting something strange and surprising.

I blinked. "Yeah. I know. So?"

"So he's . . . he's who he is, and I'm who I am. People like us aren't *friends*. We're passing acquaintances. Maybe. If we're not busy hating each other all the time."

"Ah." Raj was a Prince of Cats; Quentin was the son of some unidentified noble family. They weren't the sort of people who should have become friends. But they had. I liked to think I had something to do with that, although, if I were being honest, I had to admit that a psychopath named Blind Michael had more to do with it than I did. As a Prince of Cats, Raj had been pretty sequestered until Blind Michael kidnapped him. If that hadn't happened, we might never have met at all. It's funny how people can change your life without meaning to. Even the fucked-up, crazy people leave everything different when they go away.

Well, Raj wasn't getting off the hook that easily. He might be missing, but he wasn't free of us yet.

We were at the mouth of the faculty parking lot. The Luidaeg's car was nowhere in sight. I squinted around at the few open parking spots before giving up and turning to Quentin. "Okay, where'd you park?"

"Over here." He led me to a seemingly empty space under one of the big oak trees that dropped dead leaves and acorns with impunity on the vehicles below it. After glancing around to be sure we weren't observed, he waved his hand. The brief smell of heather and steel rose around us, and the illusion that had been concealing the car popped like a soap bubble.

"Very good," I said. Quentin's illusions had been improving steadily since he finished with the worst parts of puberty and settled in to maturing into an adult Daoine Sidhe. I wasn't in charge of that part of his education— Daoine Sidhe illusions are so far beyond me that I would have been barely more than useless—but Sylvester was doing an awesome job. I'd have to tell him so, the next time I got the chance.

Normally, Quentin would have taken a moment to preen and look pleased with himself. Instead, he smiled wanly and offered up the keys. "I didn't want to bother Walther for a parking pass when he was working with dangerous chemicals."

"Hey, what's the point of having magical powers if you can't use them to avoid parking tickets?" I took the keys before handing him the cooler. "Don't drop this."

"I won't," he said. That seemed to exhaust our possible conversation; we were both silent as we climbed into the car. He put the cooler on the floor, anchoring it between his feet. I fastened my seat belt, stuck the key in the ignition, and started the car. Time for us to go.

We drove away from campus and down Shattuck Avenue in that same frozen silence. Quentin didn't even turn the radio on—something that was practically unheard of in my experience. I stole a few glances in his direction, but decided not to push the matter. He'd talk when he was ready, and we were both going to need our strength for what was ahead of us.

Possibly sooner than I'd thought. I hit the brakes when I saw the police cars parked outside Bridget's house. Quentin yelped as he was thrown forward against his seat belt. "Ow! Hey!"

"Sorry. Sorry." I took a deep breath, steadying myself, and drove on until I saw an open space about halfway down the block, sandwiched between a red sports car and a silver-gray VW station wagon. I eased the Luidaeg's car up to the sidewalk and killed the engine, not bothering with a don't-look-here.

Quentin checked the cooler to be sure its contents were intact before twisting in his seat and staring, wide-eyed, at the police cars behind us. "Toby . . ."

"I saw them."

"What are they doing here?"

"I think we're about to find out. Leave the cooler." I undid my belt, leaning over to open the cooler and pull out one dose of the power-dampener goo. I tucked it into my jacket pocket, ignoring Quentin's puzzled look, and climbed out of the car. Quentin followed, and together we walked along the sidewalk to Bridget's house.

The door was standing open. I heard voices as we came up the walkway—Bridget's and two others, both unfamiliar. The owner of one of those voices appeared as we walked up the porch steps: a frowning, brown-haired man in a Berkeley Police Department uniform.

"Can I help you?"

I forced myself to smile. "Hi—I'm a friend of Bridget's. She asked me to come over?" Hopefully, the fact that I looked faintly worried despite my smile would work in my favor. Anyone who was actually a friend of Bridget's would look worried if they found the police in her house. Quentin didn't say anything, but he stepped closer to me, letting his obvious youth speak for him. He was the right age to be one of Chelsea's friends from school.

We must not have looked *too* suspicious, because the officer didn't reach for his handcuffs. He just shook his head, and said, "Ms. Ames is not prepared for company at the moment. Perhaps you should come back later."

"Who's there?" Bridget appeared behind the officer, blinking when she saw me. "October. I wasn't expecting you until later."

"I thought you could use a little help." My eyes flicked to the officer and then back to her. "What's going on?"

"It's been long enough since Chelsea disappeared that I can file a credible missing persons report," said Bridget.

There are times when I think I'll never understand the human world. Maybe if I'd grown up as a part of it, but now ... there's no way. In Faerie, if a child disappears, you don't wait forty-eight hours before you move. You go out and you get them back, unless they've been taken by something too powerful for you to defeat. And that doesn't happen often these days.

"What?" asked Quentin, sounding honestly confused.

"Oh," I said, surreptitiously nudging him with my elbow. He stopped talking. Good squire. "So she's not sleeping over at Brittany's house?"

Bridget shook her head. "No, she's not."

The officer didn't ask who Brittany was. It's a common enough name that it was safe to assume every girl in America knew at least one "Brittany" well enough to sleep over at her house.

"Damn," I said.

"My thoughts exactly." She placed a hand on the officer's arm. "Can we finish taking my statement, Officer Daugherty? October's been a great comfort to me." Bridget didn't blink or hesitate as she lied to the policeman; she kept her eyes on his the whole time, and her tone was steady. She must have been thinking of her excuse since they showed up on her doorstep.

"We can wait on the porch," I offered.

Bridget shot me a relieved look. Officer Daugherty slowly nodded.

"If your friends don't mind waiting, I believe we're just about done."

"Thank you." Bridget took her hand off the officer's arm, turning to me. "I won't be a minute," she said.

"Okay," I replied.

Officer Daugherty didn't say anything. But he closed the door before he turned away.

Quentin and I retreated to the edge of the porch, sitting down on the low stone wall that separated it from the rest of the yard. "Why did she call the m—" He paused, catching the word "mortal" before it could quite escape his lips.

"Kids can't just disappear anymore; people notice," I said, pitching my voice low enough that they wouldn't be able to hear me inside. "One of Chelsea's friends probably called them as soon as she went missing. It just took until now for them to take the report seriously."

Quentin frowned again, clearly not understanding the situation. That was okay. I wasn't sure I understood it myself. I just knew enough about mortal police work to know that this was all according to procedure.

There are times I really wish I'd joined the police force. I would have access to better materials, more backup, and a hell of a lot more forensic training. Then I realize I'd also be bound by rules like the ones that kept these officers from showing up until Chelsea had been gone for more than a day. I'm pretty sure I wouldn't be able to handle that.

About ten minutes passed before the front door opened and Officer Daugherty emerged, followed by a black-haired female officer. They nodded politely as they passed, but that was the extent of their interaction; either Bridget had managed to really sell the idea that we were friends of hers, or they still weren't treating Chelsea's disappearance as a kidnapping. That was probably for the best, at least for them. There was no way they'd be able to follow her into Faerie. Not if they wanted to walk away from this case alive and reasonably sane.

Bridget appeared in the doorway a few seconds later. She beckoned us into the house. Once we were inside, she shut the door and demanded, "What are you doing here?"

"What were the police doing here?" I countered. "We said we'd help."

"I called them when I was still trying to believe the faeries hadn't come and carried my little girl away," she said, glaring at me. "I couldn't stop them coming in when they finally deigned to show up."

I took a deep breath, counting to ten before I said, "Okay. I'm sorry they took so long."

"I'm sorry *you* took so long!"

Counting to ten wasn't going to be enough. I was actually grateful when Quentin stepped up next to me, scowling at her, and said, "We had to make sure we could *catch* Chelsea when we managed to find her. Unless you just wanted us to wave while she went teleporting by? Because we could do that, I guess."

"Your parents aren't going to thank me for what I've done to your manners," I informed Quentin, not bothering to hide my amusement. Finally calm enough to turn back to Bridget, I said, "Look. We are doing the best we can. We are calling in every favor and every ally that stands even the slightest chance of helping us out here. But we're not miracle workers."

"Then what's the point of being magical creatures?" asked Bridget, still glaring.

"We get a discount at Starbucks," I said. "We're going to find your daughter, Bridget. You need to start believing that, and you need to tell me exactly what she said when she called."

"She said she was in Seattle."

Sweet Oberon preserve me from the blindness of mortals. "Yes," I said. "You told us that. But what, *exactly*, did she say?"

Bridget took a shaky breath, clearly forcing herself to calm down. Then: "She said she was in Seattle—Seattle, Washington—and she'd managed to get away, but only by going as far as she could in one jump." There was a quaver in her voice. I couldn't blame her for that. "She said they were chasing her—"

"Did she say anything about who 'they' were?"

"Just that there was more than one person. Not all of them can chase her—that's how she was able to get away at all. They thought she was asleep and left her with people who couldn't follow when she opened a door." Bridget gave me a stricken look. "How many of you *are* there? I thought Faerie was fading."

"Sometimes I want to shake J. R. R. Tolkien for that one," I said. "Faerie never 'faded.' That was something Middle Earthy. The citizens of Faerie just got tired of being used for our pots of gold and magic shoes. We disappeared for our own good. There are more of us than you think." Not as many as there used to be but, from the look on Bridget's face, a lot more than she was comfortable with.

"So you can take our children whenever you want, and there's nothing we can do to stop you?"

I took a breath. "I'm going to skip the part where you never told Etienne you were pregnant—which was sort of you taking *his* chance to be a father away, the way you've been afraid Faerie would take your chance to be

a mother—and go straight to saying no, there's not.
There never has been. Some fae befriend the mortals;
some play tricks on them for fun. Some of us steal children. Some of us get them back. Now, please. Did she say
anything else? Anything she might have seen, or
smelled ... ?" Chelsea wasn't accustomed to being
around other fae. The scent of their magic wouldn't be
background noise to her yet.

"She said she was scared." Bridget straightened. She
was still glaring at me. I was starting to think of that as
her default expression. "My little girl is scared. If you're
not going to bring her home to me, what good are you?"

The fact that I was being lectured by an angry human
woman who'd already hidden a changeling from her fae
parent once wasn't escaping me. I just didn't know what
I could do about it. I looked at Bridget as calmly as I
could and said, "If you have information, call. We'll do
whatever we can to be sure that Chelsea is found safely,
but we're not here for you to abuse."

"Don't challenge me, Fair One," she said sharply.

I sighed. "I'll challenge you all I want. What are you
going to do, call the police and tell them the faeries took
your kid? You'll wind up under psychiatric evaluation,
and Chelsea will still be missing."

"I can tell the police *you* took her."

The threat was made with absolute calm. I had to
pause, considering the nerve it took for her to stand in
her living room, with no one to save her if she screamed,
and threaten me. She didn't know what Quentin and I
were capable of. All she knew was that we weren't human. And that didn't change the part where she was
threatening me. One unfortunate downside of my continuing involvement in the mortal world: I'm actually
vulnerable to threats in a way that, say, Tybalt isn't. If the
police wanted to come for me, they knew where I lived.

Quentin started to open his mouth. I signaled him to
stop before he could say something we'd both regret. Instead, I said, "You could do that. Hell, they might even
pick me up, make my life difficult for a few hours. But

since there's nothing to tie me to Chelsea before she disappeared, they won't be able to hold me. All you'll manage to do is endanger her further by taking me away from my work and guarantee that when I *do* find her, I won't be feeling that charitably toward you. Is that really how you want this to go?"

Bridget's face fell, bravado dissolving as she started to cry. "I just want my daughter back," she said. "Please. Please, get me my daughter back."

I sighed. "I've already told you I'll do what I can. That's all I *can* do. And you need to stop treating me like the enemy, okay?"

Mutely, Bridget nodded.

It was hard not to feel bad for her. When I played faerie bride, I always knew my child might not be human enough for the mortal world. The threat of a lifetime spent in the Summerlands was something I considered, seriously, before I slept with Cliff. Bridget didn't have that. She thought she was going to have her child forever, and once she realized there was a risk—once she realized Chelsea wasn't human—she took the steps she thought she needed to take in order to protect her daughter.

Reaching a hand into my pocket, I produced the jar of power dampener. "This is why we came. If Chelsea teleports home, dump this on her. It will nullify her powers temporarily—long enough for you to call me and let me come to make things right."

"It stops fae magic?" asked Bridget, a new light in her eyes as she reached for the jar.

I didn't give it to her. "Let's be clear about this. You have one shot. *One*. If you don't take it, if Chelsea comes here and you've used this stuff for something other than stopping her, you will never see your daughter again. Do you understand? This isn't a tool you can use to get your revenge. This is a way to save your little girl."

The light went out again. Bridget nodded. "I understand."

"Good. Don't make me regret this." I placed the jar in

her hand before I turned to Quentin. "Let's go. Bridget, we'll call you if we learn anything. Until then, don't do anything stupid." I paused, a thought occurring to me. "Have you warded your house against the fae? You know, with things like your frying pan?"

"Yes, I have," said Bridget. "Wouldn't you?"

"Probably, but you need to take it all down. If there's any chance you've hit on something that works, it's going to keep Chelsea from letting herself in, and that's the opposite of what we want."

"I will," she said.

"Good. Oh, and Bridget?" Quentin looked at me, bemused. I kept my eyes on Bridget. "If Chelsea comes back, call me. Don't try to run. We'll find you. I'm sorry, but you can't hide anymore. It's time to deal with all the things you were running away from in the first place."

I didn't wait to hear what she would say to that. I simply turned to the door, gesturing for Quentin to follow me, and stepped out into the cool air of the Berkeley morning. Our charms were attuned; Raj was missing; and somewhere, a group of people were working together to keep a changeling girl captive. It was time for us to find out exactly why.

TWELVE

"GET YOUR CHELSEA-CHASER OUT," I said, once Quentin and I were safely in the car. "The Luidaeg said they'd lead us to her. Let's see if we can figure out how that's going to work."

"Raj—"

"We'll find him. Chelsea's the one who might destroy Faerie, so we'll find her first."

Quentin nodded. "Okay." He dug a hand into his pocket, pulling out the charm. He frowned at it. "Is it supposed to do something? It's just glowing."

"I don't know. The Luidaeg didn't give me the instruction booklet. Shake it or something, see what it does."

"*Shake it?*" Quentin looked at me as if I'd just grown a second head before shrugging and shaking the sphere. It went from white to foxfire green. Then, with a chime like bells, it turned bright red and jerked toward the windshield, dragging Quentin's hand with it. His seat belt pulled him up short before the charm could slam itself— or my squire—into the glass.

"O-kay, that's new," I said. "Which way does it want us to go?"

"That way." Quentin pointed with his free hand. "It wants us to go that way."

"I love really specific navigation charms," I said, and started the engine.

The Luidaeg's charm led us along surface streets to Martin Luther King Jr. Boulevard, where we had to slow down to account for the increase in traffic. It kept on glowing as we took the entrance to I-880, heading toward the South Bay. I frowned. "Quentin?"

"Yeah?"

"Here." I tossed him my phone. "Call April. I want you to ask whether she's noticed anything unusual in the last couple of days. Weird lights where they're not supposed to be, unfamiliar magical signatures, stuff like that."

Quentin blinked. "You think we're going to Tamed Lightning?"

I indicated the highway with a wave of my hand. "It's starting to look that way."

"Huh," he said, and dialed.

The County of Tamed Lightning is located in the mortal city of Fremont. Like many more recently founded fiefdoms, they don't have a proper knowe; instead, their holdings are consolidated in a shallowing, which also serves as the corporate headquarters for their software design company. It's a County filled with crazy idealists, and they're weird even by the most generous of Faerie standards. I met them when they had a small serial killer problem, one that got their former Countess—Sylvester's niece, January—killed. Her adopted daughter, April, took over, and has been running the whole mess ever since.

It probably says something about me that I find dealing with April O'Leary soothing. She's the only one of her kind in Faerie, and she thinks most of the traditions and rituals that control the other purebloods are ridiculous. Sometimes it's nice to have someone look you in the eye and tell you that no, it doesn't matter whether you say "thank you" or not; it matters whether you remember to pay the DSL bill. Really, I like just about everyone at Tamed Lightning, even Alex, despite the fact that he once used his Gean-Cannah fascination powers to seduce me.

My relationships are complicated, even when they're with people I think of as allies.

Quentin lowered the phone. The Luidaeg's charm was still glowing red. "April says things have been moving around when no one was looking for the last several days, and she wants to know how we knew. She also says they'll set up two of the employee break rooms for us, in case we need a place to crash."

"Last time we slept there, you got kidnapped and nearly thrown off a catwalk. Oh, and shot. We mustn't forget the part where you got *shot*."

"Yeah, but they had really good donuts, so I guess it balances out."

I snorted laughter. My stomach grumbled, reminding me that while Quentin might have had breakfast, I still hadn't. "Donuts would be awesome right about now. I'll hit a drive-through as soon as that thing takes us off the freeway."

Quentin looked at the glowing charm. "Do you think this thing will lead us to Raj, too?"

I hate lying to him. I try not to do it when I have any other choice. "I don't know," I said. "I'm hoping so. If not, it should lead us to Chelsea, and that means we'll be able to get her to help us figure out where he wound up." I took my eyes of the road long enough to shoot him a reassuring glance. "I'm sure he's fine. Raj is tough, and he managed to get away from Blind Michael without my help. He's not going to let a little unexpected teleportation throw him."

"I hope you're right."

"So do I," I said. I started to look back to the road, and paused, the rearview mirror catching my eye. I frowned. "Quentin? That car behind us. How long has it been there?"

880 between Berkeley and Fremont is always a mess. Most people change lanes frequently, trying to win those few extra seconds. All of them were behaving nor-

mally ... except for the neutral-looking white sedan following us at the exact recommended legal distance. He'd been there long enough that he should have passed me, or at least changed lanes when he realized I was never going to speed up. Instead, he was just tooling along down the road, following at an unvarying distance.

"I don't know." Quentin looked at the rearview mirror rather than twisting in his seat. I was proud of him in that moment. There was a time when he would have turned his whole body around, telling our tail—if it was a tail—that we suspected we were being followed. "Want me to cast a don't-look-here on the car?"

"Too risky. If he *is* following us, he's going to notice us vanishing, and we don't know if he's human or not. Do you think you can manage a hide-and-seek?" Hide-and-seek spells are what come after the don't-look-here in the arsenal of magic aimed at hiding in plain sight. They're a bitch to cast, but when they work, they're almost impossible to notice.

I can cast hide-and-seek spells if I have to, but they take a lot out of me, and they're not the sort of magic you should attempt while driving. Quentin, on the other hand, is Daoine Sidhe. The spell would be easier for him, and there wasn't the additional risk of him losing control of the car. With a hide-and-seek, anyone who was looking at the car would continue to see it ... right up until they lost sight of us for some reason. It didn't matter if they looked away or we went around a curve, the end result would be the same: we'd vanish, and we wouldn't be visible to them again until the spell was broken. It wasn't a perfect solution, but if we were actually being followed, it was better than leading our pursuer straight to Tamed Lightning.

Quentin closed his eyes, the smell of heather and steel gathering around him as he ducked his head. He sang six bars from the song we'd been listening to earlier—the one about the man and the boat—and the magic burst around us, leaving the car smelling like a Bath and Body Works air freshener. I glanced his way and decided that was one comparison I wouldn't make out loud. He wasn't in a position to appreciate it.

"Now what?" he asked, slumping in his seat.

The sedan was maintaining the exact same following distance. "We stop for coffee," I said, and shifted over a lane. The sedan did the same thing. We were definitely being followed.

Not for long. The exit to downtown San Leandro involved going around a wide curve, and we were blocked from view several times before we reached the surface street. I promptly pulled off to the side, twisting around to see the other driver's reaction to our disappearance.

He hit the gas as soon as he saw that we were "gone," accelerating toward the street up ahead. He must have thought he could catch up with us. I watched intently as he blew by. For one second, I had a clear view of his face. I froze.

It was Officer Thornton from the SFPD.

"What the fuck is he doing here?" I whispered.

"Toby?"

I shook my head, looking back to Quentin. "That guy was one of the officers on duty when I got picked up the other night."

Quentin frowned. "Why would he be following us now? And to Fremont?"

"I haven't the slightest idea. But I do know one thing." I started the car again. "I really, really need a cup of coffee."

Getting food was complicated by the fact that with the hide-and-seek spell on the car, we couldn't use the drive-through. I eventually had Quentin wait in the car with the Luidaeg's still-glowing charm while I ran into the McDonalds for a sack of cheeseburgers, fries, and faux-apple pies. He got a soda large enough to qualify as a health hazard. I got a coffee large enough that I was in no position to throw stones. Officer Thornton was still nowhere to be seen when I returned to the car, handed Quentin his share of lunch, and got back on the road.

The drive to Fremont is boring under most circumstances. The roads are wide and reasonably well maintained—by California standards, anyway—and you don't usually encounter people driving like complete idiots. That changes when you're trying to eat lunch, drive an invisible car, and follow the directions of a magical snow globe at the same time. We nearly got side-swiped by a semi, and several single-passenger vehicles tried to merge, not into us, but close enough that I wasn't comfortable. I wound up drinking my coffee through Quentin's extra straw, muttering dire imprecations about my fellow drivers.

"You know they can't see us, right?" asked Quentin, amused.

"Shut up."

"I don't think it's fair to call them names if they can't even *see* us."

"Shut up, or you're walking."

Quentin just laughed. I didn't say anything, but I was relieved. With Raj missing and Chelsea's mother threatening police action—and at least one officer already trying to tail us—I couldn't imagine that laughter was going to be much of a priority in the days ahead.

We had just reached the Fremont city limits when the charm in Quentin's hand changed from red to its previous white. The air in the car went strangely flat, like something was being discharged. Quentin frowned, giving the charm a vigorous shake. Its color didn't change.

"I think it's broken," he said.

"I don't." My coffee was almost gone. I sucked the last of it through the straw before dropping it into the empty McDonalds bag. "Chelsea's moving again. Wherever she is now, it's not here, and it's not close enough for us to be drawn there. She was in Seattle before, remember?"

"So where is she now? Tokyo?"

"Wherever she is, let's just hope she's safe." I moved over a lane, heading for the freeway exit.

"Are we going to turn around?"

"Nope." I reached over to steal a few of his remaining fries. They were cold. I ate them anyway. "She stayed in one place long enough for us to get this far. So either she's managed to find a safe house near here, or her captors are here, and they're going to drag her back."

"That's a pretty big assumption," he said dubiously.

"It's what I've got right now. Besides, I want to talk to April. She's a teleporter, and more, she's a computer system. Maybe she can do some sort of magic . . . math . . . thing and tell where Chelsea has been."

Quentin shot me an amused look. "Magic math thing?"

"Shut up."

"I don't think I've ever heard of the magic math thing. How does it work, exactly?"

"Shut up *twice*." Inwardly, I was beaming. Quentin's reaction was exactly what I'd been hoping for: entertained, relaxed, and not tangled up with his concern about Raj. I was worried, too. That didn't mean we could lose sight of the larger problem. As much as I hated to even have the thought, if I had a choice between saving Chelsea and saving Raj . . .

Who was I kidding? I'd save Raj, and Faerie would pay the price. I'm a lot of things, but rational where the people I love are concerned has never been one of them. I just hoped it wasn't going to come to that.

Quentin snickered as I pulled off the freeway. Time to get ourselves over to Tamed Lightning and see what kind of help we could get from the locals.

The San Francisco Bay Area claims to be a single place, much like the United States of America claims to be a single country. In reality, the Bay is divided into four regions, maybe more. There's San Francisco, with its high fogs and deep-sunk roots. There's the East Bay, industrial city, and the deep East Bay past the Caldecott Tunnel, where the suburbanites dream of something past the hills. Fremont is in a different country entirely: the South Bay, land of technological advancements, stucco buildings that fade into the landscape like ghosts, and heat that bakes the pavement even in relatively temperate weather. If there was any place on the planet designed to be infiltrated by fae pretending to be human while they ran a computer company, it's Fremont. No one was ever going to look there twice.

We pulled up in front of the pseudo-medieval gate to ALH Computing less than twenty minutes after we got off the freeway. The fact that they could have that gate at all was one more illustration of how perfect a city Fremont was for them. None of the fae in San Francisco would have dared to install a doorway that looked like something out of a BBC drama about King Arthur. We'd have been too afraid of getting caught. The fae in Fremont just assumed they'd be written off as geeks . . . and they were right.

The portcullis spanning the gate slid upward as we approached, signaling that we'd been recognized and welcomed. I drove through, shuddering as we passed under the points of the portcullis itself. The first time Quentin and I went to ALH, that portcullis—or one like it—tried to kill us. It was only able to do that because someone had used magic to tamper with the control systems, and that someone was long dead. I didn't care. The portcullis was still a damn big piece of metal, and I knew firsthand how much damage it could do to a car.

"I hate that thing," Quentin muttered. He waved a hand, releasing the hide-and-seek that hid us. The smell of heather and steel filled the car.

"You and me both, kid," I said, and kept driving.

The driveway wound gently down to the parking lot. The cats that had decorated the place on our first visit were gone; the Queen of Cats they'd been gathered to mourn had long since been avenged, and they had scattered on whatever strange errands drive the felines of the world. Two people were waiting for us outside the main building when I pulled up to the curb.

One was tall and blonde, with the pointed ears and delicate bone structure characteristic of the Daoine Sidhe: April O'Leary, the least Dryad-like Dryad in the world. Whatever she looked like originally—probably small and lithe, with green hair and skin like bark—she looks like her mother now. There are worse ways to remember the people you love.

The woman next to April was unfamiliar. She was shorter, with sleek black hair pulled into a high ponytail, a pleasant smile, and eyes that were black from side to side, like polished jet. She was clearly of Chinese descent, and she clearly wasn't human. Beyond that, I had no idea what she was.

I waved as I got out of the car. "Hey, April. Sorry to drop in on you like this."

"I was online," she said, with a hint of amusement in her tone. That alone represented a huge leap for her. When we first met April O'Leary, she didn't understand the concept of "humor" as it applied to other people. These days, she actually makes jokes. Bad ones, but still jokes. "What is the purpose of your visit?"

"It's kind of a long story. Can we come inside?"

April nodded. "Of course."

Quentin glanced at me. I shrugged. Apparently, April wasn't planning to introduce her friend. The polite thing to do would have been to ignore the other woman until she was identified or chose to identify herself.

I've never been good at polite. "Hi," I said, offering her my hand. "I'm October Daye, and this is my squire, Quentin. Sorry if we interrupted your meeting."

"You interrupted nothing of any import, I assure you; just a tour." She took my hand, shook once, and let go. "Li Qin Zhou. It is a pleasure."

"Hi," said Quentin.

Li Qin looked like she belonged at Tamed Lightning. She was wearing gray slacks and a white cotton tank top, with plastic flip-flops that showed off her electric green pedicure. She looked back and forth between us, still smiling. "The timing is fortuitous; I was hoping to meet you. I've heard so much about you. I apologize for not creating the opportunity before. I've been traveling, and I've only just returned to California."

"Business? Pleasure?"

"Mourning," she said. A flicker of pain crossed her

face. "My wife died. I wasn't there. I needed some time to put my world back together before I could come home."

"I'm sorry," I said, the words feeling lame in my mouth. "How long ago?" I might not know what this woman was, but I knew she was pureblooded; there was nothing human about her. If I breathed deeply enough, I could taste the undiluted black tea and white hydrangea ghost of her magic. Purebloods measure time differently than changelings and humans do. Li Qin could easily have been mourning someone who had died a century before.

"Two years next week," she said, and smiled again. "But that's not why you're here."

"I'm sorry for your loss," I said. Turning to April, I asked, "Can we go inside? We're here on a case, and I need to bring you up to speed."

"Certainly." April cocked her head, looking as if she were listening to something I couldn't hear. April is the eyes and ears of her fiefdom; if she looked like she was listening to something, that's because she almost certainly was. She blinked and straightened up again. "Alex is the only one in the building, and he is occupied with hardware restoration in the main server room. We should be undisturbed in the main cafeteria. Li can take you." With that, she was gone, leaving the scent of ozone hanging in the air.

"I still hate it when she does that," said Quentin.

Li Qin laughed. "Follow me," she said, and waved for us to accompany her into the building.

As always, access to the fae side of Tamed Lightning involved going through the over-refrigerated reception area and from there to the labyrinthine maze of cubicles that served as the company's primary workspace. Being staffed entirely by fae meant the middle of the day was a dead time, and we walked through a tomb that would become a thriving business when the sun went down.

Li Qin walked as if she knew where she was going, not hesitating as she led us through the maze and out the door on the far side, to the lawn that stretched between the company's two main buildings. We had crossed into the Summerlands when we entered the reception area, and we had left the mortal daylight behind; when we stepped outside, we were greeted not by sunlight, but by the clear bright glow of three full moons and countless silvered stars. It's always twilight trending into nighttime in the Summerlands.

"So have you known April long?" asked Quentin, filling the silence with words. That's a habit he's picked up from me. He was a lot more stoic when we first met.

"Yes," said Li Qin. "Inasmuch as it matters, you could say I've known her all her life."

"She's a good kid," I said. I took a peek into my pocket as we walked across the lawn, checking the Luidaeg's charm. It was glowing passive white. Wherever Chelsea was, it wasn't nearby. "She's done a pretty good job with this County."

"She has. Jan would be proud of her." Li Qin pushed open the door into the next building, holding it as Quentin and I walked past her. "April has been a fantastic Countess. I always knew she would be, given the opportunity."

"I appreciate your faith." Somehow, it wasn't surprising to hear April's voice coming from behind us.

"What did I say about sneaking up on people?" asked Li Qin.

"That I should do it only when it was funny." There was a faint inrush of air as April vanished, reappearing in the hall about six feet ahead of our little group. She turned to me. "I have started a fresh pot of coffee. I remember that this is essential to your normal operations."

"I love you right now," I said gravely.

April smiled.

Five minutes later, the four of us were settled in the cafeteria, Quentin with a can of Dr Pepper and a platter of sandwiches from the vending machine, me with an entire pot of coffee that I didn't have to share. Li Qin was making tea on the other side of the room when April looked at me, cocking her head to the side again, and asked, "So what is going on?"

One of the nice things about dealing with April is her lack of subtlety. There was no need to beat around the bush with her. "We have a missing half-Tuatha changeling. The last sign we had of where she might be going put her somewhere in this area. You're the only teleporter I know who lives out here, and I was hoping you might help us."

"Ah." April frowned. "Why is it vital she be found? Perhaps she has simply taken a vacation."

"That seems unlikely, since she's ripping holes in the fabric of Faerie. She's gating all the way into the sealed lands, and that's not good."

There was a clanging sound from the other side of the cafeteria. We turned to see Li Qin staring at us, the teapot lying at her feet in a spreading pool of liquid. Quentin and I stared at her. She stared back. Finally, slowly, she said, "You have to find her. You have to find her *now*."

"Yeah, we know," I said. "That's why we're here. She—"

"You don't understand," Li Qin interrupted. "The shallowing has been unstable all day. I thought it was being cranky. I didn't know someone was actively undermining reality. If you don't find her, if you don't *stop* her, knowes are going to start collapsing ... and they're going to start collapsing soon."

"Oh," said Quentin faintly. "That's new."

"Yeah," I agreed. "That's very new."

Crap.

THIRTEEN

LI QIN TOOK A BREATH, composing herself. "This isn't new," she said. "This is old. This goes all the way back to when Faerie was first setting roots into the mortal world."

I frowned a little. "Sorry, but I have no idea what that means. I skipped my remedial Fairyland history classes."

"I see why Jan liked you." Li Qin picked up her teapot. She set it on the counter and reached for a towel. "The Summerlands are the only realm of Faerie directly connected to the mortal world. That's why all knowes are anchored there. It's like building houses by digging holes in the skin of an orange—they touch on both the orange and the air, but are really suspended between them, fully part of neither. Do you understand?"

"No," I said.

Quentin shook his head. "My theory lessons haven't gotten that far yet."

"All right, then, to put it more simply: knowes and shallowings exist because the Summerlands are connected to the mortal world. Normally, teleporters move through the space between the anchors, and that makes the ties between worlds stronger by making the open spaces part of the binding. Like a spider weaving a web around a few solid sticks. A teleporter who's ripping through, on the other hand . . ." Li Qin knelt, beginning to wipe up her spill. "She's forcing her way through the places where the worlds are directly connected, and that can damage the connections. A knowe can exist severed from one world, provided it has a sufficiently large foundation in the other. A knowe severed from both worlds will crumble, and anyone inside will be lost forever."

"Wow," I said. "That's basically the cherry on top of this week's sundae of suck. Got any more good news for us?"

"Duchess Riordan has recently withdrawn the majority of her forces from our border," said April.

I paused, trying to catch up with her change of subjects. "What does that have to do with anything?" I asked finally.

"It changes the status quo. Changes, while interesting, often have negative consequences." April vanished again, reappearing next to Li Qin. She grabbed a towel of her own and dropped to her knees. "Riordan has never, in my records, committed to a troop movement of this size without royal orders or intent to commit invasion."

". . . Huh." I refilled my coffee cup, using the action to buy me a few seconds to think.

Tamed Lightning is a relatively new County; April is only its second regent. It was formed by taking unclaimed land from between two Duchies, Shadowed Hills and Dreamer's Glass. Sylvester, who ruled Shadowed Hills, didn't mind. Treasa Riordan, the Duchess of Dreamer's Glass, minded a lot. She didn't approve of anything that encroached on her borders, or made her plans for long-term expansion more difficult. She was paranoid, greedy, and aggressive toward her neighbors—in short, a classic Daoine Sidhe regent. There's a reason they hold so many fiefdoms. They're good at it, sure. But they're also willing to step in and take what they want, when they want it, without caring who gets hurt in the process.

To illustrate my point: January O'Leary died partly because she was blind to what was going on in her own fiefdom and partly because she knew that if she took herself out of harm's way, Riordan would steal her lands. Walk away for a minute, walk away forever. April was right. There was no way Riordan would be moving her people without a good reason.

"April," I said, slowly. "Do you think you could take a charm to Dreamer's Glass for me? I don't need you to find Chelsea, but I need to know if it changes colors."

"I am sorry, but I cannot." She straightened and tossed her tea-soaked towel onto the counter, where it landed with a splat. "Riordan has warded the boundaries of her land against me. I can enter only when I am physically transported, and once inside, I cannot return to my primary server through normal means. I dislike travel on her land for that precise reason."

"That, and the part where she'd hold you hostage if she thought she could get away with it." I pinched the bridge of my nose. "We need to get into that Duchy."

"Perhaps I can help with that," said Li Qin. "I am still afforded certain privileges there, much as it pains Riordan to extend them to me."

"Why?" asked Quentin. "I mean why privileges, not why is Riordan a pissy bitch. I mean, we knew that part. She's a pissy bitch because she's a pissy bitch."

"The first rule of Tautology Club is the first rule of Tautology Club," I muttered.

Li Qin smiled sadly. "I am the widow of the former regent of Tamed Lightning. By tradition, all neighboring fiefdoms owe me seven years of hospitality, should I choose to claim it. That includes Dreamer's Glass."

Quentin frowned. "But I thought January was the only—ow!" He turned to frown at me. "Why did you kick me?"

"Because otherwise you would have eaten your own foot," I said. I turned back to Li Qin. "I'm sorry for your loss."

"You said that already," she said, not unkindly. "Still, I would be glad to accompany you to Riordan's Court, if you think it would assist."

"I do." I topped off my coffee before I stood. "April, can you do me a favor and watch for signs of someone you don't know teleporting into Tamed Lightning? Her magic smells like sycamore smoke and calla lilies. It's pretty distinct."

"I can," she said. "What shall I do if I am able to locate her?"

"Try to intercept her, if you can. See if you can convince her to stop running." I wasn't sure Chelsea was capable of stopping. Still. If April could manage it—if she could match her jump for jump, at least within the range of the ALH servers that allowed the cyber-Dryad to take solid form—it would be a huge step toward ending all of this.

"Understood," said April.

"I need to get my purse and some slightly less insulting clothes," said Li Qin. "Can you wait here for me?"

"Unless Chelsea appears in the cafeteria, we've got nowhere else to go," I said. I paused. "Besides, there's a phone call I should make."

Quentin gave me a curious look. "Who?"

I unzipped the top pocket on my leather jacket and extracted my cell phone. "I need to let Tybalt know what's going on," I replied.

"I will keep Quentin entertained until your return," said April. Knowing her, that could take the form of anything from math problems to violent video games. Knowing Quentin, he could take it. I nodded to her and walked out of the cafeteria a few steps behind Li Qin.

Once we were out in the hall, she turned left, vanishing. I walked over to the far wall and leaned against it. The Court of Cats doesn't have telephone service, and reaching their King can require some pretty circuitous tactics. Flipping my phone open, I dialed the house.

The phone rang three times before a sweet female voice said, "Hello?"

"Hey, Jazz." May's girlfriend, Jasmine—Jazz for short—is a Raven-maid, a diurnal skinshifter. Unlike the rest of us, she doesn't get cranky when she's forced to stay awake past dawn. "I need you to do me a favor."

Her tone shifted, becoming all business. "Sure, Toby," she said. "What do you need?"

"I need to get a message to Tybalt. Can you flap over to Golden Gate Park for me?"

"Of course."

"Great. Tell him we followed Chelsea's trail to Fremont but lost track of her before we got here. Quentin and I are heading into Dreamer's Glass. Riordan has been behaving oddly, and I want to find out whether that's due to her having something to hide, as opposed to her usual bat-shit crazy. I think I'm going to need backup. I bet he'd like some things to hit."

There was a pause before Jazz said, "Are you actually *asking* for backup?"

"I just said that, didn't I?"

"Oh, thank Oberon. I'll tell him. Where should he meet you?"

I decided to leave that one alone. "Tell him to head for the main building at ALH Computing. I'm pretty sure he can't get in via the Shadow Roads, but he's been here before—he should know where to come out. I'll tell Countess O'Leary that he's coming. She'll know when we've been gone for long enough to need someone to extract us."

Was I being paranoid in assuming there was a chance Riordan was going to try to detain us against our will? Yeah, probably. That didn't mean I wasn't also right.

"I will," said Jazz firmly. "Open roads and kind skies, Toby."

"Open roads," I said, and hung up.

Quentin and April were sitting at the table when I returned to the cafeteria. He was busy shoving sandwiches into his mouth as if he had no idea where his next meal was going to be coming from. She wasn't eating; instead, she was solemnly explaining the plot of a movie that sounded like the sort of thing May likes to watch on

Saturday nights when there's nothing better for her to do. Giant mutant fruit bats featured heavily.

Both of them turned when I stepped into the room. Quentin swallowed, not bothering to chew, before asking, "Did you get through?"

"Jazz is taking him a message and letting him know we may need backup. If all goes well, we won't wind up stranded in Dreamer's Glass while Chelsea brings the world down around our ears."

"You always say the most optimistic things." He stood, pausing only long enough to shove his last two sandwiches into his coat pockets. "It was good to see you again, April."

"It was good to see you as well." April didn't stand; she just disappeared and reappeared next to me. "I am glad you were able to meet my secondary parent."

"Me, too," I said. It was odd to think of Li Qin as having been married to Jan, largely because it was hard to imagine Jan being married to anyone not made of circuitry and computer code. I guess we're all more complicated than we look on the surface. As for why Quentin, who had been a Ducal page, hadn't known about her . . . Li Qin didn't seem to have a title of her own. Right or wrong, that would have made her irrelevant to the local political structure. If she hadn't been married to Sylvester's niece, he might have heard of her anyway, but Sylvester was oddly protective of information where Jan was concerned. That particular quirk kept finding new and surprising ways to bite us in the ass.

The door opened, and Li Qin stuck her head into the room. "Are you ready?" she asked. She had changed into her "slightly less insulting clothes," leaving her ready for either a Renaissance Faire or a semiformal Court appearance, depending on how you looked at it. She was wearing a floor-length red brocade skirt a few shades darker than her rose-pink peasant blouse, with a waist-cincher corset in a red so deep that it was almost black. Her hair was loose around her face, hanging down below her shoulders, and she was wearing an illusion that made her seem human, adding whites to her eyes and slightly softening her face.

I blinked. Quentin blinked, too, and he said what I was thinking: "How did you lace yourself into that thing without help?"

"Velcro," said Li Qin serenely. "If you would come with me, I'll take you to the next stop on your chaperoned tour of the South Bay."

"I always enjoy visiting crazy despots," I said. "Let's roll."

"Bye, April," said Quentin.

"Good-bye," said April, and disappeared.

We didn't see anyone as we walked back to the parking lot. The engine had barely had time to cool off. Li Qin took the front passenger seat without comment, apparently assuming that as navigator, she got to ride shotgun. I raised an eyebrow at Quentin. He shook his head. Even after all his time with me, my squire still had sufficient manners not to argue with a lady.

"Head for San Jose," said Li Qin, once I was in the car with the engine started. "I'll tell you where to turn when we get closer."

"Got it." I pulled out of the parking lot, the shadows of the eucalyptus trees ringing the company grounds dancing over my windshield like ghosts. The portcullis was up when we approached, and it dropped only after we were safely through. Quentin and I both sighed with relief.

Li Qin watched this with clear, if tired, amusement. Then she said, "I understand you were made Countess of Goldengreen?"

"Yeah, but I gave the title up. Dean Lorden is in charge of the County now." More power to him. I'd hated being a Countess. I wasn't equipped for it, and if I'd kept my fiefdom, I would probably have done some serious damage. Dean, on the other hand, was raised in a noble household. His mother, Dianda, was the Duchess of Saltmist, and when she wasn't playing scary mermaid games, she ran a pretty good Duchy. She'd taught her sons to rule, even knowing that only one would ever inherit in the Undersea. Lucky Dean, he tripped over one of the rare land nobles who wanted her holdings about as much as she wanted a hole in the head. Maybe less.

"Good," said Li Qin. "The fact that you had power and chose to give it up will tell Riordan that you're either without ambition or dangerously unbalanced. Either way, you should be interesting enough not to throw out unheard."

"What about me?" asked Quentin.

"You're my squire, so clearly your folks are cool with you hanging out with a loony slacker," I said amiably. "That makes you pretty harmless, politically speaking."

"I'm not sure how I feel about that," said Quentin.

"For today, embrace it," advised Li Qin. "It may be what makes this a fruitful meeting."

"Good old Duchess Riordan." I shook my head. "That's the problem with feudalism. You never get to vote the crazy ones out."

"Don't," said Li Qin, with sudden sharpness. I glanced her way, surprised. She shook her head. "Don't make the mistake of writing Treasa Riordan off as crazy. If you want madness, visit the Court at Golden Gate. Riordan has something a lot more dangerous."

"What's that?" asked Quentin.

"Ambition." Li Qin said the word like it was coated in poison, something to be thrust away as quickly and as firmly as possible.

"Charming." I glanced Li Qin's way again as I drove. She was frowning. "Sorry."

"I offered," she said.

"Still." I sighed. "So, new topic. Not to be rude or anything, but I'm pretty up on my fae taxonomy, and I've never seen a member of your race before. What are you?"

"That's because not many of us live in North America, and most of the ones who do are in Southern California, Montreal, or Texas. We had a colony in San Francisco, but we moved to more stable ground shortly before the 1906 earthquake." Li Qin shook her head. "We're called Shyi Shuai. We . . . read luck, for lack of a better way of putting it."

That explained how they'd been able to move to stable ground before the earthquake, rather than joining the exodus from the Bay Area that followed it. "Huh," I said. "Neat." I meant that, too. Now that I had the taste of her bloodline filed in my memory, I'd be able to identify any other Shyi Shuai purebloods or changelings I might encounter. "Who claims you?"

"Maeve," said Li Qin. She gave me a sidelong look. "Now, to be polite, I must ask you the same question. Your squire is Daoine Sidhe. April informs me you're not, although she says you once told her you were. What are you, and who claims you?"

"In my defense, I wasn't lying at the time; I was misinformed," I said. "I'm Dóchas Sidhe. My mother, Amandine, is our Firstborn, and Oberon was her father, so I suppose technically he claims us. No one else has put in a bid, anyway."

"Dóchas Sidhe?" Li Qin frowned. "That's familiar, somehow."

"What? Where did you—"

"I don't know. I think . . . the Library. I came here from Southern California a long time ago, to study there. I wanted to chart the genealogy of the Shyi Shuai in North America. I think that's where I heard that name before. I'm sorry." Li Qin shook her head, frown deepening. "I don't really remember. It was a footnote, if that."

"Right," I said, and fell silent, pondering. The Libraries are the repository of fae history, going all the way back to the beginning. They're invaluable resources . . . if you can get a pass, something that's not always easy. I'd never even bothered to try. The librarians don't let many people past their doors, and as a changeling, I was automatically at the bottom of their list.

Quentin's had time to learn how to recognize my "I'm thinking, leave me alone" silences. He leaned forward, poking his head over the back of the seats, and asked Li

Qin, "So why'd you stay up here, if you just came to study?"

"The usual reason," said Li Qin. "I met a girl. Fell in love. Decided to stick around while she did a variety of insane, occasionally impossible things. Got married. Adopted a Dryad. Did my best to live happily ever after."

"Oh," said Quentin. Then he asked the one question I wasn't sure how to word: "Why weren't you here?"

"Because Jan asked me to leave," said Li Qin. "The situation was ... complicated. My luck was tangled, and everything I could see, or get Yui to scry for, said it was tangled because it contained a potential death—my death. We agreed it was best for me to go and see some family in Montreal while I worked past the knot. By the time I heard what had happened, it was too late. I couldn't even come to the funeral."

Yui had been Tamed Lightning's Kitsune alchemist. If she told Jan that Li Qin had to leave or die, Jan would have listened. I still winced. "I—"

"Please don't say you're sorry for my loss." A smile ghosted across her lips. "Twice was more than enough."

"I lost my boyfriend recently," I said quietly. "It's not the same thing, but it's in the same family. I can't imagine losing a spouse."

"Pray you never have to," she recommended, and turned to look out the window, plainly signaling that she wanted a break from the conversation. It was something I was more than happy to give her.

Connor was a Selkie, and I was a relatively weak changeling when we met. We always knew we wouldn't have forever, even if everything in the universe went our way—and that's something that never happened, for either of us. I lost him too soon, but I always knew on some level that the loss was coming. Jan and Li Qin were both purebloods. They had every reason to think they had forever, or at least the next best thing. Losing her like that must have seemed impossible. Sadly for all of us, it wasn't.

"Take the next exit and follow the signs to the Museum of Science," said Li Qin, breaking the silence that had fallen over the car. I nodded and followed her directions.

Downtown San Jose looked disturbingly like downtown in a hundred other American cities, a mixture of towering office buildings, obscenely large hotels, green patches of park, and museums meant to titillate and enthrall the tourists, causing them to spend more money before heading for home. The Museum of Science fit right in, tucked as it was between a chain restaurant and a park that promised dire fines for anyone seen walking a dog.

"Pull into the parking garage, and head for the lower level," said Li Qin.

A machine at the mouth of the garage gave me a piece of paper with a timestamp on it and lots of small print telling me how much it would cost if I lost my ticket. I was starting to think San Jose existed solely to charge me for things I didn't know were against the rules.

The parking garage was about half-full, but I drove past the open spots on the first two levels anyway, heading for the bottom. "Now what?"

"Now drive into that wall." Li Qin pointed at a patch of blank concrete.

"Wouldn't be the first time," I sighed, and hit the gas. There was a faint electric tingle as we passed through the seemingly solid stone and into the Summerlands. I immediately stepped on the brake, looking around. "Um."

"Weird," said Quentin.

"Welcome to Dreamer's Glass," said Li Qin.

We had driven out of a parking garage and into . . . a parking garage. This one was constructed in what seemed to be a natural cavern; the walls I could see were ragged stone, and the ceiling was so high it disappeared into shadow. Globes of glowing witchlight floated about twenty feet up, casting their rays down on the jarringly mundane grid of white lines painted in the middle of the cavern floor, marking out the parking spaces. Most of them were full.

"You want to park in one of the spaces marked with a poppy," said Li Qin. "Riordan is very touchy about people using their assigned spaces."

"Poppy meaning . . . ?"

"Visitor, not hostile, not yet allied, still has to pay for parking."

I sighed. "Wow. I love hospitality."

No one came to greet us as I parked the car. That made me more nervous. Everything I'd ever heard about Dreamer's Glass told me we should have been surrounded by an army by now. Instead, we were alone.

"I don't like this," said Quentin.

"You're not meant to," said Li Qin. "Just drop your human disguise and get out. It'll all be clear in a moment."

"I hate it when people say things like that." I let my illusions go as I opened the car door. From the sudden blend of scents in the air, I knew Li Qin and Quentin were doing the same.

I had barely finished standing when a man appeared in front of me, tall, thin, and translucent as clear water poured into a human-shaped mold. He was holding a sword as clear as the rest of him, its point only a few inches from my throat. I froze. I could see more of the spun-glass fae appearing out of the corner of my eye. They weren't teleporting. They were just becoming visible.

"Guess we got that army after all," I said, and breathed in sharply, hoping it would be taken as a sign of fear.

The sword at my throat didn't waver. "What is your business?" demanded the man, in a voice only slightly more substantial than the rest of him.

"We're here to request audience with Duchess Treasa Riordan," I said. I knew the taste of his heritage, even if I couldn't see him clearly: Folletti. Their race hailed from the Cloud Kingdoms, where it was easier for someone who was essentially a living piece of the wind to get by. They only came to land to sell their services to the highest bidder. In this case, it must have been Riordan. Somehow, knowing that she had invisible guards didn't make me feel any better about being there.

Li Qin walked around the car to stand beside me, unbothered by the translucent men with swords. "I am allowed, under the mourner's flag, to visit these lands and claim hospitality."

"Well, sure, honey, but that doesn't mean you get to go bringing guests." The new voice was female, more solid than the whispering tones of the Folletti. I turned to see a Daoine Sidhe woman in jeans and a black T-shirt with "The Careful Application of Terror is Also a Form of Communication" printed across the front. Her only jewelry was a ruby choker, red against the white of her throat. "Sergio, you can take your boys and go back on patrol. I've got these ones."

"Yes, Your Grace." The Folletti in front of me slid his sword back into an unseen sheath, sketched a bow, and vanished. The other Folletti did the same. My hair was ruffled by a sudden wind, and the taste of their presence vanished from my mouth.

"Hello, Treasa," said Li Qin. "You're looking well."

Duchess Treasa Riordan looked more than well. Like most Daoine Sidhe, she looked radiant, even dressed like she was getting ready to make a munchies run before a night of cramming for exams. Her shoulder-length hair was a shade of red so dark it verged on black and shattered the light into prismatic shards when she moved. Her features were exquisite, and her figure could have convinced a fashion magazine that jeans were the only appropriate attire for the season. Gorgeous isn't uncommon in Faerie. Still, I sometimes think I see certain people so often that their beauty stops affecting me the way it should. I wasn't having that problem with Riordan. Just looking at her made my heart hurt a little bit.

"And you're looking like you're taking advantage of mourner's rights. I'm counting your hours, Li. One minute over, you're on my land, your ass is mine." Duchess Riordan said this as calmly and pleasantly as a normal person might ask her guests if they wanted a cup of coffee.

"I am aware," said Li Qin, taking it in stride.

"Just so we're all on the same page here." Duchess Riordan turned to me and Quentin. Her eyes were an impossible shade of frosted lilac, like flowers that had been left outside during a cold snap. "And you are?"

"October Daye of Shadowed Hills, Your Grace." I bowed. Being a knight means I don't have to curtsy unless I want to. Bowing was equally appropriate, and it would hopefully make me look like I was a little dense when it came to courtly behavior, rather than making me seem rude. Riordan was an unknown factor.

"Really? You're Amandine's daughter?" Riordan's frosty purple eyes searched my face with new intensity before she passed judgment: "I thought you'd be taller."

"I get that a lot," I said, even though I didn't. Quentin moved to my other side. I gestured to him with one hand. "This is my squire, Quentin."

"Milady," said Quentin. His bow was deeper than mine and scrupulously formal. He was a Ducal page before I acquired him. Certain habits die hard, and no matter how hard I try to shake them out of him, I have to admit that sometimes they come in handy.

"Hmm," said Riordan. The look she gave him was as assessing as the one she'd given me, but it was the sort of assessment most people reserve for livestock and expensive appliances.

Quentin was growing up. He was handsome enough, if I stepped back and forced myself to think of him that way, but that wasn't what mattered. What mattered was that he was a pureblood Daoine Sidhe, trained in the courtly arts, and approaching marriageable age. For a woman like Riordan, the fact that he came from a family low-ranked enough to allow him to be squired to a changeling—and one from an unknown bloodline, at that—was probably a bonus. What I knew about her told me that she wasn't a woman who shared power well.

I wasn't the only one who understood what that look meant. Quentin swallowed hard, looking uncomfortable, and shifted to put himself just a little bit farther behind me. Smart kid.

"Now, then. I'm sorry I wasn't here to greet you as soon as you pulled in, but I was just wrapping up a raid when the border alarms told me we had company." A smile spread across Riordan's face. I didn't trust it one bit. "I'm glad to see Sergio and his boys didn't damage any of you. Folletti can be so endearingly enthusiastic, don't you think?"

"Raid?" I asked.

"You play *World of Warcraft*?" Quentin asked, almost at the same time.

"Sure do, sugar. On the internet, nobody knows that you're an all-powerful faerie monarch, now, do they?" Riordan's smile turned briefly more believable.

"All-powerful" was stretching things a bit, but hey. We were in her domain; if she wanted to be delusional, I wasn't going to argue. "Your Grace, Li Qin is here because I wanted to request an audience with you. We're trying to locate a missing changeling. I was hoping one of your people might have seen her."

Riordan's eyes narrowed. "Are you implying something, honey?"

"No, not at all. I just figured someone as connected and well-informed as you would be aware of anything strange that happened in your Duchy, and there are signs she went this way, at least for a little while." I was laying it on a little thick. That probably wasn't a bad idea.

"Hmm," said Riordan, managing to sound interested and annoyed at the same time. It was a neat trick. "All right, then, if you were willing to endure her company," she waved a hand at Li Qin, who held her silence, and her small, polite smile, "just to see me, I suppose I should let myself be seen. Li can show you where I keep the guests I don't feel like dealing with. The Folletti will escort you to my receiving chamber in twenty minutes." She turned to walk away.

"But you're here now," I protested, before I thought better of it.

Riordan looked back over her shoulder at me, and winked. "Gotta log off, honey. Otherwise, the guild will get annoyed with me, and you're not worth that much. Ta-ta." That appeared to finish things, at least for her; this time when she walked away, she didn't look back.

"That was . . ." I said, and stopped, unsure how I could finish that sentence without bringing the Folletti down on my head. The fact that Riordan had left us standing in a big, empty room potentially full of invisible men who were hanging out just outside the range of my ability to find them wasn't escaping me.

"I usually go with 'bracing,'" said Li Qin. "Jan usually had a few other things to say, but she was smart enough to save them until we were home. Still, we have permission to be here now. Come on. I'll show you to the foyer."

Li Qin was short enough that keeping up with her was easy. Keeping myself from walking too fast and leaving her behind, now, that was hard. It didn't help that Quentin was practically glued to my side, looking around as though he expected Riordan to leap out and propose shacking up at any moment.

"So," I said, as we walked. "That was different. Given the way you're dressed, I expected something a little more, you know. Traditional." Probably including the traditional changing room just inside the knowe, where I could have cast an illusion over my own jeans, jacket, and T-shirt.

Li Qin laughed. "Riordan is *very* traditional, at least when it comes to making sure her guests know who's in charge. If I dressed like this every day, she'd expect me to wear casual clothing when I came to see her. She wants people to be uncomfortable. That way, they never forget she's in control."

"Cute," I said.

"Believe me, you've only scratched the surface." We had reached the wall of the cavern, which looked like smooth, unbroken stone. After our arrival from the park-

ing garage, it wasn't really a surprise when Li Qin just
kept going, disappearing into the gray without a ripple. I
looked at Quentin, shrugged, and followed her through
the wall.

The cavern-slash-garage was huge the way mountains
or oceans are huge—naturally, and without trying to
make a point through sheer size. That was the only thing
it had in common with the hallway on the other side of
the wall.

The entry hall of Riordan's knowe was decorated in
what I could only describe as early Victorian bordello as
reinterpreted by the creative team behind the *Lord of
the Rings* movies. The globes of glowing light from the
cavern were here, too, dancing a slow weaving pattern
between chandeliers laden with candles that burned a
steady green. At least they didn't flicker. Hanging tapestries covered the walls, all depicting Riordan. Riordan
sitting in a throne during formal Court, looking majestic
and wise. Riordan on a white horse, leading a charge in
some unidentified battle. Riordan in a meadow, gazing
thoughtfully off into the distance.

"Whoa," I said. "Medieval political propaganda."

Quentin didn't say anything. He didn't need to. The
way he was wrinkling his nose said everything for him.

Li Qin chuckled. "It takes most people like that the
first time. When Jan started sending me here to negotiate
for peace along our borders, I thought she was mad at
me. This way." She started down the hall. The thick, or-
nately patterned carpet muffled her footsteps entirely.

That carpet ... the pattern was vertigo-inducing
enough to make my stomach turn if I tried to look at it
while I walked, leaving me with a choice between the
horrible tapestries—bad—and the dancing globes of
light—just as bad. I settled for staring straight ahead, trying not to look at anything but the back of Li Qin's head.

Maybe talking would help. I cleared my throat and
asked, "So she just lets you run around the knowe? Even
though you're from Tamed Lightning?"

"When January was alive, refusing me a host's courtesies would have been an aggressive act. Riordan is never aggressive unless she's confident of having the upper hand. We were always small, but an unprovoked move against us would have brought Shadowed Hills into the fight, on our side. She wasn't going to risk it." Li Qin kept walking. "Now that I'm a widow, etiquette states she can't refuse me any privilege I had while I was still the wife of a Countess. It's a useful, if slightly stupid, arrangement of manners."

"Seven years from the death of a spouse or child, if you're the parent or consort of a noble," said Quentin. I glanced his way. He shrugged. "There's a book we have to memorize."

"Yet one more reason for me to be glad I was never a child of the nobility." Daughter of a Firstborn, yes; noble, no. My mother doesn't have a title. I guess no one ever thought she needed one.

"Here we are." Li Qin stopped at a door that would have been almost tasteful, if it hadn't been for the gilded crown molding that surrounded it, like a giant picture frame. It swung open at her touch, revealing a room that appeared to have been decorated entirely in white velvet. Six *shades* of white velvet. It was like a whipped cream explosion.

"Wow, this just gets classier all the time." I started toward the door, and froze. The air currents in the hall had shifted when Li Qin opened the new room; not much, but enough that the natural airflow was bringing me different scents.

I smelled sycamore smoke and calla lilies.

"Chelsea," I whispered.

"Toby?" Quentin looked at me, eyes wide. "What's up?"

I didn't answer. Instead, I dug a hand into my pocket, pulling out the Luidaeg's Chelsea-chaser. It was blazing a bright fire-engine red. Quentin gasped, pulling out his own charm. It was the same color.

"She's here." I looked up, toward Li Qin. "Can you cover for me?"

"Until the time of your audience, yes. After that ..." She shrugged helplessly. "I'll do what I can, but I don't recommend attracting the attention of her guards."

"Yeah, I'll do my best." I reached into my other pocket, dug out the car keys, and tossed them to Quentin. "You know what to do."

His mouth dropped open as my meaning hit home. "You can't seriously mean to—"

"Go running off alone so that if one of us winds up getting snagged by Riordan's invisible goons, the other one can keep looking for Chelsea and Raj? Yeah, I can." I forced a smile. It didn't feel sincere. I didn't care. "Besides, what's the worst that can happen? You keep Li safe. I'll be back as soon as I can."

With that, I turned and walked away, letting the Luidaeg's charm lead me deeper into Riordan's knowe, where hopefully, Chelsea—and through her, Raj—would be waiting.

FOURTEEN

THE DEEPER I WENT into Riordan's knowe, the more obvious it became that she took her decorating tips from a Vegas casino, with dashes of the Moulin Rouge thrown in to spice things up. There was no neon, probably because she couldn't get it to stabilize in the Summerlands. Globes of witchlight and those damn green candles more than made up the difference.

There was one nice thing about the place: it was so garish that there was no chance I'd start going in a circle. I would have needed to be blind to wind up in the same room twice without knowing it. The Luidaeg's charm pulled me onward, glow intensifying until it hurt to look directly at it. I caught hints and wisps of Chelsea's magic, like the ghosts of sycamore trees and lilies. It was almost faint enough to be my imagination, but the charm was glowing, and I trusted the Luidaeg's magic.

The carpets in the knowe muffled my footsteps, which meant they were doing the same for anyone else who happened to be wandering the halls. If I hadn't been paying such close attention, I might have missed the sound of someone talking up ahead. I froze. I didn't know who it was, but I knew that they weren't with me; neither Li Qin nor Quentin would have been speaking that openly while they walked around Riordan's knowe, and they probably wouldn't have been wandering around unescorted.

I pressed myself against the wall, planning to hide behind the nearest tapestry. The fabric buckled under my weight, sending me plummeting. I managed to clap my free hand over my mouth before I landed on my ass. All that escaped from between my fingers was a faint squeak, barely audible even to me. The red light from the Luidaeg's charm cast a bloody glow on the room I'd fallen into. It was a small antechamber, barely bigger than a closet. It was the most plainly decorated room I'd seen since we arrived in Dreamer's Glass, all bare walls and uncarpeted hardwood floor. That was a relief.

I climbed to my feet, moving slowly to keep from being heard by whoever was coming down the hall. The voice that was coming closer outside the tapestry, on the other hand . . . I wrapped my fingers tightly around the Luidaeg's charm, dimming the glow as much as I could. Enough still seeped out to make the walls look bloody. I closed my eyes.

"—you, she's in my damn receiving room. I don't know what you're intending to do about this, but our deal did *not* include me having unexpected guests." Riordan sounded annoyed. She would probably have been more annoyed if she'd known I was there. Since I didn't hear any other voices, I assumed she was on the phone. "I want you to fix this. I don't care what it takes, you fix it. I have things to do."

There was a pause while the person on the other end of her call answered. Riordan's snort was so loud that she had to be passing directly in front of the tapestry concealing me.

"Oh, is that so? Look, Mister, you're going to have a much bigger world of trouble than I am if you don't take care of this, and take care of it *now*. I have more to worry about—"

Her words faded into unintelligibility as she moved on down the hall. I stayed frozen until even the faint echoes of her voice were gone. Then I let out a breath, straightened, and unwrapped my fingers from around the Luidaeg's charm. That had been close. Too close: if I didn't find Chelsea soon, I was going to need to head back to the others.

I tugged the tapestry aside and peered out into the hall. There was no one there. Even so, it never hurts to be careful. I closed my eyes and breathed in, filtering through the scents in the air, looking for traces of the Folletti. There were none. For the moment, at least, I was alone.

The tapestry slid back into place with a heavy swishing sound as I crept out of my hiding place and resumed letting the charm tug me along, thinking as I walked. Riordan wasn't happy about one of her visitors. Li Qin was a familiar face, and Riordan would hardly be demanding someone "fix it" when Li Qin was within her rights to be here. No, she had to be complaining about me. Which brought up a more interesting question: *who* was she complaining to?

The Luidaeg's charm was dimming. It was still glowing red; it was just . . . duller, as if its batteries were going out. Or as though Chelsea was moving again. I swore softly and picked up my pace, trying to let the charm lead me to where I needed to be before I lost the trace.

I didn't hear the wind whistling through the chandeliers until the sound was almost on top of me. I whirled, staring up into the darkness against the ceiling. That's the trouble with Folletti. By the time you know where they're coming from, there's no way that you can run. And me without a big bag of coal dust to throw on them and keep them visible.

"Shit," I muttered, and started backing up. Maybe I'd get lucky and find another hidden chamber behind a hideous tapestry. Sure, the Folletti would probably see me duck inside, but it would give me a chance to get the charm out of sight, and I could always say I got lost looking for the bathroom. Most purebloods assume all changelings are stupid. There was even a chance they'd believe me.

My shoulders hit the fabric—and hands reached out from behind the tapestry, yanking me backward into the shadows on the other side. I squeaked before I could stop myself—

—and then everything was dark and cold, and I was falling, falling, *falling*—

—and we fell through a portal in the side of a wall, landing in a heap on the floor of what appeared to be an attic. My lungs were aching. I stayed where I was, trying to catch my breath.

Underneath me, Tybalt commented mildly, "While this is amusing and such, don't you think we'd be more productive if you elected to move? I ask merely out of curiosity, and not because you're cutting off circulation to my left arm."

"Oh, crap. Sorry." I scrambled to my feet, narrowly avoiding elbowing Tybalt in any sensitive spots. "Are you okay?"

"I am quite fine." Tybalt flowed to his feet with effortless grace before stooping to retrieve the Luidaeg's charm from where it had fallen to the floor. He held it out to me. "The same question might well be asked of you, you know. Whatever possessed you to think roving the halls of Dreamer's Glass unescorted would be the wisest thing to do?"

The charm was dark in Tybalt's hand. When my fingers touched it, it flickered back into foxfire light. Not red, though, not anymore. That would have been too much to hope for. "I was trying to find Chelsea."

"You nearly found the wrong end of a Folletti's blade."

"Didn't. That means I win." I tucked the charm into my jacket pocket. "That was a good save. How did you know I needed it?"

"Jasmine was kind enough to let me know my services might be required. When I arrived in Tamed Lightning, April alerted me to your destination." A small, self-satisfied smile spread across Tybalt's face. "There are no Cait Sidhe in Riordan's domain."

I blinked. "So?"

"So, when she employed my late, lamented cousin Barbara as one of her spies, she was forced to open her wards to access from the Shadow Roads. Otherwise, there was no way the espionage could have continued for as long as it did."

Barbara was one of the people who died at ALH, right around the time Jan did. At the moment, that didn't matter as much as the fact that Barbara had been Cait Sidhe. I stared at Tybalt, comprehension dawning. "Riordan didn't think to close her wards back up."

"I daresay she assumed there would never be cause." His smile became a smirk. "I do enjoy proving people wrong."

"You know, Tybalt, I could kiss you right now," I said. His eyes widened in surprise, and I barely managed not to wince. I shouldn't have said that. Kisses were nothing to joke about, especially where Tybalt was concerned. I turned quickly away, using the need to survey my surroundings as an excuse not to meet his eyes.

Wherever we were, it was clearly Riordan's knowe. Like all attics, this one was filled with things too worn to be on display and too expensive or treasured to get rid of. Unlike most attics, this one could have been used as a shrine to kitsch. Some of the things Riordan had decided were too tacky to keep on display were truly appalling, if only because someone, somewhere, had gone to the trouble of actually *making* them. Who needs a brass fountain shaped like a pissing Satyr, anyway?

Tybalt cleared his throat. "Interesting décor."

"You should see the rest of this place." I turned back to him. "Is there any chance you could get me back to Quentin and Li before Riordan reaches them?" I paused. "How did you find me, anyway?"

"For all that I must keep reminding you that I am not a bloodhound, it's true that on occasion, having a sensitive nose is a useful thing. I followed the smell of you." Tybalt sighed, looking exaggeratedly put-upon. "If you must be ferried back to your people, I suppose I can oblige. But only because you asked so very nicely, and promised me a kiss."

I raised an eyebrow.

Tybalt sighed again. This time, his put-upon expression seemed less exaggerated. "Take a deep breath."

"At least this time you're giving me fair warning," I said, and breathed in.

"Surprising you was better than the alternatives," he said. He put one hand to either side of my waist and stepped backward, pulling me into the shadows.

The more time I spend with Tybalt, the more I think that investing in some good silk long underwear would be a good idea. Sure, I'd roast most of the time, but I wouldn't be nearly as concerned about getting frostbite on the Shadow Roads.

We stepped off the Shadow Roads in the white velvet antechamber, where Quentin was pacing while an anxious-looking Li Qin sat on an overstuffed loveseat, spindling her skirt in her hands. She froze when she saw us, skirt dropping from suddenly motionless fingers. Quentin followed her gaze, turning, and relaxed markedly.

"You're late," he said. "Did you find her?"

"No, but she was here." I turned to Tybalt. "Can you wait at Tamed Lightning? I don't think I can explain you to Riordan, but I'm pretty sure we're going to need you again, real soon."

"Yes. There is, however, the matter of my payment to be settled. Tell your squire to avert his eyes, if you would be so kind."

"Why would I—"

My question was answered when Tybalt returned his hands to my waist, pulling me toward him, and pressed his lips to mine.

Passage through the Shadow Roads had left my skin cold. Not his. Kissing Tybalt was like standing too close to an open fire, all heat and the promise of pain if I came any closer. I stepped forward without thinking about it, returning his kiss with a willingness that surprised us both. Tybalt's fingers tightened on my waist, his lips starting to melt the frost from mine . . .

. . . and then he was pulling away, a smile on his face. "Enjoy your audience," he said, and stepped into the shadows, and was gone.

I stared at the wall for a moment, trying to recover my breath. My lips were still cold. I licked them. They tasted like some weird new brand of mint lip gloss. "Pennyroyal Perfection," not available any time soon from a store near you.

"Well. Your boyfriend certainly knows how to make an exit," said Li Qin. "I do hope he can get out of here without being seen."

"He's not my boyfriend, and he's good at not getting caught when he doesn't want to be." I turned back to the pair of them. Li Qin was standing now. Quentin was just staring at me. I wrinkled my nose at him. "Close your mouth before a Folletti flies into it."

He closed his mouth with a snap before saying, "That was weird."

"I know."

"I mean, really weird."

"I know that, too."

"Tybalt—"

"Quentin, as your knight, this is where I declare this conversation over. Got it?"

"Sure," he said, somewhat dubiously. "What did you find?"

"Nothing I'm going to be discussing here." There was no trace of the Folletti in the room, but I'm not Spider-Man. I can't sense danger coming without making a serious effort, and even then, my ability to feel out people's heritage at a distance is pretty tenuous. I've only had to count on it a few times. I wasn't willing to bet my life on it.

Both Li Qin and Quentin nodded their understanding. I turned to look at the door.

"It's been twenty minutes, hasn't it?"

"Don't the nobles ever make you wait to show who's

in charge where you come from?" asked Li Qin. "It's a fairly standard tactic here."

"I've encountered it a time or two," I said, as mildly as I could. Mostly from the Queen of the Mists, who isn't exactly what I'd call a role model for appropriate noble behavior. "How long do you think she's going to leave us here? We don't have forever."

As if on cue, the door to the reception room swung open, revealing—sort of—two half-solid Folletti. Both had their weapons drawn, but they weren't pointing them at us. Yet. The implied menace was sufficient.

"You will come with us," said one of them, voice barely loud enough to be audible.

When the wind orders me to do something, I do it. "We will come with you," I agreed, and gestured to Quentin and Li Qin to follow as I walked out of the room.

The translucent bodies of the Folletti distorted the tapestries and crown molding as they led the three of us down the hall. It was like being accompanied by two giant funhouse mirrors, both set permanently to "warp."

We stopped at a large set of double doors, surrounded by more of that ubiquitous crown molding, and built on a scale that made me wonder if Riordan had looked at the doors in Shadowed Hills and thought, "Mine should be bigger." They were so massive that I wasn't even sure they could be opened. One of the Folletti ghosted forward and turned what looked like another bit of crown molding in a full circle. One of the bottom panels in the right-hand door swung outward.

"I guess they can't be," I murmured.

The other Folletti turned to frown at me. "What was that?"

"Nothing," I said.

Still frowning, the Folletti led us through the panel and into Riordan's receiving room.

After the rest of the knowe, I'd been expecting something over the top and almost laughable. I definitely hadn't been expecting what was there. The room was large, easily on a par with the ballroom at Shadowed Hills. Globes of witchlight floated near the ceiling. There were no chandeliers, and the globes moved freely, according to some undefined pattern. The floor was simple stone, and the walls were bare, except for a banner at the very far end of the hall, directly behind Riordan's throne. It showed the arms of Dreamer's Glass—a crack running through silver fabric, with a lily on one side and a spindle on the other. I've never studied heraldry, but I know enough to know that the lily was probably a reference to the Lady of Shalott, who had her issues with mirrors. It was an odd choice for a Ducal coat of arms, but hey, not my business.

Riordan herself was seated on the throne beneath the banner, waiting for us. She came into clearer focus as we approached, and I realized that she'd changed her clothes. Her college girl chic was gone, replaced by a green floor-length gown that looked much more in tune with what Li Qin was wearing. Only her ruby choker remained; she wore no other jewelry. An unornamented silver circlet rested on her brow. If I hadn't seen her knowe, I would have looked at her and assumed she was a little old-fashioned, a little humble.

Since I *had* seen her knowe, I had to wonder what her angle was and what she expected to get out of it.

Riordan raised a hand, waving it languidly. The Folletti ghosted away again, becoming breezes that ruffled our hair as they flew past. The door slammed behind us. Quentin glanced at me. I nodded reassuringly, and we kept walking.

We stopped the polite ten paces before her throne. Li Qin curtsied. Quentin and I bowed. We all held our positions at the lowest point, supplicating ourselves. It was the appropriate thing to do; we were guests in Riordan's home. It still rankled, especially given what I'd heard her saying while I was in the hall—and since I wasn't supposed to have been there, it wasn't like I could reasonably ask her about it. Not unless I wanted to find out whether her hospitality extended to dungeons.

My back was just starting to hurt from having been folded over so long when Riordan said, with practiced sweetness, "You may rise."

"Your Grace," I said, straightening. "We appreciate your granting us this audience."

"It's the least I could do, sugar. You've never come to see me before, and it'd be plain rude to send you packing without letting you experience the grandeur of a formal reception." She giggled. It was probably meant to sound girlish and carefree. Instead, it sounded overly practiced, like the host of a bad PBS kid's show. "How are you finding Dreamer's Glass?"

"I've never seen anything like it," said Quentin, with absolute honesty.

Riordan beamed, clearly choosing to interpret his answer as a good thing. "I've worked very hard on this place. I'll have you know, I had a hand in decorating every single room."

"Really?" I asked. "That must have taken a lot of time."

"It was worth it." Riordan settled back in her throne, smile turning into something smug and dangerous. "Now. Why don't you explain just who it is you're looking for?"

"A changeling girl named Chelsea is missing. She hasn't had her Choice yet; she was still living with her mortal parent when her powers manifested." It wasn't a completely true statement. It was close enough, especially given my growing suspicion that Riordan was involved. "Her magic smells like sycamore smoke and calla lilies. She's shown a pretty impressive range on her gates—we don't know how far she might have traveled by now."

"Shoot, you mean you're here about a runaway? I thought it would be something worth getting worked up about. Teenagers run off, especially ones who can open themselves magic doors in space. She's probably in Los Angeles swooning over some movie star, and she'll come home when she's ready."

"I don't think so," I said. "For one thing, she's already

called home once, begging for help. Someone took her, Your Grace, and it's my job to get her back."

Riordan's eyes narrowed. "She called home? Did she speak to her human mother?"

"No," I lied. "I took the call. I was there looking for signs that might point me in her direction."

"Did you find any?"

"Not yet." I forced myself to keep looking at Riordan's face. Breaking eye contact would be a quick way to tell her something was wrong. "I was hoping she'd come here. I cast an augury that indicated she'd at least passed through." More lies, unless you wanted to interpret the Luidaeg's charm really, really broadly. But the Luidaeg is a blunt instrument, and telling Riordan she was helping us might trigger a violent response. If I were a kidnapper and someone told me the sea witch was on my trail, well. I'd be tempted to make sure that someone never had the opportunity to report back to her allies.

"I haven't seen her," said Riordan. If she was lying, she was doing it too smoothly for me to be sure about it. I suppose that was only fair. I was lying through my teeth, after all.

"If I may," said Li Qin. "The girl is young and does not know or respect the bounds of our domains. Might your guards have seen an intruder, one who came and was gone too quickly to be detained?"

"First off, *honey*, there's no 'our' in the domains around here. You didn't inherit when your little love bug went and left us." Riordan's words were delivered with a smile that did nothing to reduce their sharpness. The smell of apples and snowdrops rose in the air around her, a menacing reminder of her anger. I stiffened. She was too wrapped up in her own dialog to notice. "Second, if she'd been here, my guards would've caught her. I don't know how you do things in Tamed Lightning, but here, no one comes or goes without my leave."

"Can I leave a number for you to call if she shows

up?" I asked, trying to keep my tone level. It was essential that she not realize I recognized her magic. "We need to find her."

"Changelings run away. It happens." She kept smiling. "You did, didn't you? I remember your mama was so *mad*. This Chelsea girl is probably just doing the same thing. I don't see where it's any of my problem, to be honest."

I took a deep breath, counting to ten before I answered her. Amandine wasn't the perfect mother, and I *did* run away from home. But I was in my twenties and coming to understand that I'd never belong fully in the Summerlands, not a confused teenager who barely understood what she could do. "She's lost, and she doesn't know what she's doing," I said, as steadily as I could. "It's not your problem. Telling us if you see her is the right thing to do."

"I'll consider it," said Riordan. Her eyes flicked to Quentin, and she smiled. "Now, if one of you wanted to stay here, and maybe help me make sure I didn't get distracted..."

Quentin looked alarmed. I cleared my throat. "I'm sorry, but I need my squire with me. He's got important squire things to do. Part of his training. You understand."

"Of course," said Riordan. She didn't bother to conceal her disappointment. "If there wasn't anything else, one of my guards has reported a trespasser—not your little girl, this one didn't leave any gate traces behind—and I should be looking into that. You can leave." It wasn't an offer. It was an order.

"Yes, Your Grace," I said, bowing again. Quentin did the same.

Li Qin ... didn't. She tilted her head to the side, looking at Riordan. Finally, she said, "I understand from April that you did not attend January's funeral. A pity. It would have been nice to have you there."

"I didn't kill her, Li," said Riordan bluntly. "I didn't kill her, and I didn't invade her lands when that little abomination you call a daughter took power. How about you just be glad of that and leave the guilt trips for someone who's willing to take them?"

"As you like," said Li Qin, and curtsied. "Your hospitality is impeccable, as always."

"Yes," said Riordan. "I know." She'd followed the rules binding a host to the letter, giving no more than she had to but not withholding anything we could legitimately expect. It was a fine line to walk. She'd walked it without hesitating.

The Folletti whispered back into view around us, five of them this time, their positioning and posture clearly stating that we were supposed to go with them. I nodded one last time to Riordan, whose smile had faded entirely, before I turned to follow the Folletti. None of them said a word, not as we left the throne room and not as they walked us back through the knowe to the cavern where the car was waiting.

Quentin gave me back the keys. I unlocked the door while Li Qin paid our parking fees. Then we all put our human disguises back on, got into the car, and drove away.

FIFTEEN

NONE OF US SPOKE UNTIL we were past the San Jose city limits. Riordan might not have been spying on us when we were on the way into her Duchy, but there was no way in hell she wasn't going to be spying on us while we were on the way out. She was too clever, and too paranoid, not to keep an eye on us for as long as she could.

Li Qin turned to me once we were on the freeway. "Did that tell you what you needed to know?"

"Yeah. Riordan's dangerous because she's *not* a crazy bitch. Bitch, yes. Crazy, no." I sighed. "I think I like it better when they're nuts. At least then I don't have to worry about them using actual logic against me."

"Is she involved?" asked Quentin. "She was sort of creepy, but . . ."

"Her magic smells like apples and snowdrops. I smelled that combination in the Court of Cats. I don't think Riordan went there herself—but I think her magic did. Does she know how to make blood charms?"

Li Qin nodded. "Yes. It's how she sets her wards so firmly."

"I figured." Blood charms were a uniquely Daoine Sidhe way of getting around normal rules. Blood carries power; that includes magic, and it's possible to "loan" or steal magic temporarily if you know how to properly work the blood. Evening Winterrose was always fond of blood charms. If Riordan was the same way, she'd be able to use them to boost her power, borrow abilities from others, and make wards that were both stronger and more specific than anything I could manage. In short, she had a big advantage.

I shook my head, trying to clear the first tinges of fatalism away, and continued, "Also, I never told her Chelsea was a teenager, and I never said which of Chelsea's parents was human."

Quentin paused. "What?"

"When I said Chelsea had called home, Riordan asked if she spoke with her human *mother*. Not 'human parent.' She knew which parent would have been there to pick up the phone."

Silence fell in the car. Finally, Li Qin said, "None of this is proof."

"See, the nice thing about not being a member of the nobility anymore is that I don't *need* proof. I just need to be right. The knowe smelled like Chelsea's magic; I smelled Riordan's magic in the Court of Cats; Riordan knew which of her parents was mortal. And there's more." I took a breath before launching into a description of the phone call I'd overheard while I was hiding in Riordan's hall.

When I was done, silence fell again. It lasted longer this time, until Quentin said, "I don't like her very much."

"Yeah, well." I took my left hand off the wheel long enough to rake my hair out of my eyes. "Join the club, okay?"

"No one likes Treasa very much," said Li Qin. "It's part of her charm."

"She has charm?" I asked.

"No," said Li Qin, and laughed.

I shook my head and hit the gas harder. I wanted to get back to Tamed Lightning. I wanted to be sure Tybalt had been able to get out of Dreamer's Glass without getting caught. And I wanted a cup of coffee really badly.

My priorities may be strange sometimes, but they were good enough to make me drive almost thirty miles over the speed limit all the way to Fremont.

The smell of hydrangeas and black tea rose from Li Qin's side of the car. I glanced over to see her playing cat's-cradle with a piece of string, lips moving silently. Whatever she was doing didn't involve casting a don't-look-here or a hide-and-seek; I couldn't feel any illusions on the car. But no one pulled us over, either.

The portcullis was up when we reached ALH. I drove through. Li Qin stopped her cat's-cradle as the portcullis began to descend, letting her hands drop to her lap with a relieved sigh. I slanted a glance her way. "What was that?"

"I bent our luck. Kept the police from noticing you were speeding, kept any of Riordan's spies who might have tried to follow from getting close enough to hear what we were saying." Li Qin smiled a little. "It seemed like the best course of action."

"Better than a speeding ticket." I pulled into a space toward the front of the lot, and blinked at the empty sidewalk. "Huh. I expected April to come meet us."

"She's probably distracted by the company you sent her." Li Qin unfastened her seat belt. "Let's go rescue him."

"Good idea," I said, and followed her, with Quentin at my heels.

We walked through the reception area into the knowe and were starting to make our way through the cubicle maze when I heard voices up ahead. "Déjà vu," I muttered. Voices in the cubicle maze greeted me when I first came to ALH. Li Qin looked pleased and started walking faster, making me and Quentin pick up the pace if we wanted to keep up with her. For someone short, she sure could move.

April turned as we came around the corner into the cube maze's central meeting point, a quizzical expression on her face. Tybalt, who was sitting on the edge of the desk she'd been facing, didn't rise. He just looked toward us and smiled.

I let out a breath I hadn't been quite aware of holding, some of the tension slipping out of my shoulders. "Is there coffee?" I asked.

"Hello to you as well, October. You're looking lovely, or at least not incarcerated, which is a definite pleasure, given where I left you." Tybalt waved a hand toward April. "Countess O'Leary was explaining the functionality of her server systems to me. Fascinating stuff."

It says something about how much practice Tybalt has had in the art of sounding interested when he isn't that I didn't realize he was kidding until he winked at me. "No arrests," I said. "Riordan is involved in Chelsea's disappearance, even though I don't have any way to prove it to someone who could make her give Chelsea back. Now. Coffee, and then we have to hit the road."

"Where are we going?" asked Quentin.

I paused, digging the Luidaeg's Chelsea-chaser out of my pocket. It was glowing a neutral white. I sighed. "I don't know. Maybe we're not going anywhere. If we don't know where she is, there's no point in chasing after her, now, is there?"

"If you do not chase, I can provide coffee," offered April.

"Coffee would be fabulous," I said. "Let's go."

April nodded, and disappeared, apparently deciding that walking to the cafeteria would be a waste of her time. Li Qin started for the door, motioning for Quentin to join her. He glanced at me, then glanced at Tybalt, and followed her without looking back a second time. In a matter of seconds, the two of us were standing alone in the cubicle maze.

"Um," I said.

Tybalt lifted an eyebrow, looking amused. "'Um?'" he echoed.

"Nice weather we're having."

"I was unaware that you were interested in the weather." He slid off the desk. "I am, however, aware of at least one thing."

"What's that?"

"I was proud of you today." Tybalt stepped closer. The

smell of pennyroyal and musk was suddenly strong. "You were cautious. You were careful. You hid when you were given the opportunity to hide, and you allowed me to assist you. You have no idea how relieved I am."

"Tybalt, this isn't—"

"Is your charm glowing?"

I glanced down before I thought better of it. "No," I admitted.

"Then while this may not be the best time, it is almost certainly the only time we're going to have. You've been frightening me lately, October, and more than me. Your lady Fetch has been concerned as well. The risks you've been taking—"

People telling me not to do stupid things and get myself hurt was sadly familiar ground. I narrowed my eyes, straightening. "The risks I've been taking are my risks to take."

"You don't believe that. Fortunately for both of us, I know what it sounds like when you try to lie to yourself by lying to me." Tybalt's voice was soft. "You have responsibilities in this world, whether you meant to take them on or not. To your squire, to my nephew, to your Fetch. To every friend and every enemy you've ever made." He paused before adding, "To me."

"Tybalt . . ."

"I've stood by and watched you throw yourself against the walls of the world, because I hoped the impact might shake the sense back into you. We do not raise the dead by mourning them so fiercely that we join them. I wish we could. It doesn't work."

There was something deeply sad in his tone. "How would you know?"

"Oh, October." Tybalt sighed, reaching out to tuck my hair behind my ear. He left his fingertips there, resting them against my skin. "Do you truly believe you are the only one, ever, to have lost someone you cared for? To have given something up because to hold it would destroy the very thing you treasured? You're not as alone as you think you are."

Tears welled in my eyes. There was a moment when I could have stepped into his arms, into whatever he was trying to offer me. But he was Tybalt, and Connor was gone, and it felt like letting myself move would be a betrayal, no matter how much I wanted it. I stepped away instead, leaving Tybalt's hand hanging empty in the air.

"We'd better catch up with the others," I said. "They're going to be wondering where we are." I turned before I could see the look on his face and went striding toward the door to the lawn between the buildings.

He didn't follow me outside. I didn't know whether to be glad or not. I crossed the lawn to the other building. The afternoon was waning toward evening, but ALH was still deserted as I walked toward the cafeteria. That struck me as odd. As a functioning computer company, there should have been people. I pushed open the cafeteria door, and asked, "Where is everyone?"

"Everyone presently in the knowe is in this room, with the exception of Tybalt, who is on the lawn," said April. She was perched on the edge of one of the tables. Li Qin and Quentin were sitting more normally in chairs, each with a mug of liquid and a sandwich.

"Okay, that's what I asked, but that's not what I meant," I said, stepping into the room. "Shouldn't people be at work by now?"

"Ah!" April nodded understanding. "Under normal circumstances, they would be. Since these are not normal circumstances, I have given everyone the night off. I would prefer to avoid bloodshed if possible. It has been difficult to attract replacement staff after the last time."

"Yeah, well, murder and mayhem do tend to upset most people." I walked to the coffee machine, pausing only to take a mug from beside the sink. "Coffee."

"Perhaps that will make you less unpleasant," said Tybalt.

I jumped, whirling to see him standing next to the vending machine, arms folded, glaring at me. "Maeve's bones, Tybalt! Just because April teleports everywhere, that doesn't mean you have to start doing it, too!"

"What? You mean it irritates you when I appear and disappear in the middle of conversations?" He unfolded his arms, but kept glaring. "I'm pleased to see we still have a few things in common."

"I can't talk to you right now." I turned my back on him, picking up the coffeepot and filling my mug instead. "April, telling everyone to stay home was smart. Now we just need to figure out our next smart move."

"Can it be not dying?" asked Quentin. "I like not dying."

"Yeah, it can." I sipped my coffee, taking that moment to recenter myself before I turned back around to face the others. Tybalt was still there. That was something, anyway. "So we have not dying, finding Chelsea, and finding Raj. The last trace we had on Chelsea put her in or around Dreamer's Glass. We've got nothing on Raj, except for knowing that wherever he is, he doesn't have access to the Shadow Roads." I paused. "Tybalt. The Shadow Roads. What do they connect to?"

"Ah, so now you can talk to me? Truly, I am honored."

I sighed. "Okay, maybe I deserved that. I'm sorry. I mean the question seriously. What do the Shadow Roads connect to?"

Tybalt frowned. "The shadows, of course. Their anchors are in the Courts of Cats; the Kings and Queens keep them open with our presence. Without us, our subjects would be as trapped as those of the Divided Courts."

"Raj isn't a King yet. Can he hold the Shadow Roads open on his own?"

"For a time, yes."

"What if he were in a place where Cait Sidhe hadn't been in a really, really long time? Would he be able to open the shadows then?"

Tybalt's frown deepened. "No," he admitted. "Raj is a Prince, and a strong one, but I couldn't have held the shadows at his age."

"Would you know if he was nearby, but not exactly in the same place? Like if you were in a knowe, and he was right outside?"

"Yes. He is a Prince of Cats. I always know when someone with his potential is near."

"Got it." I turned to the table where Li Qin, April, and Quentin waited, watching me with puzzled expressions. "Quentin, I know what has to happen next, and you're not going to like it."

He sighed. "You're leaving, aren't you?"

"I am, and I need you to stay here, so you can call me if the charm changes color. We don't have to stay together, and it seems to react to proximity. I don't want us to miss another chance to catch Chelsea."

"What if you're in San Francisco when it lights up? It'll take you like two hours to get back here."

"No, it won't." I turned to Tybalt. "Will you take me? I think I may know how to find Raj, but I'm going to need someone with access to the Shadow Roads."

Tybalt's lingering frown faded into a look of resignation. "We're going to talk later."

"I guessed that part." I finished my coffee in one long drink. "April, keep an eye out. Quentin, don't get yourself killed."

"I'll do my best," he said.

"Good." I walked over to Tybalt. "We need to go to Shadowed Hills."

"Then you need to hold your breath." He put his hands around my waist, a little tighter than strictly necessary, and he stepped back, into the dark.

I don't know how the Cait Sidhe navigate the Shadow Roads, any more than I know how they can breathe there. They must be able to, at least a little. Tybalt is in good shape, yes, but there are limits. He kept one hand on my waist, removing the other and twining his fingers with mine. Then he turned me around, and pulled me in his wake as he began to run.

Experience had made it strangely easy to trust him as he pulled me away through the absolute blackness and freezing cold. Whatever else I might be feeling, however confused I might be, I trusted him to bring me safe out the other side. I trusted him to—

I trusted him. Qualifiers were meaningless. Worse yet, he was right; I'd been pushing everyone away as hard as I could since Connor died, trying to isolate myself in order to protect my heart against further damage. Losing a lover and a child on the same day was more than anyone should be asked to bear. But how much could I ask my friends to bear? How much could I expect them to take before they said, "Fine, if you want to push us away, we're going"?

Our emergence back into the light caught me by surprise. Tybalt kept running for a few more feet, letting us bleed off our momentum. Then he let me go, turning to face me. "Toby," he said, surprise and delight coloring his voice. "You've stopped making yourself heavier than you need to be while we're running."

"What?" I blinked, feeling the ice crystals on my eyelashes stick together. I reached up to wipe them away. "What do you mean?"

"This time, while we ran, you didn't think about how dark the shadows were, or how afraid you were of being lost there."

"How do you—?"

"Because you came easily, and look." He waved a hand. "We're here."

We were standing on a stretch of grass surrounded by sculpted wild rose hedges. They formed an elegant walking maze, cutting wide avenues through the greenery. Fountains and benches were studded here and there, offering convenient places for people to sit and talk, or rest their feet a little while before continuing on. The shape of the great hall was visible on the other side of the maze, somehow managing to loom across the scene without becoming menacing.

"We are," I said. "Come on."

The maze was meant for idle wanderers, not for people who wanted to spend an entire night snared in a labyrinth. We made it through the hedges quickly, emerging onto a swath of lawn. Ahead of us was a gray stone patio, and doors from there led into the great hall. I didn't approach. Instead, I stopped where I was, motioned for Tybalt to be quiet, and listened.

He watched with amusement as I turned to one side and then the other. Finally, I pointed to the left. "This way."

"And why, precisely, is this way superior to any others?"

"Because this way leads to Luna," I said, and started walking.

Luna Torquill is many things. A Duchess. A Blodynbryd—sort of like a Dryad, only connected to rosebushes, not trees. But above everything else, she's a gardener. Always has been and probably always will be. And because she's a gardener, even though Shadowed Hills has groundskeepers, she can often be found in the location of the most noise in the yard.

We came over a low rise to find ourselves facing a vegetable garden being harvested by half a dozen Hobs, a few Brownies, and one delighted Cornish Pixie, who was picking ears of corn from stalks nearly fifteen feet high. It didn't matter that it wasn't harvest season. This was Luna's garden. It would ripen when she wanted it to. Luna herself was on her knees in a patch of strawberry plants, plucking berries from beneath the broad, flat leaves. Some were the normal red. Others were white with the faintest blush of pink, or so dark they seemed black.

"Luna?"

She straightened at the sound of her name. By the time we finished our approach, she was standing, and her gloves were in the basket with the berries. "October," she said, sounding surprised. "And Tybalt. What are you two doing here? Is everything all right? Sylvester is inside . . ."

"We're not here to see Sylvester," I said. "We're here to see you." This was the tricky part. I needed her to help us. I wasn't yet at the point of telling the Torquills what was going on.

"Me?" Luna blinked again. "Why me?"

"We need access to the Rose Road," I said. "It's sort of an emergency."

As a Blodynbryd, Luna had access to the Rose Roads, which ran, near as I could tell, between the Summerlands and places where the walls of the world had worn thin. I had taken the Rose Road from Shadowed Hills to the Luidaeg's apartment once, and once into Blind Michael's lands. Those places weren't necessarily lost—in fact, they were, by definition, found. They were also outside the normal passages of Faerie. If we wanted to find Raj, we needed a miracle. This seemed close enough for me. I might as well risk it all on the liminal spaces.

Luna's eyes widened, pink eyelashes making her expression of shock almost comic. It's taken me a long time to get used to her new coloring, snow white and rose red where she used to be shades of brown. Sometimes, it's still a little strange. "What do you need the Rose Road for?"

"We've sort of misplaced Raj. I think if we can get between realms, we might be able to get a fix on him." I hoped, anyway.

Luna frowned. "I can't just open a road with no end. You have to have a destination."

Destination. Right. "Send us to your mother," I suggested.

"I don't know . . ." said Luna uncertainly.

"Milady of Roses, you know October wouldn't ask if it were not of direst importance," said Tybalt. He smiled hopefully. "Please? It would be a great favor, to both of us, and I am sure all will be made clear, given time enough."

Time enough, and us managing not to die. "Please?" I echoed, trying my hardest to look ingratiating. I probably managed to look deranged.

Fortunately for me, Luna has always been responsive to derangement. "If you get yourself killed, Sylvester will never forgive me," she said. That was when I knew I'd won. If she was making dire statements about what I could or couldn't do to myself on the Rose Road, she was going to send me.

"I know," I said.

"Just so long as you do." She bent to retrieve her gardening shears from the basket of strawberries. She opened the shears, using them to snip off a foot-long lock of her pink and red hair. The smell of roses was suddenly strong, and grew stronger as she shook the cut hair.

Somewhere in the middle of the motion the curl straightened, taking on overtones of green. And then it wasn't hair anymore, but a long-stemmed white rose. She held it out to me. I took it, managing not to wince when the inevitable thorns bit into my fingers. The edges of the petals began turning red, the color spreading inward like blood spreading through white silk.

"Both of you," she said, gesturing for Tybalt to take hold of the rose as well.

"As you like," he said, and wrapped his fingers around mine. The red began spreading faster, taking on a deeper hue. The smell of pennyroyal and musk rose around us, and I realized that the other things I smelled—roses, and fresh grass, and blood—weren't just part of being in the garden. Luna's rose-red magic was rising, and my own cut grass and bloody copper was answering the call.

"Breathe in," said Luna. Tybalt and I did as we were told. "Good. Now breathe out, turn around, and start walking."

It was no surprise to turn and see the gateway, even though there had been nothing there but grass when we arrived. It was shaped like a wicker trellis, with red and white roses growing around it in such vulgar profusion that they almost concealed the structure underneath. Beyond them, a tunnel enclosed by roses stretched into the distance. The only safe place to walk was the narrow dirt path between the creepers and the thorns, and even that was occasionally crossed by fallen branches, making the way hazardous to all but the most cautious traveler.

"Walk quickly, but walk with care," said Luna. "Don't look back. If you look back, you'll have to go back the way you came or risk falling off the Road, and I won't be able to retrieve you if you wind up somewhere you didn't mean to be."

"Got it," I said. "Is there anything else we need to know?"

"Don't let go of the rose until you're off the Road, and don't let it out of your sight until you're absolutely sure you're not going to need it anymore."

"I do so love how all magic comes with its share of dire warnings and unclear requirements," sighed Tybalt. "It's like being on the stage, only there's no director, and the understudies have all died of typhus."

"On that charming note, see you later, Luna. Here's hoping we don't die." I kept a firm grip on the rose as I started forward. Tybalt walked alongside me, his steps paced to mine, and together we passed through the archway. I heard it close behind us. We were on the Rose Road, and we were alone. The only question was what we were going to do next.

SIXTEEN

I DUG THE LUIDAEG'S CHARM from my pocket as we walked, holding it in front of me. It was still in its neutral state, although the reflections off the roses around us tinted it pale pink. "Chelsea's not near here," I said. "Do whatever hoodoo you need to do to know if Raj is nearby."

"Hoodoo?" said Tybalt, sounding amused. "I'm the King of Cats, October, not the King of Goblins."

"And you don't live in a labyrinth, but that doesn't mean you can't make like a Henson character and start scrying for our missing boy. Also, how have you even seen that movie? Does the Court of Cats have cable?" I kept walking. "This thing will eventually dump us in Acacia's backyard. I'm hoping we can get a lead on one or both of the kids before we get there."

"But Chelsea is your priority."

"No," I said. "Raj is. Chelsea's in trouble, but she can get herself out of it. Raj is somewhere he can't get out of. I don't leave people behind."

There was a moment of silence. I risked a glance to the side. Tybalt was watching me, an odd, thoughtful expression on his face. He looked away when he saw me looking.

"Well, then, I suppose I must rise to your example."

He waved his free hand in the air, the smell of penny-royal swirling around us before converging in the space just above his palm. He cupped his hand, and a globe of what seemed to be solidified shadow dropped into it. "Here. This will tell us if there is only a thin wall between me and my nephew."

"Good." I kept walking. "Hey. Can I ask you a question?"

"My dear October, we are bound by an enchanted rose made from the hair of a Duchess, and my blood is covering your hand. You can learn anything you wish to know about me merely by licking your fingers." Tybalt laughed a little. "Yes. You may ask me a question."

"Back in the Court of Cats, you said you made a mistake when you took Raj as a nephew. What did you mean?"

"You have an uncanny ear for the things I most wish you would forget, while willfully and continually forgetting the things I wish you would remember," said Tybalt dryly. "I had a choice, when Raj's parents brought him to me. I could do as they asked, take him as a nephew and let them stay by his side. Or I could do as my father taught me, take him as a son, raise him as my own, and drive them as far from my territory as I could."

"Oh." We kept walking. Finally, I said, "I don't like Raj's dad. He's kind of an asshole. But I'm glad you let him stay with his son. I think it says something good about your character."

"I appreciate your approval," said Tybalt. Then he laughed. "Had I known it was as easy to get as all that, I might have confessed my softheartedness years ago. Really, October, you should provide a list of ways to reach your good side. It would be a kindness beyond measure."

"I'm not that complicated," I protested.

"As someone who has to deal with you on a regular basis, I beg to differ," said Tybalt. "At times, I suspect you're doing it intentional—" He stopped in the middle of the word. He stopped walking at the same time, jerking me to an unexpected halt. The rose thorns bit deeper into my fingers. I yelped.

"Dammit, Tybalt! What gives?"

"I'm afraid I owe you an apology," said Tybalt, eyes wide. He held up his ball of shadow. Ball of mostly shadow—swirls of bluish light were moving through it, appearing and disappearing like eels swimming in brackish water. "He's near. Not here, but . . . near."

"Where?"

Tybalt nodded toward the nearest tangled wall of rosebushes. "That way."

"Then let's go."

He shot me a surprised look.

I smiled. "I trust you. Now open up those shadows, and let's bring our boy home."

Tybalt nodded. Pulling back, he threw his ball of shadow at the roses. It stuck where it hit. Then it dissolved, blackness spreading over branches, thorns, and flowers alike to create a black "doorway" in the wall. I could feel the chill radiating out of it.

There was a time when Tybalt only got me into the shadows by surprising me or jerking me off-balance. That time has passed. I walked with him into the dark willingly, the rose still joining our hands. For a moment, the light of the Rose Road shone in from behind us, illuminating nothing, but making that nothing a little easier to see. Then the way behind us closed, and everything was blackness.

We stopped walking and just stood there in the dark, not moving. I forced myself not to breathe and tried not to shiver too hard. The cold of the Shadow Roads was somehow worse when we held still, as though that immobility really allowed the frost to catch hold and begin gnawing its way inside. Even the blood on my fingers was freezing; I could feel it turning to ice.

Finally Tybalt whispered, "This way," and pulled me forward. There was a horrible wrenching, twisting sensation, as if the shadows were pushing back against us, as if we were going somewhere we weren't meant to be. It became almost painful, and still Tybalt kept pulling me forward. I gritted my teeth and kept going, trusting him to know what he was doing. The twisting became a tearing, and the cold became a burn, and just as I was about to scream—

—the darkness broke around us, and the tearing sensation stopped.

Tybalt dropped my hand, letting go of the rose in the process, and bent forward to rest his hands against his knees, panting. I straightened and looked around, still holding the rose. We were . . . I didn't know where we were. We were someplace I had never been before. There was one thing I knew, though, all the way down to the core of my being.

This wasn't the Summerlands.

The sky was the deep, impenetrable blue of true midnight. The stars were bright; I didn't know any of the constellations. We were near the edge of a cliff; I could see more cliffs gleaming white as bone to either side, descending sharply to the equally white beaches below. They contrasted well with the absolute blackness of the ocean beneath them. Far out on the bay, a lighthouse swept its light smoothly across the waves.

"Where the fuck are we?" I breathed.

"I don't know," wheezed Tybalt. "Remind me to beat my nephew for making us come here."

"No," I said. I turned to look behind us. The land stretched into a wide moor. Beyond that, hills, some crowned with the familiar, irregular shapes of castles. The air smelled like heather, flowering bloom, peat, and the sea. What it didn't smell like was the modern world. No pollution, no smog, no traces of combustion engines. Wherever we were, it was a place that had been sealed away long before the technological revolution changed things. "I get to beat him. I figured out how to get us here. That means I have dibs."

"Why are you an adherent to logic only when it results in the commission of violence?"

"What can I say? I know what I like." I turned again, this time continuing until I'd completed a slow circle. The lighthouse turned, the waves swept in and out, the sedge on the moor rippled in the breeze ... but that was all. Nothing else moved, nothing else stirred. "You're the one who can sense Raj's location. Where is he?"

"You make me sound like a machine."

"You complain when I use you like a bloodhound. This is a step up." The thorns on Luna's rose were sharp enough to be a distraction. I pushed it into the tangled mess that was my hair, forcing it down until the flower snagged and refused to move farther. That would keep it until we needed it again.

Tybalt chuckled, still sounding winded, and pushed himself upright. He looked around thoughtfully before stepping away from me, moving off the hard-packed sand at the cliff's edge to the border of the moor. He bent, plucking a yellow-flowered sprig of broom. "I know where we are," he said, a wondering edge to his voice. He straightened, turning to offer me the broom like it was the most precious thing the world had ever known. "This is incredible."

I took the broom—it would have been rude not to—and tucked it behind my ear before asking, "Well? Where are we?"

He stepped closer. The hot smell of pennyroyal and musk baking off his skin overwhelmed even the smell of the sea. "Annwn," he whispered. "We're in Annwn."

My eyes widened as I swallowed my instinctive denial. Chelsea was weakening the walls of the world. The Rose Roads followed their own rules. Who was to say that right now, with all those factors working together, we couldn't get around the gates Oberon had erected and find our way someplace we absolutely weren't supposed to be?

Annwn was one of the deep realms. It used to be accessible by sea from half a dozen other homelands and by gate from a few more. It was a port country, worked by seafaring folk, ferrymen and sailors and traders who liked the unpredictability of the land, as wild as the First-born who made it, Arawn of the White Stag. It was a verdant farmland, one of the few deep realms that ever knew seasons. And no one had walked there or breathed its heather-sweet air in over five hundred years.

"Whoa," I said.

"Yes. Very much 'whoa.'" Tybalt turned, scanning the landscape. Then he pointed out into the moor and said, "There. That's where we need to go."

"Because Raj is there or because you want to watch me go tromping around in a field full of sticker bushes?"

He smiled a little, still looking tired. "Oh, don't be silly, October. This is Annwn. There will almost certainly be thistles."

"This gets better and better," I said, and together we tromped into the heather.

We were on a mission—the glow of the Luidaeg's charm was a constant reminder—but it was hard not to get distracted by the sheer alien novelty of the landscape, a place as unfamiliar to me now as the Summerlands were, when I was a little girl, I could have spent hours just looking at the stars, trying to guess what the people who used to live here made of them. Instead, we had to keep walking, fording through the waist-high brush as we tried to find the place where Raj had gone to ground.

True to Tybalt's prediction, there were thistles scattered through the heather and broom, their bright purple flowers only providing a little bit of warning before their prickles bit into my ankles or hands. "I think the landscape is out to get us," I muttered, after the fifth stealth attack.

"Almost certainly," said Tybalt. "A knowe, allowed to go fallow, will lash out at one who enters it. Why should a realm be any different?"

That gave me pause. When I went to claim the knowe at Goldengreen, it fought back. Not because it wanted to be left empty but because it was hurt. It had been abandoned, left alone, and it was angry. Our hollow hills are alive, in their own slow way, and just like any living thing, they have feelings. Why would a realm be any different?

Answer: it wouldn't. "Oak and ash," I muttered. "I hope Raj is okay."

"As do I," said Tybalt.

We walked faster after that. The moor seemed endless, but eventually the brush began to thin, the formerly hard-packed ground turning soft and marshy under our feet. Tall stands of bulrush made their appearance, some of them growing higher than Tybalt's head. Finally, Tybalt stopped, looking straight at one of the patches of bulrush.

"All right," he said. "You may emerge. Quickly, if you please; the ground is damp, and I would prefer not to sink."

There was a moment of silence. Then the bulrushes rustled, and a boy-sized missile flung itself at us, zigging at the last moment to slam into me. If Tybalt hadn't been standing there so calmly, I might have reacted with violence. As it was, I simply braced myself, and when Raj made impact, I wrapped my arms around him, letting him bury his face against my shoulder.

"You came you came you came," he was saying, the words so fast and jumbled-together that they were practically a chant. "I didn't think—I wasn't sure—I didn't know—"

"Hey. Hey!" I unwrapped my arms and grabbed his shoulders, pushing him out to arms' length. He went reluctantly, but he went. That was all I could ask for. "We'll *always* come. You got that? If we have to move heaven and earth—"

"Or find a route into a realm that's been sealed for centuries," interjected Tybalt.

"—we will," I finished. "Do you understand me? We'll *always* come for you, Raj. You're family. We look out for our own."

Raj nodded, eyes wide and swimming with tears. Then he ducked out from under my hands and slammed into me again, resuming his embrace. At least he didn't start chanting again. I looked over his head to Tybalt.

"We got him," I said.

Tybalt nodded. "Indeed. Allow him his distress. Even for a Prince, this must have been . . . trying." He looked around. "I know where we are, and I doubt I would have taken this so calmly at his age."

The idea that Tybalt was ever a teenager was almost enough to make me start laughing. Instead, I snorted and said, "Now that we have him, we should probably be getting out of here."

Raj pushed himself back enough to look up at me. "How?" he asked, an edge of panic in his voice. "I tried and I tried, and I couldn't find the shadows. They wouldn't come."

"That's because there has been no King here to remind them of their place," said Tybalt.

"Besides, we had help." I pulled the rose from my hair, only wincing a little when the thorns sliced my fingers. Healing fast has its perks, but it also means I never get numb; I had fully recovered from my first bout with the thorns, and round two hurt even more, if that was possible. "Luna opened a Rose Road for us. Hopefully, we can figure out a way to pry it open again from here."

"Hopefully?" echoed Raj. "You mean you don't know?"

"Look at it this way, kiddo. At least now, if you're going to be stranded, you're not going to be stranded alone. Plus, hey, think about all those empty castles. We can totally take one over. Paint the whole thing pink."

Raj smiled a little. "Where are we going to get pink paint?"

"We'll improvise. We're clever that way." I tightened my hand on the rose, getting as many thorns to pierce my skin as I could. The smell of cut grass and copper filled the air. I looked toward Tybalt. "What's our shadow status?"

"I can feel them, but I haven't been here long enough to anchor them properly." He frowned. "This is an . . . interesting dilemma, I must admit."

"Then let's do this the hard way." I held my hand out to him, half the rose stem protruding from my fist in invitation. He nodded and closed his hand around it. The smell of Luna's magic suddenly mingled with our own, as the Rose Road we had so recently stepped off of remembered that we had been going somewhere.

I wasn't sure it would work. Luna had told us not to drop the rose, not to leave the path. But we never dropped the rose—it was on me the whole time—and we didn't leave the path, not really. We just took a shortcut through the shadows and the brush, something idiots in fairy tales have been doing since the beginning of time.

Maybe it was the fairy tale impossibility of our situation; maybe it was the blood in the air giving me the strength to push while Tybalt pulled. Whatever it was, the smell of roses got stronger, and the wicker trellis wove itself together in front of us, opening on the long, rose-lined tunnel.

"Fantastic," I breathed. "Raj, take hold of my jacket. I don't want to lose you in here."

"I have a better idea," he said. He stepped back, jumped into the air, and landed on my shoulder as an Abyssinian cat, the smell of pepper and burning paper clinging to his fur. He wrapped his tail around my neck, yawning in that casual way cats have, and settled down to purr loudly in my ear.

"Sure, I'll carry you," I said. I looked to Tybalt. "Is he this respectful to you?"

"Believe it or not, my dear, he's more respectful of you than he is of almost anyone else."

I glared. Tybalt laughed, and kept laughing as we stepped onto the Rose Road.

The binding Oberon used to seal the deep realms must have been incredibly strong. We were barely through the door when it slammed behind us, with a ripping, tearing noise that made it sound like the whole thing had been torn right out of existence. I forced myself not to look back, mindful of Luna's warning that looking back could screw everything up. Raj had no such compunctions. I felt him twist as he stared at whatever was behind us. He meowed, somehow managing to make the sound bewildered.

"Just stay on my shoulder and hold on," I said, and began to walk. Tybalt kept pace beside me. Our fingers, still clenched around the stem of Luna's rose, were tangled up enough that we were almost holding hands, if your definition was generous enough. I found myself wishing for a generous definition. Ears red, I tore my eyes away from the rose and looked toward the Luidaeg's charm, instead.

It was still glowing starlight neutral.

"I hope Quentin's having better luck than I am," I said.

Raj meowed.

"He's back at Tamed Lightning, waiting to see if Chelsea—that's the girl who accidentally knocked you into Annwn, and she's going to be really sorry, once she stops being freaked out and ripping holes in everything—shows up there. He'll call me if she does." Both my hands were full. I frowned and added, "Not that I'm sure how I'm going to answer my phone if that happens."

"Always the practical one," said Tybalt. He stopped walking, pulling me to a halt as well. "This is where we entered."

"Are you sure?"

He shot me an amused look. "I find it refreshing when I notice the smell of blood before you do, little fish. It reminds me of old times."

"I don't think I enjoyed them as much as you did," I shot back, and breathed in. Now that I was looking, I could see splashes of blood on the thorns, and smell the mingled traces of Tybalt and myself. "How do we get out of here?"

Tybalt considered for a moment before he said, "Let go."

It made sense. It fit what Luna had told us to do. I still frowned before nodding. "I guess so," I said, and opened my hand. Tybalt did the same, and we watched as the rose fell, a little more slowly than normal—gravity apparently doesn't work the same way on magical roses—to land on the thorny ground.

Then the Rose Road collapsed around us, fading into nothing in an instant, and we were back on the lawn at Shadowed Hills, standing on a low hill. The vegetable garden was in front of us, and even the clean air of the Summerlands smelled dirty somehow, tainted by proximity to the mortal world. After Annwn, the pristine seemed polluted.

Tybalt reached out with his bloody left hand and wrapped it around my bloody right one, this time twining our fingers properly, with no rose to get in the way. My cuts were already healing. His weren't, and he held me all the same. Raj was purring again; the Luidaeg's charm was still glowing pale and inert.

"Well," I said, looking at the garden, where Luna and her staff were still working. "That's not something I do every day."

Tybalt just laughed.

SEVENTEEN

LUNA LOOKED UP before scrambling to her feet, nearly upsetting her basket of strawberries. "You're back!" she exclaimed. Her gaze flicked to our bloody hands, then to the cat sitting on my shoulder. Where her eyes settled, however, was on the sprig of broom behind my ear. Her skin was already the stark white of newly fallen snow. Somehow, she still managed to go pale.

"Where have you been?" she asked, voice down to a whisper.

"Annwn." I didn't have any hands free, and so I had to disentangle my fingers from Tybalt's in order to reach up and pluck the broom from my hair. I held it out toward Luna. "No people, lots of hedges."

Her fingers trembled as she walked forward and took the broom from me. "This isn't possible," she said. Her head snapped up. "It isn't *possible*."

"We have a Tuatha changeling tearing holes in things," I said. That seemed safe enough. She wasn't going to jump straight from "Tuatha changeling" to "Etienne." I wouldn't have. Sylvester might, if Luna told him about this, but it was a risk I had to take. "Raj got sucked through one of those holes. That's why we needed the Rose Road. We were hoping we could find a way to track him if we could get between the Summerlands and the islets. We found it."

"Mixing magic often has its unexpected rewards," said Tybalt.

Luna didn't say anything for several minutes, but her eyes were suspiciously bright as she stared at the sprig of broom. Finally, she said, "I was there when Grandfather evacuated Annwn. It was never a populous land; most of those who lived there immigrated to escape their lives in other, more rigidly ruled places. They wept when the walls were sealed. I think some of them are crying still . . ." She shook herself as though she was trying to clear away a memory she'd never wanted to keep. "You shouldn't have been there. Those doors were sealed for a reason."

I looked at her—my liege's wife, a woman I once thought of as a second mother—and all I felt was tired. The fractures between us started forming when she knowingly sent me to die in her father's land. They've only grown deeper since then. Luna comes from a different Faerie, an older one, and I don't understand it. It's as alien to me as the Summerlands would be to Bridget. Watching Luna's reaction to a bit of broken broom, I realized I was glad. I didn't want to understand that world.

"My nephew was on the other side of those doors," said Tybalt frostily. "I was not willing to leave him stranded to salve your sense of what is and is not proper." He turned to me. "I should return him to my Court. His father will be worried."

"I'm coming with you," I said, almost before I realized I was going to. Tybalt blinked. I smiled. "I need a way back to Tamed Lightning, remember? I left the car there."

"Ah, yes," he said. "Expediency."

"October, surely you can't intend—" began Luna.

I looked back toward her. "Luna, I am begging you, think before you finish that sentence. I'm tired, I'm covered in blood, and I'm probably not going to get a nap for a long time. So don't tell me not to rattle any more doors looking for our missing changeling. I owe it to her parents to bring her home." To her parents, and to Faerie itself if the Luidaeg was correct in her warnings.

Luna frowned, rose-pink eyebrows furrowing. "You should leave well enough alone."

Frustration overwhelmed my good sense, and I snapped, "Raj wound up on the other side of those doors *because* of the changeling I'm looking for. You say your grandfather sealed those doors? Well, she's *unsealing* them, and she's going to get a lot of people killed if I don't stop her." Luna gaped at me, and she was still gaping as I offered my hand to Tybalt. "Let's go."

His smile was weary but so bright that it seemed to light up the twilight. He took my hand, cautioned, "Breathe in," and pulled me with him as he stepped backward, into the shadow of a hedge. I let myself be pulled, and together, the three of us fell into shadow.

Raj was a warm weight against my neck as we ran through the darkness of the Shadow Roads, his claws dug deep into the leather of my jacket. He could have made this run himself, but after what he'd been through, I wasn't going to ask him to do that. He was small enough for me to carry, at least for now.

The distance between Shadowed Hills and the Court of Cats seemed substantially shorter than the distance between Tamed Lightning and Shadowed Hills. I wondered whether the Shadow Roads worked like the passages between the mortal world and the knowes, with every use making the next use just a little easier. The Shadow Roads didn't run between knowes very often, but they always ran back to the Court of Cats.

We stepped out of the shadows and into the high-walled alley I used to think of as the Court itself before I was granted access to the true Court of Cats. Cats—both mortal and Cait Sidhe in feline form—lounged on crates and garbage cans against the alley walls, although there was no stink of trash or decay in the air. A pile of mattresses was pushed up against one end of the alley.

The other was shrouded in darkness, hiding this temporary gathering place from the mortal world.

I shoved the Luidaeg's charm back into my pocket as I wiped the cold from my eyes. "Hop on down, Raj," I said. "We're home."

He meowed piteously.

"Right." I sighed, and freed my hand from Tybalt's in order to scoop Raj from my shoulder and place him, carefully, on the ground. He stretched. Then he stood up, returning to his human form in a swirl of pepper and burning paper. "Feeling better?" I asked.

"No," he said glumly. "But I'm home."

"Yeah, well. We're a full service operation."

Raj looked at me, glass-green eyes solemn. "I thought I was going to die there."

"You didn't. But you should get some sleep. You've been through a lot, and—"

I didn't get to finish that sentence. Raj's father, Samson, came stalking from the shadows of the alley. His hands were balled into fists, and his pupils were narrowed to hairline slits, making him look alien and strange. "You," he spat, angling toward me. "What are you doing here, whore? You have no right to passage in these lands."

"You really don't like me, do you?" I asked, trying not to let my irritation show. "What have I ever done to you? I saved your son. Twice now. Doesn't that at least warrant not calling me a whore every time you get the chance?"

"Consider your answer carefully, Samson," said Tybalt, in a mild tone. "I find myself awaiting your reply with great interest."

Samson glared. Then he turned to Raj, dismissing us. "Are you injured?"

"No, Father, I—"

Samson's backhand caught Raj across the cheek, snapping his head to the side. He made a startled mewling noise. I started forward before I realized I was going to move and stopped as Tybalt's hand closed around my upper arm, holding me in place.

"No," he said, very softly. "You cannot intervene."

"I hate your rules," I muttered, but stayed where I was. Raj was a teenage boy. He was my unofficial squire. And he was also a Prince of Cats, and that meant some battles, he had to fight on his own.

"Sometimes," said Tybalt, "so do I."

Raj turned back to his father, eyes wide. Then he straightened, gathering himself with a visible effort. He was tired. He'd been through a lot. Coming home and getting challenged by his father probably hadn't been included in his plans for the day. "You do not strike me," he said, practically spitting out his words. "I am not yours to strike."

"You are my son."

"I am a Prince of Cats."

Samson sneered. "What Prince needs a changeling *whore* to rescue him? You should have called the shadows. You should have brought yourself home triumphant and unaided, rather than begging like a kitten in the night for rescue."

"I did the best I could," said Raj.

"You didn't do enough."

There was a moment where things could have gone very, very badly—even worse than they already were, and they weren't going all that well. Raj looked at his father, measuring him, clearly assessing his chances of winning. Samson glared back.

And finally, Raj smiled. "I can beat you," he said. "I've been able to beat you for a long time. You know that too, or you wouldn't be goading me. I love you, Father. I don't like you very much. I think maybe you shouldn't come around me for a little while." He turned to Tybalt. "May I be excused? I want a bath and a nap and a meal, not necessarily in that order."

Tybalt inclined his head. "Rest," he said. "I will be away; the Court is yours until my return."

"Yes, Uncle." Raj's eyes remained on Tybalt. He seemed to be paying no attention to anything else. Yet when Samson's hand lashed toward his face again, he grabbed his father's wrist without hesitation. Raj wasn't a big kid, maybe five foot six and thin as a rail despite the amount I knew he ate. Samson still struggled against his grip like it was iron.

"Let me go," he commanded.

"No," said Raj. He sounded exhausted. "You brought me here because I was going to be stronger than you. Because you wanted to have power, and this was the closest you could come. You didn't save Mother when she got sick—you wouldn't let me feed her, because you said future Kings couldn't show favors. That's how you see Kings. That's not how I see them. That's not how the people I trust see them. I don't have to listen to you." He let go of Samson's wrist, pushing him away at the same time, so that he went stumbling backward.

Samson started to step forward again. Tybalt was suddenly between Raj and his father. I hadn't even seen him start to move.

"Your challenge has been refused, Samson," he said quietly. "Now trouble the boy no further, or you'll answer to me."

Samson's eyes narrowed. He looked past Tybalt to me, hissed, and spun on his heel, stalking toward the shadows. He stopped just before stepping into them, saying, "You will regret this." Then he was gone, leaving Raj, Tybalt, and me alone in the center of the alley.

The cats on the crates and cans lining the walls watched us with unblinking interest, as though this was the sort of entertainment they expected to receive every afternoon. One yawned and began washing himself.

I shook my head. "Sometimes I'm not sure whose politics are worse, you know."

"All politics are terrible," said Tybalt. He looked to Raj. "Go rest in my quarters. Your father is a fool, but even a fool will think twice before troubling you."

"And if you want to head for my place when you wake up, May will be happy to let you order pizza," I added. "She's worried about you."

Raj smiled a little. "Okay. See you both later." He

darted in and hugged me before turning to run into the shadows opposite the ones his father had disappeared through. He should have run right into the wall. Instead, he ran through it, and he was gone.

I pulled the Luidaeg's charm out of my pocket. It was still glowing neutral. Chelsea wasn't nearby. "Can you get me back to Tamed Lightning?" I asked, stepping closer to Tybalt. "I should get back to Quentin and the car and let him know Raj is okay. He's got to be worried by now."

"How angry do you think he'll be that we went to Annwn without him?" asked Tybalt.

I laughed, a little unsteadily. This close, his presence was distracting. "On a scale of one to livid? Livid times ten. That's the sort of field trip nobody likes to be left out of."

"Perhaps we should have sent a postcard before departing. 'Deserted heaths are lovely, it's probably best you aren't here.'"

I laughed and was still laughing when Tybalt took my arm and led me back into the shadows. They were no warmer this time than they'd been before, but they felt safer. I was getting more comfortable in them, and more at ease with the fact that Tybalt had me—he had me, and there was no way he was going to let me go while we were out there in the dark. Tybalt would never let me go. Maybe it was time for me to come to terms with that idea.

We ran together through the shadows. The blood on my hand was freezing again, but that didn't matter; I could wash it off when we got back to Tamed Lightning. And after that—

I never finished the thought. Something slammed into us, knocking my arm out of Tybalt's hand. I cried out before I remembered how thin the air was on the Shadow Roads. Tybalt roared . . . and the roar of another Cait Sidhe answered him, followed by another, and another. We were surrounded by his subjects. In the dark. Where I couldn't see, or help him fight them.

Tybalt threw me onto the Shadow Roads once, to save my life. I nearly died of hypothermia and lack of oxygen. I couldn't help remembering that as snarls and the sounds of flesh hitting flesh filled the darkness. I tried reaching toward the sound, hoping to find something I could grab onto, but my hands found only emptiness and cold.

Then the claws found my arm, and there was sudden heat as my blood ran down my skin, filling the air with the smell of copper. Maybe that's how Tybalt found me. He grabbed my outstretched arm, hissing, "Run," with an urgency raw enough to be almost as frightening as the idea of being stranded on the Shadow Roads. He jerked me forward. I felt something pop inside my wrist, a single white-hot flare of pain. Then we were falling, so fast and far that I wasn't sure we'd ever hit the bottom. The sound of roaring grew distant behind us.

"Hold on," whispered Tybalt. The roaring faded into silence—we were too far away to hear them. That seemed to be what he'd been waiting for. He wrapped an arm around my waist, pulling me close, and leaped out of the darkness, into the light.

We punched back into the human world on a suburban street lined with pastel-colored houses and broad-leafed mulberry trees. The air smelled like roses and jasmine and was almost warm enough to break through the cold trying to work its way all through me. My arm was still bleeding, but sluggishly, already starting to heal. Tybalt staggered and collapsed as his feet hit the sidewalk. I managed to catch him, sliding an arm under his, and looked around.

There was no one in sight, and the curve of the street meant that we had a moment of privacy. California road planners sometimes seem to have a phobia about straight lines. We were lucky; it was early enough in the afternoon that most adults were at work and most kids were still at school. We might not have long before that changed, but for the moment, we were alone. "Hey—hey! Stay with me here, big guy. What the hell was that?"

"That, my dear October, was an assassination attempt," he wheezed. He was shivering more than I was, and ice was caked in his hair and eyelashes. How hard had it been to fight on the Shadow Roads without losing track of me? He was a King of Cats, but not even a King of Cats has access to infinite resources. "Someone, I fear, has decided to depose me."

"What the—" We were too exposed. If anyone passed us, the blood would catch their attention, and we'd wind up with a lot of explaining that we weren't equipped to do. "Come on." I shifted my arm to balance most of Tybalt's weight against me as we staggered down the long driveway of the nearest house.

"This happens," he said, without real authority; he was trying to convince himself as much as he was trying to convince me. "It will be fine. I just need to catch my breath, and I will crush this insurrection. *I* will be fine."

"Liar," I said, with as much warmth as I could muster. "No one who's bleeding as much as you are gets to say that to me."

"They're all flesh wounds."

"Isn't every wound a flesh wound?" I kept us moving until we were in the shadow of the garage. The climbing ivy that was doing its best to strangle the surrounding structures hid us from the street. I eased him to the pavement. "There's no car in the driveway, and the shades are drawn. We should be safe for now."

"Not for long," said Tybalt, closing his eyes again. "Whoever has decided to challenge for my throne will follow. We cannot stay here."

"And we can't go anywhere else, either. So just breathe."

Something rustled in the bushes. I whipped around, grabbing the knife from my belt. If the Cait Sidhe who attacked us on the Shadow Roads had already found us, we were toast, but I'd be damned if I wouldn't take as many of them with me as I could. Tybalt couldn't fight yet. That just meant I needed to do the fighting for him.

A cream-colored Siamese cat stepped out onto the

pavement, tail curved in a question mark. Smoke-blue markings defined its paws and face. It barely spared a glance in my direction as it walked over and stepped into Tybalt's lap, meowing loudly.

The sound seemed to serve as a summoning. Cats poured from the bushes on every side. Tabbies, calicos, and tortoiseshells, white cats and black cats, striped marmalade cats, and more. They leaped over whatever obstacles were in their way to twine around Tybalt, batting him with their paws and meowing. For a moment, I was afraid I was seeing a Cait Sidhe funeral—that he'd died for real this time and wouldn't be coming back.

I relaxed when Tybalt opened his eyes, tilting his head toward the Siamese. "Ah," he said, sounding weary but amused. The Siamese meowed. He nodded. "Yes, I feared that was the case. I would appreciate that very much, if you would be so kind."

That seemed to satisfy the Siamese. It jumped out of his lap and ran for the street, a river of cats racing behind it. They were gone in seconds, some hiding in bushes, others sitting in full view on porches or the sidewalk. This was a California suburb. Thanks to no-kill shelters, healthy feral populations, and crazy cat ladies, no one would think twice about them.

No one but me. I turned to Tybalt, one eyebrow raised in question.

He smiled. "That was my opposite number, Shade. She keeps mostly to herself, but she felt the disturbance when we fell off the Shadow Road. She had heard rumors of the coming challenge to my authority, and while she is not allowed to interfere on my behalf, she does not support the challenge. Her Court will watch this area while we rest. If anything comes, they'll hold it off as best they can and make sure we're warned. My opponent made that permissible when you became involved. They should never have touched you. October . . ." His expression sobered. "October, I'm so sorry."

"It's all right." I walked over and sat down next to him. "I think I understand."

If Shade was Tybalt's opposite number, that made her a Queen of Cats. Kings and Queens of Cats never live together. They don't share Courts, they don't share territory, and they don't—according to gossip, anyway—share beds. Every Court of Cats has a single regent who rules according to his or her own laws. Queens tend to be more private than Kings, but they pay attention to what happens in their lands. Failure to notice a King of Cats showing up would probably lead to her having a very short reign.

Tybalt closed his eyes, sighing. "I don't think I can do that again today. Not even if . . ."

"I understand that, too." I dug the cell phone out of my pocket, looked at the display, and scowled. "My battery's dead. We're not calling for help."

"That would have been too convenient."

"I guess that's true." I replaced the cell phone in my pocket and put my hand on his knee. "Thank you anyway. For everything. For trying."

Tybalt put his hand over mine and didn't say anything about being surprised by my thanks. We sat in silence for several minutes. His fingers were cold and had barely started to warm up when he spoke again. "Did I ever tell you about my wife?" His tone was light and conversational, as if he were commenting on the weather.

I didn't have to feign surprise. "I didn't know you were married."

"I'm not married anymore. It was a long time ago."

That was oddly reassuring. I pushed the thought away. "I'm not sure this is a good time to—"

"This is the *only* time." The weariness was back in his voice. "You know as well as I do that we may die here. If those who attacked us follow our trail before my strength returns, we won't be able to run. There are ways of tracking where someone goes when they travel in shadow."

"You'll get better."

"Not if they kill me properly. And you won't get better regardless."

I frowned, biting back further protest. "Okay. No. You never told me about her."

"We met over two hundred years ago, in New York. Her name was Anne O'Toole." His lips curved into a smile I'd never seen before, soft and wistful and almost longing all at the same time. "She was Irish when it wasn't fashionable to be Irish, and a woman when that wasn't fashionable either. She was all impulse and sharp words." He opened his eyes, looking at me. "I think you would have liked her. You're similar in some ways. Mostly in your habit of charging headlong into danger while swearing you're doing no such thing."

I looked at him but said nothing. After a moment he looked away, still smiling.

"We hated each other, of course. She thought I was arrogant and boorish. I thought she was common and dull, like every other human. But we ... learned otherwise, and I loved her. She burned so bright—she raced through every day like she knew they wouldn't last. She wanted me to remember her." He stopped.

The cats yowled in the distance, marking out their territory. I brushed my hair away from my face with my free hand and asked, "Did she know?"

"That I wasn't human? Of course she did. She wasn't stupid." The implied criticism of Cliff stung. "She knew before the first time she let me touch her. She said she loved me all the more for knowing I'd be here after she was gone. I was her immortality, she said. 'The Sidhe have always been immortal for the sake of the Irish,' that's what she told me. And she laughed, and I laughed, because I was young and foolish and in love, and she was never going to die."

"What happened?" The words seemed too bald, but I knew he'd never finish his story without prompting. We'd sit in silence until it was time to run again, and whatever demon he was trying to cast out with his recollection would stay with him.

"She died." This time his smile was bitter. "She became pregnant, as women do, and it proved too much for her. Medicine of the time was ... the human world lacked the skills she needed to survive. The Cait Sidhe have no talent for medicine, and I couldn't find a healer among the Divided Courts who'd tend my 'mortal slut.' I begged. I bent my knee and I *begged*, like any penitent. And still they refused me."

"I'm so sorry," I whispered.

"Anne died in my arms, and the only mercy of it is that she was gone before she knew the baby wouldn't live. I buried my wife and daughter, and I swore I'd never trust the Divided Courts again, or love anything that came from the mortal world."

"Tybalt . . ."

"That's why I hated the changelings for so long. It was a changeling that killed my wife, intentionally or not, and doubled that . . . that pain by leaving me alone."

I started to pull my hand away, but he caught it, pulling me back. "I wanted to hate you. Amandine got to keep her mortal lover and have her mortal child, even if she lost them eventually. I wanted to hate you because you made me think of Anne."

"What changed?"

"I fell in love."

Four words, simply stated, and impossible to believe. "You can't mean that."

"Can't I? It's been a long time since I've loved someone, but I know what it feels like. When you turn from me, it hurts. When you think badly of me, I think badly of myself. When you do stupid, suicidal things, I want to slap you upside the head and demand to know how you can be so brilliant and so blind at the same time." Tybalt's expression was calm. "If that's not love, what is it?"

"Why are you telling me this?" I whispered.

"Because we're probably going to die today." He waved his free hand toward the street. "I've always tried not to lie to you; I've seen how you react when others do. Dying without telling you how I felt would be lying. I've been patient. I've given you time to recognize my feelings, and I've seen you choose a man who loved the girl you were, not the woman you are. Now he's gone, and I can't be patient anymore. I love you, October. I'll be sorry if we die here, but I won't be sorry I helped you ... and I won't be sorry I finally told you."

"Tybalt ..."

"Cats never regret anything," he said, and he turned and kissed me.

The lingering chill from the Shadow Roads fled as my body reacted without consulting my mind, leaning forward and returning his kiss with a degree of eagerness almost as surprising as his admission. We'd kissed before, but those kisses weren't like this one. Nothing had ever been like this one. He kissed me like a man who knew he'd been condemned to die and had chosen me in lieu of his last meal.

One hand stayed on mine, pinning it to his knee, while the other hand laced through my hair, pulling me closer. A flicker of common sense asked what I thought I was doing—there were people coming to kill us, Chelsea was missing, and Riordan was planning Oberon-knows-what, yet here I was, kissing the King of Cats like a human teenager sneaking out in the middle of the night.

Tybalt's thumb outlined the true edge of my ear through the gauze of my human disguise. I dropped the illusion, letting him touch my skin without magic getting in the way. At the same time, I placed my free hand against his cheek and leaned closer, until there was no space left between us. We were generating a stronger heat than I would have expected, and it wasn't sudden. No, it wasn't sudden at all. So many things he'd said and done were starting to make sense to me, and as we pulled each other as close as skin would allow, all I could do was wonder what had taken us so damn long.

A cat screamed from the direction of the street, the sound cutting off as abruptly as it started. Tybalt and I were on our feet before the echoes faded. My heart was pounding, fueled by hormones and adrenaline. That sounded like a response to fear, not an intentional signal, and one glance at Tybalt confirmed my fears. His eyes were narrowed, lips drawn back to expose his teeth. He flexed his hands, and his fingertips extended into claws. There was no more running.

I drew my knife. I spared a brief, wistful thought for my sword, but didn't dwell on it; there wasn't time. We were going to stand. And we were going to die.

The rest of the cats had stopped their calling, leaving silence in their wake. Shade was only willing to defend us so far. That was fine. This wasn't her fight. This was mine, and my only regret was that Tybalt was going to go down with me.

"Come on, you bastards," I said. "Let's get this over with."

As if that were the signal they'd been waiting for, Cait Sidhe—some familiar, some not—poured out of the shadows. They formed a ring around us, hissing, snarling, and flexing their clawed hands. Tybalt hissed. The largest, a tiger-striped pureblood I recognized as a member of Tybalt's guard, hissed back.

"I warned you," said Samson's voice. I turned to see him smiling at us, lips pressed thin. "You could have put her aside, but you let her interfere with the smooth running of the Court. You were weak. You deserve to fall."

Tybalt didn't even look. "You will never be King."

"My son will."

"And how? You know he isn't ready to take the throne. What would you do? Take it for him and hold it against all challengers, you and your little band of traitors? You would pervert Cait Sidhe law so much as that? Because there *will* be challengers, Samson. There are always challengers, when the King is weak."

Samson snarled. "My son will be a stronger King than you ever were, and who are you to speak of perverting the law? You perverted it the day you brought her here." He jerked his head toward me. "My son will heal this Court. He will *be* the law."

In that moment, I realized just how far gone Samson really was. He could never be King, but he had rationalized away the rules until he actually believed he had a right to what he wanted—Raj as a puppet King of Cats, with himself as the power behind the throne. He didn't know his son very well; Raj would never let himself be used that way. I was about to say something nasty when the smell of calla lilies hit my nose. I jerked the Luidaeg's charm from my pocket, eyes widening as I saw that it was burning a brilliant red, brighter than it ever had before. "Tybalt . . ."

"Please do me a favor, October. Fight first, argue later."

I turned, eyes searching the underbrush—there. Standing to the left, behind the ring of Cait Sidhe, looking utterly lost and terrified: a dark-haired teenage girl with eyes the color of freshly minted pennies. Only three men stood between her and us.

I had an instant to make my decision, and I made it. Grabbing Tybalt's arm, I lunged toward Chelsea, shielding his body with mine as much as possible. My wounds would heal in a matter of minutes, as long as they weren't fatal. His wouldn't.

My lunge had been surprising enough that we were almost out of the ring before the nearest Cait Sidhe snarled and raked his claws across my belly, freeing a flood of warmth down my front. It felt like more than just blood was trying to slip out of me. I forced myself to keep running. My wounds might heal fast, but no one ever said they wouldn't hurt.

Chelsea's eyes widened as she saw us running toward her. The smell of smoke and lilies grew stronger, her magic writhing through the air. She was getting ready to jump again.

"Chelsea, wait!" I shouted. "Take us with you! Your mother sent us!"

If I thought her eyes were wide before, it was nothing compared to what they were now. The blood loss was slowing me down. Tybalt surged forward, dragging me with him, and we reached Chelsea just before the smell of smoke and lilies became thick enough to be cloying. I slumped forward, my vision going blurry—and then it was the world that was going blurry, and it was the world that was gone, replaced by the short-lived, furious shrieks of the Cait Sidhe.

And everything was the smell of smoke and lilies, and there was blood everywhere, and I closed my eyes and let the darkness—the darkness, and Chelsea, who was finally found now that I was on the verge of being lost—carry me away.

EIGHTEEN

EVERYTHING SMELLED LIKE BLOOD and nothing hurt when I opened my eyes on the star-splashed Annwn sky. The inside of my mouth tasted like blood and bracken—not the most appealing combination ever. I pushed myself to my elbows, trying to swallow the taste away, and realized I was lying on top of something Tybalt-shaped.

"Crap!" I rolled to the side, landing on my ass in the brush. Since nothing hurt, I looked down at myself, doing a quick check for injuries.

Claw marks shredded the front of my shirt, revealing pale strips of skin behind dark brown fabric that had been white when I put it on. My jeans were three shades darker than they'd been earlier, and my head was spinning. I heal fast. These days, I can recover from damn near any injury that doesn't kill me. That doesn't make me invincible, and the amount of energy it had taken my body to knit itself back together was clearly taking its toll.

I looked up again. "How long—?"

"I don't know," said Tybalt, sitting up and smiling at me. It was a pained, weary expression, but it looked real. "I was unconscious for the first part of it. Before you panic further, my injuries were superficial, unlike yours.

Please try not to get yourself gutted again. It's hard on my heart." He closed his eyes.

He was lying. I could smell too much of his blood for him to be telling the truth. And there was nothing I could do about it without getting us out of here. "We were both going to get worse than gutted if we didn't run for— Chelsea!" I scrambled to my feet. My head throbbed, protesting the movement. "Where did she go?"

"Here," said a meek voice. I spun to see the dark-haired girl with Etienne's eyes standing waist-deep in the heather, a wary, hopeful look on her face. "Did my mother really send you?"

"Your mother *and* your father," I said.

Her eyes widened. "My what?" she squeaked.

Okay, maybe that wasn't the best approach. I'm never the most subtle person in the world. Massive physical trauma and blood loss turn out not to help. "Chelsea, look—"

"Are you working with the people who stole me?" she demanded. The smell of her magic was beginning to curl through the air around us.

If she jumped, not only would Tybalt and I be stranded in Annwn until we could find a way out, but we might never find her again. And Tybalt wouldn't heal like I did. "Chelsea, wait. Please, wait. We're not with the people who took you, I swear. We're trying to help." I pushed my hair back, showing her the point of my ear. "If we were kidnapping you, would I be showing you what I really am?"

"A better question: would she have felt the need to bleed quite so much to lend her claim veracity?" Tybalt climbed stiffly to his feet. At least he could stand. "While my dear companion is occasionally dense, she is rarely stupid to the degree that sort of gesture implies."

"Nice 'rarely,'" I said.

He inclined his head. "I felt that truth would be better received than polite falsehood."

Chelsea giggled. It was a short-lived sound, and when I looked back to her, she seemed faintly stunned, as if her laughter were somehow surprising. She'd lost her glasses somewhere, between the kidnapping and the running away. Without them, her resemblance to Etienne was clear. No one who knew him would be able to look at her and not guess they were related.

"I'm October," I said. "You can call me Toby. Most people do."

"I don't, as a rule," said Tybalt.

"That's because you're not people," I said. "This is Tybalt. He's a King of Cats. You can ignore most of the things he says."

"I would bow, but given my current condition, I fear I would injure myself," said Tybalt. "It is a pleasure to meet you at last, Miss Chelsea. You have quite a few people direly concerned for your well-being."

"What—what are you?" The smell of Chelsea's magic faded. "You're not like the ones who . . . you're not like *them*." It was clear from the way she stumbled and stressed her words that she was talking about her kidnappers. "But you're not human, either. You're like me."

"Tybalt's what we call 'Cait Sidhe'—the fairy cats. Which explains the attitude. And the eyes."

"Meow," said Tybalt, deadpan.

I snorted, and continued, "I'm Dóchas Sidhe."

"You're Sidhe?" Chelsea asked. "Mom always said my dad was one of the Sidhe, and they'd come for me if we weren't careful." Her face fell. "I guess I wasn't careful enough."

"We're related," I said, inwardly cursing Etienne—again—for getting involved with a folklore professor. Human folklore gets too much right and too much wrong at the same time. It's hard to tell people you're not planning to curse their cows and steal their children when every fairy tale they've ever read tells them that's exactly what you're planning to do. "Your dad isn't Sidhe, Chelsea. He's Tuatha de Dannan, and he's very worried about you right now."

Chelsea's eyes narrowed. "If he's so worried about me, where has he been my whole life?"

"That's something you're going to need to talk to your mother about. Just please, trust me." I looked to Tybalt. He was still bleeding, but not as much; I hoped that was a good thing. Turning back to Chelsea, I said, "We really appreciate you getting us out of there before, Chelsea. Do you think you could take us somewhere a little less totally deserted? My friend needs medical attention."

"I didn't know I was going to get anyone out of anywhere!" she protested. "I don't even know where I'm going half the time! I just wind up there, and then people grab me, or try to stick me with needles, or tell me they're my friends and don't I want them to keep being my friends." She spread her arms, gesturing to the landscape. "I don't even know where we are now, but did you see those stars? This isn't Earth! We're not on Earth anymore!"

"Annwn," said Tybalt. "Some call it the land of the dead. Some call it the land of the blessed. Many centuries ago, a part of Faerie called it home."

Chelsea froze. "We're in Fairyland?" she whispered.

"You've been in Fairyland for a while, Chelsea," I said. "It has a lot of different parts. The Court of Cats, for one, and the Fire Kingdoms, for another."

"Is that where all the lava came from?" she asked.

"We wouldn't call that the Snow Kingdoms," I said, earning another of her brief-lived smiles. "You're opening doors deeper and deeper into Faerie, and you have to stop. It's not safe for you. It's not safe for anyone."

"Is that why there's no one else here?"

"Among other reasons," said Tybalt.

"I can't control where we go. Mostly I wind up in places I've already been, whether I want to go there or not. We could wind up right back where we were, with those people who were trying to hurt you before." Her eyes widened again. "Why were they trying to hurt you? What did you do?"

Maeve preserve me from the mood swings of high-strung teenage girls. "We didn't *do* anything," I began. "We . . ."

"I pursued an association with a woman outside my Court, and some of my subjects took umbrage," said Tybalt. I stopped talking. He continued, "It is an unfortunate truth of the Court of Cats that we do not, as a rule, play gently with one another. When I did not oblige their request to focus my attentions on them, and them alone, they decided the appropriate course of action would be to depose me, that I might be replaced with someone more agreeable."

"They tried to kill you because you liked a girl?" asked Chelsea.

Tybalt looked toward me. "Yes," he said mildly. "They did."

I reddened. Turning my attention back to Chelsea, I said, "We *need* to get out of here. Please, can you at least try?"

"We could end up anywhere," she said miserably. "Totally anywhere."

I paused. Chelsea hadn't been coming to find us, but she'd found us all the same, just when we needed a miracle to get us out of the situation alive. She'd managed to take us back to one of the only truly safe, empty places in Faerie. Annwn had no resident monsters, not since Oberon sealed the doors.

And Li Qin, back at Tamed Lightning, bent luck.

"Try," I said.

Chelsea swallowed. Then she raised her hands, the smell of sycamore smoke and calla lilies gathering around her. When she spread her hands, a circle appeared, apparently cut out of the air. Through it, I could see the lawn at Tamed Lightning, complete with picnic tables and frothy white lace-o'-dreams growing in the grass where you would normally expect to find mortal clover.

"Thank Oberon," I muttered. "Come on. You, too, Chelsea. There are some people here you should meet, and we can call your mother and let her know that you're okay." And I could go out to the car while she was still calm, and get some of Walther's power-dampening solution before she could jump away again.

We'd found her. We needed to keep her if we possibly could.

Tybalt was first through the portal, largely because I shoved him. He gave me a look that was half amusement, half aggravated dignity and stepped onto the lawn on the other side. I followed. Once I was through, I turned to beckon to Chelsea.

"Come on," I said.

"Okay," she replied, and stepped through. I *saw* her step through. She entered the glowing circle just as Tybalt and I had.

Unlike the two of us, she didn't emerge out the other side.

The portal remained open for a moment, showing the moon-washed fields of Annwn. In that moment, I smelled apples and snowdrops. Then the portal vanished, leaving us looking at the rear of the company's main building.

"Well," I said. "*That* didn't work." *Riordan has her. Riordan has her again, and I can't tell Tybalt, because he needs medical care, and he needs it fast . . .*

"No," said Tybalt. "It did not." He grimaced. "Loath as I am to distract from the important business of resuming our wild goose chase, might we find some soap and water first? I need to wash these cuts before I run the risk of infection."

"We're finding you a first aid kit," I said firmly, taking his arm. "Come on. I think there's one in the cafeteria." If there wasn't, April would notice our arrival and come to find out what we were doing back. She could tell me where to find some bandages and antiseptic cream.

There are times I wish Faerie had more healers, or that my particular healing talents extended to people other than myself. Since I still can't stand the sight of blood, I'm basically useless for anything more involved than smearing Neosporin on a scrape and calling it good.

Tybalt wasn't quite staggering, but he was close. I tried to tighten my grip on his arm without being too obvious about it. He shot me a sharp look. "I am not going to drop dead on the lawn. It would be crass to die without at least saying hello first."

"Oddly, not that reassured." I kept pulling him along. "Samson tried to *kill* us."

"Yes," said Tybalt dryly. "I noticed."

"No, I mean—he really tried to kill us. Both of us. Not just you, which would be forgivable under the Law." Succession in the Court of Cats is often fatal. As a consequence, the Cait Sidhe are considered exempt from Oberon's Law as long as they stick to killing each other. A Cait Sidhe killed by another of his or her kind isn't considered a murder victim so much as, well . . . bad timing. If Samson had killed me, on the other hand . . . "Even if the Queen wanted to hand out fiefdoms and cookies, I'm pretty sure Sylvester would insist on something being done."

"Among others, yes. You have a surprising number of willing noble patrons. Even so, you must understand . . . Samson allowed you to be brought into the line of fire not because he thought he could get away with it, but because he didn't care." Tybalt's expression turned grave. "The intent was almost certainly to send us both running into the shadows, where our deaths would go unremarked—and my death would be less likely to reverse itself." Seeing my bewilderment, he explained, "A King or Queen who dies on the Shadow Roads—not after falling off them, but truly on them—remains dead. The magic that restores us can't find us in the dark."

I blinked. "That must have been a fun one to learn."

"If it were not so, I could never have killed my father."

My eyes widened before I could stop myself from reacting. Tybalt was a King of Cats. I'd always known what meant—that sometime in the past, he'd killed someone to get his throne—but I'd never really thought about it before. I hadn't wanted to.

Tybalt shot me a very small, very tired smile. "I'm done with secrets between us, October. If I am asking you to let me court you—and to court me in return—I cannot pretend to be other than I am. I am a King. Kings gain their thrones in certain ways."

I blinked again. This time, I didn't have any words to follow the gesture. Admissions of love are one thing. One strange, scary, unexpected, potentially insane thing, but still, they're self-contained. They can be ignored, if they have to be; they can be politely forgotten by both parties and never spoken of again. It didn't seem likely, given the circumstances. It was still an option. Courting, on the other hand . . .

Formal courtship is common among the older pure-bloods, played at by the younger purebloods, and practically unheard of among changelings. It's somewhere between the Victorian ideal of calling cards, chaperones, and romantic failure to even hold hands, and the fairy tale ideal of glass mountains, dragon-slaying, and the occasional curse. The whole concept was terrifying.

Tybalt clearly realized he'd managed to unsettle me. His next words made it plain that he didn't understand *why*: "I thought you knew what I was."

"I did," I said. "I mean, I do. I mean . . . I don't know what I mean." *I mean, I don't know why you'd want to court me. I mean that I don't know how to court you. I mean that I don't know whether I want to be courted.*

I meant a lot of things. I just didn't know how to say any of them.

"Please tell me when you acquire the knowledge," said Tybalt. He stepped away from me long enough to open the door into the next building. His shoulders were squared, and the effort that it took for him to stay upright unassisted was impossible to miss. I ached to help him. I didn't move. Not until he had the door fully open and was gesturing for me to step inside.

"I will," I said.

He followed me through the door and didn't object when I took his arm again, shifting so he could lean on me.

"I promise not to make a habit of this," he said.

"Tell you what. You don't make a habit of this, I won't make a habit of getting myself gutted, how's that?"

His eyes went to the slashes across the front of my shirt. "I believe I can agree to that."

"Agree to what?" inquired April, with what sounded like genuine curiosity. We both turned to see her standing a few feet away, head cocked to the side as she waited for our reply.

I frowned. "Why don't I smell ozone?"

"Answering a question with a question is inefficient," said April. "You do not smell ozone because I am not functionally here. This is a projection." Then she smiled — an expression so joyful and sincere that it made my heart ache. She looked like her mother when she smiled like that. "Do you like it?"

"It's very nice, April. It looks just like you." April was made of solid light, rather than anything messy like flesh or bone. She'd always been questionably physical. This was just one more step along that illogical progression. "Where are the others, please? Tybalt's injured, and I need to get someone to help me clean him up."

"You have also been injured," noted April. "The amount of blood on your clothing indicates a blood loss of approximately—"

"Please don't calculate how much of my blood isn't actually inside my body right now," I interrupted. "I really, *really* don't want to know. Where are Li and Quentin?"

April frowned. "In the cafeteria. I will alert them to your arrival." She disappeared, as silently and scentlessly as she had appeared in the first place.

"Oh, Tamed Lightning, is there *anything* you can't make creepier?" I paused, and added, "Don't answer that. Come on."

Tybalt and I walked to the cafeteria in the sort of silence that spoke, very loudly, to the effort he was making to stay on his feet. I wanted to suggest he shift to feline form and let me carry him, but I was afraid if he did that, he wouldn't have the strength to shift back. Eventually, the bright blue cafeteria door came into view. Quentin pushed it open a second later and held it for us, a worried expression on his face. That expression deepened when he got a good look at my clothes.

"Toby . . . ?" he said, in a small voice.

"I'm okay," I said. "Could probably use some cookies and orange juice, but I'm okay. Tybalt needs help."

"I assure you, I am less injured than I appear," said Tybalt. "I am simply conserving my strength while I recover from the effort of holding October's intestines inside her body."

Quentin looked between the two of us, paling. Then he stepped aside. "Li's getting the first aid kit." He looked past us to the hall. "Where's Chelsea?"

"Why would Chelsea be here?" I asked, leading Tybalt into the cafeteria. He was leaning on me harder all the time, and I could smell fresh blood again. He was bleeding somewhere under his clothes from an injury I hadn't seen. That wasn't good.

"Because I bent your luck and hers together," said Li Qin. She was spreading the contents of a first aid kit out on one of the room's oddly shaped white tables. "She should have gone right to where you were."

"She did," I said. "That's why we're alive."

"What?" Li Qin looked up, and paled. "Oh, sweet Titania . . ."

"Hasn't been seen in a long time, and wouldn't help us if she were here," I said grimly.

"I think I might want to take one of those seats," said Tybalt, in a thoughtful tone. "They seem pleasant. They seem like a good place to wait while the room stops spinning . . ."

Then he collapsed.

People in real life never collapse like people in the movies, who always seem to fall like trees, or slump gently into whoever's trying to support them. Tybalt pitched forward and folded up at the same time, turning from a man who was at least trying not to knock me over into more than a hundred and eighty pounds of dead weight.

I yelped, scrambling to get a better grip on him. All I succeeded in doing was cushioning his fall as he bore me down to the cafeteria floor.

"Toby!" squawked Quentin. Li Qin said something in startled-sounding Chinese. Then both of them were next to me, working together to try to pull Tybalt off the floor.

Between the two of them, they were able to lever him off me. I scrambled out from under him, terrified that every move I made was just going to make things worse. He didn't move. I took off my—his, it was his to begin with, and, oh, Maeve, he couldn't die on me—took off my jacket and folded it into a pillow, sliding it under his head before fumbling with blood-sticky fingers for his pulse. It was there, but it was nowhere near strong enough for my liking.

"We need a healer," I said, standing. "This isn't going to be fixed with aspirin and gauze."

Li Qin looked sick. "We have no healer. The closest we ever came was Yui, and she . . ."

"Died the same time January did, I know." Tybalt wasn't moving. The closest healer I knew of was Jin, at Shadowed Hills.

Shadowed Hills.

"I'm an idiot," I said. "Quentin, give me your phone. Mine's dead." Quentin fished his phone out of his pocket and tossed it to me. I clicked it open, scrolling to the contacts. As I expected, Shadowed Hills was second on the list.

The phone only rang twice before Etienne picked up, beginning, "Shadowed Hi—"

"I need you to grab Jin and get to Tamed Lightning *right now*," I interrupted. "It's an emergency."

Etienne hesitated. "October? I don't . . ."

"Tybalt's hurt! Don't argue with me, just get over here."

"I can't run off with the Duke's personal physician without better reason than a friend of yours being injured."

"How about he got hurt because we were looking for

your daughter, huh?" That wasn't strictly true. For the moment, it was close enough. Etienne didn't say anything, and so I pressed on, saying, "There's no healer here. I can't drive him to a place where he can get cared for. Duchess Riordan is one of the people who snatched Chelsea, and she has her right now. Now please, get Jin, and get over here." I glanced at Tybalt. He was so still . . . "Please. We don't have much time."

"Tell Countess O'Leary to open the wards," said Etienne. Then the line went dead.

I clicked Quentin's phone shut, handing it back to him. April was nowhere to be seen. I cleared my throat and said, as calmly as I could manage, "April, I need you."

There was a popping sound, accompanied by the strong smell of ozone, before she said, from behind me, "Yes?"

There was a time when that would have been enough to make me jump. How times have changed. "I need you to open an exception in the wards," I said, turning to face her. "Sir Etienne is going to be teleporting in, accompanied by an Ellyllon healer. I apologize for inviting them without checking with you first, but it's an emergency."

"Ah," said April. Her gaze went to Tybalt. She frowned. "Is he damaged?"

I nodded, trying to deny the sinking feeling in my chest. "I think he is, yeah," I said. "Can you please open that exception?"

"Of course," said April. "I do not want anyone else to leave the local network. We are too sparsely distributed." Then she was gone, leaving the air to rush back into the place where she'd been standing.

I stayed where I was, eyes going to Tybalt. He hadn't moved. There was a bloody fingerprint on his cheek that I recognized as my own, standing out in vivid red against the pallor of his skin. Mine. This was my fault. If it hadn't been for me distracting him, Samson wouldn't have decided Tybalt was neglecting his Court. Tybalt wouldn't have been running through the shadows; he wouldn't have been vulnerable to an attack. He got hurt because of me. This was mine, and I had to own it, just like I had to own what happened to Connor. This was my fault.

"October." Li Qin touched my wrist. I whipped around so fast I almost hit her; the wind from my motion actually ruffled her hair. She looked at me impassively and said, in a low, firm, tone, "This is not your fault."

"What—how did you—?"

"I'm not a mind reader, but I spent quite a few years married to the kind of woman who thinks the best way to adopt a daughter is to break the rules of nature. Jan took responsibility for everything that happened within a mile of where she was standing. In the end, I think that's what killed her." A flicker of sorrow crossed Li Qin's face, only to be wiped away by sternness. "You don't have much in common with her, and that's for the best—she could never have done the work you do—but you share her fondness for taking blame. You didn't do this."

I took a breath, letting it slowly out before I said, "I guess we'll see about that. I'll let you know whether it's my fault or not when we know whether or not he's going to live."

"He's going to be okay," said Quentin. "He has to. He's *Tybalt*. You'd be all weird and irritating if he wasn't around."

"Weird and irritating?" I raised an eyebrow. "What gives you that idea?"

Quentin shrugged. "That's already how you get when he isn't around."

The smell of cedar smoke and limes swirled through the air, saving me from needing to reply. I turned to see Jin stepping through a circle in the air, her gauzy mayfly's wings buzzing anxiously until it looked like she might actually leave the ground from sheer nerves. It wasn't going to happen—adult Ellyllon are too heavy to fly without using magic—but it was the sort of reflex that told me how little she enjoyed traveling via teleportation portal.

Etienne stepped through behind her, closing the portal with a wave of his hand.

"Where's the—" Jin began, and stopped when she saw the state of my clothes, her eyes going wide.

Etienne was less restrained. "Maeve's teeth, October, did you bleed to death and just not notice? You've got more blood outside than you have room for inside!"

"Hello to you, too," I said, too relieved to get annoyed. "Jin . . ." I didn't know what to say, so I didn't say anything at all. I just stepped aside, pointing mutely toward Tybalt. He still wasn't moving.

"Ah," said Jin softly. Her wings stilled their buzzing as she studied Tybalt, assessing his condition from a distance. She's been Sylvester's personal physician for a long time—long enough to see most of the damage that a body can sustain and still survive. So it was more than a little unnerving when she shook her head and said, "You should have called for me sooner."

My mouth went dry. "What are you saying?"

"I'm saying you should have called for me sooner." She stepped toward me, reaching out to touch my wrist, much as Li Qin had. Unlike Li's touch, hers sent a wave of serenity washing over me, dimming and dulling my fear. Ellyllon can secrete both sedatives and stimulants through their skin. It's what makes some of them such great healers, even as it makes the rest of them such great hedonists.

I glared at her, or tried to, anyway. With her artificial calm spreading through my body, the most I could manage was faint peevishness. "Don't drug me."

"Would you rather I knocked you out? Because I could do that. And I will, if it looks like you're going to interfere." She took her hand away, leaving tingles of chemical peace dancing over my skin. "Etienne, Quentin, get over here. I'm going to need the two of you to help me lift him onto the table. I need him higher."

"Sure," said Quentin, moving to join her. Etienne didn't say anything. He just went.

Li Qin was abruptly at my side, taking my elbow and

turning me away from the sight of Jin and her makeshift assistants descending on Tybalt's unmoving form. "Let's make some coffee," she said, soothingly. "Wouldn't you enjoy that? You like coffee."

"Yes, I do," I agreed. My voice sounded distant. I was aware, in an almost academic fashion, that I should be more upset than I was—that I should be doing something to help, not going to fix myself a cup of coffee. Now that Jin wasn't adding to the calm, I could feel the shape of it in my blood, smooth and foreign. I could remove it if I wanted to. I might not have seen that if I hadn't been so relaxed, but I was too calm to get in my own way. If I wanted it to stop, it would.

And that was why I couldn't want it to stop. The only thing I could do to help Tybalt was stay out of the way and let Jin do the job I'd begged her to come to do. If he was going to be saved, she was going to be the one who saved him, not me. Not even a hero can do everything.

Li Qin led me to the coffee maker, where my current serenity turned the process of grinding beans and pouring water into something slow and ritualistic. It was like watching my friend Lily, the Lady of the Tea Gardens, setting up a formal tea service. Only this time, the end result wasn't going to taste like licking the lawnmower.

"You like strong coffee," observed Li Qin.

"Don't sleep much," I said. "Need the caffeine."

"Jan didn't sleep much either. She always said she could sleep once she was dead." Li's voice didn't quaver. She kept watching me, smiling just a little. "I suppose that means she's well-rested by now."

"Jan was weird," I said, pouring coffee into my cup. The part of me that was still aware that insulting a dead woman's memory might not be a good idea cringed. The fact that Li Qin was Jan's widow just made it worse.

But Li Qin didn't seem to mind. Her smile didn't waver as she agreed, "That's very true. Everyone in Tamed Lightning is weird, one way or another."

Living flesh being sliced open makes an unmistakable sound. Raw meat being cut is a kissing cousin, but it doesn't really compare. Living flesh fights back. It *resists* in a way that dead things can't, muscle and bone fighting against the invasion of the knife.

The thick, wet sound of someone being cut open hit my nerves like a cattle prod. I didn't drop my coffee cup—it would take a lot more than shock, fear, and hope, all mixed into a sick cocktail, to make me drop a perfectly good cup of coffee—but I did go stiff, my fingers locking on the handle until I would have sworn I felt the porcelain bend. Jin's peace fled as quickly as it had come, chased out of my body by adrenaline and my own rising magic.

"That's gross," said Quentin.

"Never become a doctor," said Jin.

"I wasn't planning on it."

"Good," said Jin, and started to sing.

The Ellyllon songs are strange things. They're unique every time, because they bend to suit the needs of their subject matter. Ellyllon can sing both harm and healing, and what they can't sing away, they can at least dull down. Jin kept singing long enough for me to raise my shaking hand, drink an entire cup of coffee without tasting a drop of it, and pour myself a refill.

Jin stopped singing. Silence fell . . . and in the silence, Tybalt coughed.

"And that's how you perform home surgery," said Jin.

I forced myself to move slowly as I put my cup down on the counter, barely registering the suddenly silent Li Qin, and turned around to face them.

The first thing I noticed was the blood, which covered the surface of the white plastic table and pooled on the industrial-blue linoleum floor. The second thing, oddly enough, was the glitter. A thick haze of silver and green glitter shimmered in the air around them, making them look like they were having a small, quiet, horror-movie-themed rave. Etienne and Quentin were standing on the far side of the table that Tybalt was lying on. Jin was standing in front of the table, blood coating her arms to the elbows, soaking into her shirt, and even covering the bottom half of her face.

And Tybalt, for all that he still looked pale and unwell, was struggling to sit up, eyes open, and looking back at me.

"Massive internal bleeding," said Jin, tilting her chin up so that she was talking to no one in particular. "Damage to the liver and spleen. Three broken ribs, one of which managed to puncture a lung, which, let me tell you, takes talent. Also a cracked femur—shouldn't have been walking on that—and a pretty severe concussion. Congratulations. It's a nice, macho death, which nobody gets to die today."

"For that, I thank you," said Tybalt, swinging his legs over the edge of the table, gripping it hard for balance as he stood.

Jin glared at him. He was more than a foot taller than she was, but she still managed to look imposing as she gestured for him to sit back down. "No walking! No standing, no bending, no moving, no accessing the Shadow Roads, *nothing*. You don't swim for an hour after eating, you don't swan around like an idiot for an hour after narrowly avoiding death."

"Toby does," said Quentin.

"Toby is genetically predisposed to swan around like an idiot," Jin shot back. "Now *sit*."

"Must everyone behave as if I am some sort of hound?" asked Tybalt. Still, he moved to the nearest chair and sat. "I simply wished to reassure October that my condition was improved."

"She can see you. She has eyes. There is no reason for you to be on your feet."

"Elliot is going to be furious when he sees the condition of the cafeteria," supplied April. I didn't need to look to know that she was behind me. "That is a perfectly valid reason to be on your feet and potentially running away."

I didn't say anything. I just kept looking at Tybalt.

Li Qin put a hand on my shoulder, nudging me forward. "You're not the one who's not allowed to move," she said.

It only took me four long steps to cross the stretch of floor between me and the chair where Tybalt was seated. Jin moved out of the way. The blood on the linoleum made it slippery, and when my feet started to go out from underneath me, I let them, hitting the floor on my knees. Somehow, in the course of the motion, I managed to get my arms around him. Jin had objected to him standing, but she didn't object to this. He closed his arms around me in turn. I buried my face against his blood-soaked shoulder, struggling to keep my breath steady.

"Thank you," he whispered. "If you hadn't called them here . . . thank you."

"You're welcome," I whispered back.

My jeans had almost dried while I waited for Jin to finish working on Tybalt. Now, they were getting soaked again, becoming heavy with blood. The feeling of it congealing against my skin was what made me let go and climb to my feet. I rested one hand on Tybalt's shoulder, like I was afraid he'd disappear if I let go for too long. And maybe I was.

"Chelsea was here," I said, turning to Etienne. His eyes widened. There was a smear of blood on his forehead, spoiling his normally immaculate appearance. Oddly, that just made him look more like his daughter. Blood will tell. "She's the reason Tybalt and I survived long enough to get here. We were attacked in Berkeley. We were just about done for when she teleported in, and we managed to get her to bring us back here."

"Is she . . . is she hurt?" asked Etienne.

"She's scared, and she's running, but she wasn't injured that I could see. She's definitely teleporting without any problems." Teleporting, and tearing her way through doors that were supposed to have been locked centuries ago. "She brought us back by way of Annwn. I think she's starting to wear some seriously thin patches in the walls of the world."

"What?" asked Jin. She looked from me to Etienne, her wings beginning to vibrate rapidly again. "What are you two talking about?"

"A Tuatha changeling—" began Etienne, then stopped when he saw my glare. He took a breath, and started again: "My daughter, Chelsea, is missing. Her human mother reported her disappearance to me, and I retained October to locate her. Unfortunately, there have been complications."

"You involved Toby. Of course there have been complications. If you don't want complications, you buy her a bus ticket and send her to Vancouver to buy those coffee-flavored candy bars they have in Canada." Jin said this in an almost distant tone, as if her mouth were keeping itself busy while her brain tried to process what it had just heard. "What do you mean, your *daughter*?"

"Bridget," said Etienne.

Jin's eyes widened. "You got the *folklore professor* pregnant? Are you an *idiot*?"

"See, that's what I said." I blinked, leaning back against the table as a wave of dizziness hit me. "Whoa. Why is the room spinning?"

"Probably because you lost enough blood to count as exsanguination in a mortal hospital, and your body's going crazy trying to rebuild itself," said Jin. Her gaze turned accusingly toward the slashes in my shirt. "Did you decide to test just how indestructible you really are?"

"Yup," I said, as lightly as I could. "It turns out that I'm pretty damn indestructible. Me and cockroaches."

April appeared next to me in a haze of ozone and sparks. She had a bottle of orange juice in one hand and a pack of Twinkies in the other. "These will improve your current condition."

"Awesome," I said, taking my snack from her. My fingers were so bloody that it was impossible to avoid getting at least a little bit on my Twinkies. I did my best to ignore that as I crammed the first one into my mouth.

"While my dear October is preoccupied with restoring herself to a semblance of normalcy, if I may: Chelsea has been to Annwn at least twice. She opened a gateway into the Court of Cats. Her jaunts are becoming no less impossible with repetition."

"And the shallowing is becoming unstable," added Li Qin. "We've had at least five microquakes today that weren't mirrored in the mortal world."

"Seven, to be more precise," said April. "I do not know how much longer I can maintain structural integrity of the grounds. We may need to evacuate for the sake of our own safety."

I blinked, swallowing my mouthful of Twinkie before I asked, "How can you evacuate? Isn't your main server inside the shallowing?"

"It is," confirmed April. "I can survive on backup power for up to nine days before I encounter permanent systems failure. I am more concerned about our data storage and the employees in the basement, who cannot be moved into a mortal environ without raising questions we will be unprepared to address."

"Employees in the . . . oh." I stopped talking, turning my attention to my orange juice instead. It seemed safer, or at least a little less macabre.

The murders at Tamed Lightning two years ago weren't the normal kind of killings. All the victims were purebloods, and they were killed in a way that meant the night-haunts wouldn't come for their bodies. Faerie flesh doesn't decay. The last time I'd been to Tamed Lightning, all the victims save one—January, who hadn't been killed like the others, and whose body had been burned—were still in the basement, waiting for April to put together the necessary pieces and find a way to bring them back.

"Um, ew," said Quentin, clearly following the same train of thought as I was.

"It would cause complications with the mortal authorities if we were to remove them," said April, seemingly oblivious to the fact that other people might find a basement full of dead people creepy. "This is aside from the fact that they are presently unable to conceal their fae natures, you understand."

"Right," I said, and stuffed the second Twinkie into my mouth to save myself from needing to come up with anything else to say.

"Now that Toby isn't on the verge of collapsing, can someone *please* tell me how Etienne's daughter was able to open a door to Annwn? Does Sylvester know about this?" Jin paused and answered her own question: "Of course Sylvester doesn't know. If he knew, he'd be here making sure you idiots didn't get yourselves killed. Good job on that, by the way."

I swallowed without chewing, grateful for the spongy nature of Hostess products. "Etienne said he was going to tell him."

"I am," said Etienne. "I just found out Chelsea existed. I wanted to have her safely recovered before I went to His Grace with the news."

"This is a whole new level of 'better to beg forgiveness,'" said Jin. "Annwn? Really?"

"Turns out Chelsea didn't inherit the blocks that keep most Tuatha from using too much power and blowing themselves up," I said grimly, digging the Luidaeg's Chelsea-chaser out of my pocket. It was glowing a serene white, caught in its neutral state. "Quentin and I each have one of these. The Luidaeg gave us these to track Chelsea down. So far, we've managed to get to where she's been a few times, but we only wound up where she was once, when Li bent our luck to bring us all together."

"An endeavor for which I am very grateful, as it no doubt saved both our lives." Tybalt took the hand I had left resting on his shoulder, lacing his fingers with mine as he stood. "The fact remains that she is loose, somewhere, she is afraid, and she is doing a great deal of damage."

"I think we're all on board with the idea that we need to find Chelsea and get her to stop punching holes in things," I said. "We're not covering enough ground."

Etienne frowned, sudden resolve washing over his face. "I will stay," he said.

I blinked. "Excuse me?"

"I will remain with you. I can't ask you to do this for me and not be willing to help—or do you think having another teleporter won't be an asset? You have a mechanism for tracking my daughter. I *am* a mechanism for following her if she opens a door while you're in pursuit." Etienne's frown deepened. "If you're concerned about getting paid—"

"If you finish that sentence, I'll have to hit you, so how about you don't?" I shook my head. "We're glad to have you. We need all the help we can get, especially since Riordan—"

I was interrupted as the shadows behind the nearest vending machine rippled like a black muslin curtain, and Raj stepped into the room, a revolver in his hands. He leveled it on Tybalt before any of us had a chance to react. "Hello, Uncle," he said. "I'm here to kill you now."

Oh, this day just got better and better.

NINETEEN

I STARED. SO DID QUENTIN, Jin, and Li Qin. April frowned, irritation evident.

"I did not consent to your presence," she said peevishly. "Please depart, and attempt your political assassination on someone else's property."

Tybalt just smiled. He took my hand off his shoulder and stood. Then he raised my hand to his lips, pressing a light kiss against my fingers, before letting me go and walking, with the utmost calm, toward Raj.

"Tybalt, what—"

"It's all right, October," he said, and kept walking. Raj trained the revolver on his uncle's chest, the shaking spreading from his hands to his arms, until his entire body seemed to be caught in a wind that none of the rest of us could feel. Tybalt reached out and placed his hand atop the muzzle of the gun, pushing it gently downward.

Raj didn't fight him. If anything, he looked relieved. Glass green eyes brimming with tears, he looked up at Tybalt and repeated hopelessly, "I'm here to kill you."

"With a firearm? In a fiefdom belonging to the Divided Courts? My dearest boy, do you truly believe this is a fight you could win?" Tybalt's voice was soft, his words reasoned and calm. I didn't feel nearly that serene, and I wasn't the one who'd just had a gun pointed at me.

Raj shook his head. His eyes flicked to me, desperation evident in their depths, before returning to Tybalt.

"I'm sorry," said Tybalt, still calm. "I didn't hear that."

"N-no, Uncle," said Raj. He swallowed hard, and added, "I figured it was a fight I'd lose. I hoped it was."

"But you came."

"Yes, sir."

"Who sent you?"

Raj said nothing.

Tybalt sighed. "This is senseless, and we do not have the time. October?"

"Uh, yeah?"

"Can my beloved nephew, the assassin, stay with you for a short time? I fear the Court of Cats may not be safe for him at present."

I glanced toward Quentin, who shook his head, looking as baffled as I felt. Right. We were winging it again. That's my *favorite* way to deal with crazy. "Sure," I said. "Raj knows he's always welcome in my home."

"Thank you," said Tybalt solemnly. It was the third time he'd thanked me in an hour. It was starting to feel like something I could get used to. He turned his attention back to Raj and said, "If you would like, I can banish you. It would be a fitting punishment for a failed challenge to my throne. I'd prefer not to do so. I've spent a great deal of time and energy preparing you to take my place. We both know you're not ready and that you have no desire to depose me like this, without honor or the validity of fair combat. Now. What did he tell you?"

Raj's face fell. I'd only seen him look that miserable once before, the day his mother died. Then he threw himself into Tybalt's arms, heedless of the blood covering the older Cait Sidhe. "He said I had to come here and kill you, you were dying anyway and if I didn't, I'd be useless, because I wouldn't get the throne, and then he'd kill everybody! Quentin and Jazz and everybody!" He sniffled before adding, "He said Toby was already dead."

I raised my hand. "Not dead."

"Who said he was going to kill me?" asked Quentin.

"I'm pretty sure that was Raj's dad," I replied.

"He said he gutted you like a fish," said Raj. He pulled away from Tybalt, just far enough to scrub at his eyes with the back of his hand. "There was no way you'd survive that."

"Surprise," I said grimly. "Tybalt? Is this normal?"

"Not in the slightest." Tybalt pushed Raj the rest of the way away from him, holding his nephew and heir at arm's-length. "Raj, I am sorry to do this, but I have no choice. Your father has seen to that. Do you stand with him? Or do you refute him as your parent and stand with me?"

Raj's eyes went wide. "What?"

Tybalt sighed. "You were misled, and I am sorry. I allowed this to happen. I knew he wanted you to hold power because he never could, and I allowed it because I wanted you to be happy. I wanted you to know your mother's eyes. I wanted to give you what most Princes never have. I was a fool. Perhaps your father is right, and I am unfit to be King—but you are unprepared. If you are loyal to him, run. Go to him, tell him you failed and have to flee, because otherwise, I will be forced to kill you both. Do you understand?"

Raj nodded mutely.

"Good. If you are loyal to me . . . stay. Your father will be punished for what he has done, but you are still a Prince, and you are mine to punish or to pardon." Tybalt looked at Raj, hope and anguish both clear in his face. "The choice is yours. The choice is always yours."

It sometimes seems like Faerie reserves the hardest choices for the children. Raj bit his lip, glancing past Tybalt to me. His eyes widened again when he noticed my shredded shirt. Then they narrowed, his expression hardening. He turned back to Tybalt. "I won't help you kill my father," he said.

"I wasn't planning to ask you to. Believe it or not, I have long since tired of killing."

Raj nodded. "Okay."

"Just 'okay'?" asked Tybalt, raising an eyebrow.

"Okay," repeated Raj. He stepped back and knelt, seeming not to notice the blood soaking through his pants. "My King, I beg forgiveness for my actions. I was misled."

"I know, Raj," said Tybalt tiredly. "Rise."

"Being a King sort of sucks," I said.

Quentin wrinkled his nose. "So does your outfit."

"Blood is in this season." I cleared my throat. "If we're done with the political upheaval, can we move on to finding Chelsea, figuring out what Riordan thinks she's doing, and stopping Samson from turning the Court of Cats against us? Because those all seem like high-priority items, and instead, we're just standing around getting blood on everything in sight."

"You need new pants," said Quentin. "And a new shirt. And maybe new hair."

"And we're missing the point," I muttered.

Tybalt turned to face me. "Not at all," he said. "Samson has doubtless intended to have me overthrown for quite some time. He hasn't been foolish enough to force his son to challenge me, but I've heard him talking to the guards, implying that I am not fit for my position. He lacks the power to take my place. Sadly, that doesn't stop him from taking my life."

"Only Raj isn't strong enough to kill you empty-handed," I guessed. "Hence the gun."

Raj looked deeply embarrassed. He set the gun down on the nearest table, muttering, "Father didn't think I could take Uncle Tybalt without help, even if he was wounded."

"Your father is wrong about many things, but right about that much," said Tybalt. "If Raj kills me, however he accomplishes it, he becomes King. Samson's co-conspirators would then be absolved of their part in this. There is no shame in backing a revolution that succeeds."

"And if you live?" I asked.

Tybalt didn't say anything, but his smile seemed to hold far too many teeth.

I sighed, retrieving my jacket from the floor and shrugging it back on. "Okay. Raj, you're with us now. Etienne, you go with Quentin. We know Riordan's involved. I think she's using a blood charm to call Chelsea back to her. Quentin has a duplicate of the charm I showed you. Take some of the power dampening solution from the cooler in the car. You see her again—"

"I'll pour it on her," said Quentin.

Etienne and Jin blinked. I raised a hand, signaling that I'd explain later, and said, "Good. Tybalt, can you reach the Shadow Roads, or are you still too beat up?"

Tybalt looked at Jin, who rolled her eyes, wings buzzing in annoyance. "I don't suppose I can stop you from flying around like a pixie with its head cut off any more than I can stop Toby," she said resignedly.

"No, you can't," he said, looking amused.

"Hey," I protested. "I'm always careful after a healing."

Jin didn't dignify my blatant lie with a response. She glared at Tybalt instead. "Will you at least *try* to go easy on yourself for the next few days? I know it's hard. Toby's essentially a walking bad influence. But please."

Tybalt quirked a faint smile. "I bow to the wisdom of milady chirurgeon."

"Huh?" said Quentin and Raj, almost in unison.

Jin smirked. "It means 'doctor.' I'm glad someone here knows how to take medical advice."

"He's using words that are no longer recognized as valid in Scrabble," I said.

"I don't care, he's a smart cat. And before you try to tell me where to go, I'm staying here. You people are going to need patching up, I'm sure of it."

I wished I could argue with her. Sadly, she was probably right. "Fine. Tybalt and I will go to Berkeley on the Shadow Roads, see if we can pick up Chelsea's trail where we saw her last. After that—"

My phone rang.

I blinked, digging for the phone. "What the—I thought my battery was dead."

"It was," said April cheerfully. "I recharged it for you."

"Without taking it out of my pocket?"

April blinked. "Why would I need to take it out of your pocket?"

"Right." The display said it was May calling. I flipped the phone open. "Hello?"

Screaming and the sound of something being smashed greeted me, followed by the sound of May shouting, "Toby! Get over here! I don't know how long I ca—"

The line went dead.

I shoved the phone back into my pocket without thinking about it, already breaking into a run. "Tybalt! Shadows! My place! Now!"

Tybalt nodded, stepping back toward the wall. The others moved out of our way as I jumped for him; he grabbed my hands, and then we were falling into darkness.

The Shadow Roads were cold and airless, but nothing came to attack us as we ran through the black. That made it a more pleasant trip than our last one. When I inevitably faltered—I may heal like a superhero, but it takes a lot out of my body, and I hadn't eaten nearly enough to make up for it—Tybalt caught me smoothly and ran on through the dark with me cradled in his arms, holding me tight against his chest. This close, the heat from his skin was enough to beat back some of the chill. I relaxed as much as I could with blood freezing in my hair and terror pounding in my veins and let him carry me home.

I knew we were getting close when he slowed long enough to drop me back to my feet, murmuring next to my ear, "Seconds, little fish. Hold fast . . ."

And then we were bursting back out into the warmth and light of my cluttered living room, where May promptly hit me in the back of the head with my own aluminum baseball bat.

The reverberating "bong" of metal meeting bone was still audible as I dropped to my knees, no longer interested in focusing on much of anything beyond the shooting pain in my head. Tybalt snarled, a sound as inhuman as it's possible for a mostly human throat to make, and May yelped. I managed to twist around, squinting past the tears in my eyes, to see Tybalt holding her off the floor by her throat. May was scrabbling uselessly at his fingers, trying to pry them away. Jazz was in the hall behind her, face pale, eyes wide and terrified. The smell of their mingled blood hit me a split second later, washing the scene in red.

It was the blood that gave me the strength to speak, focusing past the pain as I said, "Put her down, Tybalt." I swallowed, tasting the air, and added, "It's May. Not an impostor. She bleeds right." A wave of nausea washed over me, and I stopped speaking. I really hate head injuries.

"She *hit* you," snarled Tybalt.

"She thought you were that *man* again!" shouted Jazz. There was a harsh note under her normally soft voice, like a raven's shriek. She was a skinshifter, not a shapeshifter—she'd need her cloak of feathers to transform—but some aspects of her avian nature were bleeding through. "Put her *down!*"

May didn't say anything. Talking would have required air. She just went limp in Tybalt's hand.

Tybalt sighed, looking clearly unhappy as he lowered May back to her feet and took his hand away from her throat. Livid red bruises shaped like his fingers remained behind, striping her skin. May took a hasty step backward, out of his reach. Jazz was right there to catch her, putting her left hand on her girlfriend's shoulder and glaring murder in Tybalt's direction.

The room was still spinning, and I was pretty sure that getting up was a terrible idea. I did it anyway, forcing myself first to my knees, and then to an unsteady standing position. Another wave of nausea hit me. I wobbled. "Wow, May," I said. "I think maybe you cracked my skull. Please don't do that again."

Tybalt growled, low and deep in his throat.

"Chill," I said. Moving as slowly as I could to avoid

setting off any more alarm bells in my head, I looked around the living room. It wasn't just cluttered, which would have been normal; it was *destroyed*.

The coffee table was shattered, as if something had been dropped on it from a considerable height. One of the legs protruded from the broken remains of the television set. Pictures and knick-knacks, some of which I hadn't even known we owned, were shattered on the floor, amid the confetti remains of May's gossip magazines and several of my books. Even the cat beds were shredded, bits of cloth and puffs of cotton filling scattered everywhere.

"What the hell happened here?" I asked.

"Why do you think I hit you with a bat?" May asked.

I turned to see her glaring at me. Jazz was doing the same, with a considerably more pained look in her eyes. Her right arm was dangling at her side, with a sharp new bend below the elbow. There were fingermarks on her throat, too, and I knew they weren't from Tybalt.

"It was one of *your* people," spat Jazz, that harsh croak still underlining her words. Her eyes flicked from me to Tybalt as she spoke, making it plain whose people she was referring to. "Gray hair. Green eyes. Tried to kill us both."

"Samson," said Tybalt, eyes narrowing. "He should not have done that."

"Raj's father," I explained, for Jazz and May's benefit. "He tried to kill us a little while ago. Actually, he nearly succeeded."

"Well, when he failed, I guess he decided to take out his anger on something a little more defenseless," said May. For the first time, I noticed the blood streaking the back of her blouse. May saw me looking. Her expression hardened. "He was a little surprised when I didn't die. I guess no one told him Fetches are indestructible."

"Lucky us," I said quietly.

Spike slunk out from under the nearest couch, thorns rattling like bones in the wind. It stayed low to the ground as it crept to press itself against my feet. The pain in my head was abating, or at least that's what I told myself as I stooped to gather my rose goblin's thorny body into my arms. It promptly plastered itself into my chest, making small whimpering noises. I gritted my teeth and let it nestle. The thorns hurt when they broke my skin. That was nothing compared to what I'd already been through, and the day wasn't over yet.

"Why did Raj's father come here and try to kill us?" demanded May. "Why did he try to kill *you?* Dammit, Toby, what the hell is going on? You disappear all day, you don't call, you don't tell me what's going on, and then a man I've never met before is here slamming my girlfriend into walls! Why is this *happening?*"

I swallowed hard, trying to figure out what to say. "I'm sorry" seemed insufficient. She was right. I should have been here when Samson came; I should have called and warned her that she might be in danger, if nothing else. But it had never occurred to me that he might come here, or that he'd take his anger at me out on my Fetch and her girlfriend.

"I'm sorry," I said finally, choosing insufficiency over silence. May's expression hardened further, until she might as well have been made of stone. "I didn't know he would come here. Please believe me, I had no idea."

"And I don't understand why he would," said Tybalt. "There was nothing here for him."

"We may not be Toby, but we're not 'nothing,'" snarled May.

Tybalt put his hands up. "I did not mean to imply that you were nothing, merely that there was nothing here for Samson to find. Whatever he was looking for—"

"He was looking for me," I said. All three of the other people in the room turned to me. I kept talking, saying, "The last he saw, we were falling into a hole that Chelsea tore in the world. I was pretty hurt, but he's smart enough to know that I was going to heal and you weren't. The smart thing for us to do would have been to split up, send you one way to get medical care, send me the other way to take care of Chelsea. How was he supposed to know we'd be total morons and stay together?"

"And the logical place for you to go would be here?" asked Tybalt.

May sighed. "Okay. Now we've hit something that's not her fault. It's mine. Tracking spells sometimes decide that I'm Toby. Something about me being made from her blood and bone confuses them, even though I'm not Dóchas Sidhe."

"So he used a tracking spell, it led him here, and then he got pissed when he couldn't find me," I said. "That's a big risk to take. I mean, killing me is going to open a pretty big can of worms . . ."

"But if his son has just been elevated to the throne of the Court of Dreaming Cats, he need never again enter a place where those consequences are his to face," said Tybalt. He rubbed his face with one hand, looking unbearably weary. "Milady Fetch, I beg your forgiveness."

"I'm not the one with the broken arm," said May, putting a protective arm around Jazz's shoulders. "Is he going to come back here?"

"I don't know," I said. I glanced to Tybalt, then back to the pair of them. "Call a taxi. Have it take you to Goldengreen. Count Lorden will let you stay there, and Marcia—"

"Isn't a real healer," snapped May, her arm tightening. Jazz whimpered. May loosened her grip. "I'm sorry, baby. You need a healer. She needs a healer!"

"Jin is in Tamed Lightning right now, but we can't take you both through the shadows," I said. "Even if Tybalt could carry all three of us—"

"Which I could not do, at present," interjected Tybalt.

"—even if he could, Jazz is hurt, and neither of you is used to it."

May grimaced. "I remember the Shadow Roads. The first time . . ."

"Remembering them doesn't mean your body has adjusted," I said. "It wouldn't work."

"Goldengreen doesn't even have a real healer," said May.

"Marcia does okay with a first aid kit, and she can put together a sling until we can get Jin to Goldengreen or Jazz to Shadowed Hills. With Samson on the loose out there, you can't spend an hour in a cab to get to Sylvester or two hours to get to Tamed Lightning," I said. The pounding in my head was fading, replaced by spinning as the bones of my skull knitted back together and burned through more of my body's denuded resources.

"She's right," said Jazz. She straightened a bit, standing on her own. "Goldengreen is the best place for us right now."

"Honey—"

"I mean it. We can't stay here." Jazz shuddered. "If he came back . . ."

"He won't come back."

"But *if* he came back. He'd kill us. And we can't go to a human hospital, not without getting a whole bunch of questions I'm not ready for." Jazz shook her head. "Goldengreen is the only answer. We have to go."

"I'll call us a cab. Danny will be thrilled to drive us, as long as we don't bleed on the seats," said May. Moving with surprising speed, she leaned over and grabbed my wrist, jerking me toward her. I somehow managed not to fall over as I stumbled across the floor. "Come on, Toby. You're the one who has his number memorized."

I knew the half-murderous, half-grim look on her face. I had to go with her, or she was going to start swinging. "Tybalt, keep an eye on Jazz," I said, letting myself be pulled out of the living room and across the hall into the kitchen.

May let go of me long enough to close the kitchen door. Then she turned to face me, slowly looking me up and down. "How bad was it?" she asked finally.

"If you were still my Fetch, you'd probably be feeling pretty shaky," I said. "And if Amandine hadn't shifted my blood, I'd definitely be dead. I think I saw my own intestines."

"You sure do know how to have a good time." She rubbed her face with one hand. It was a gesture so familiar that it hurt. I know May's memories don't just come from me—she has Dare's memories, too, and the memories of the night-haunt she used to be—but sometimes looking at her is like looking in a slightly sideways mirror. "How much danger are we in, October? And how much of it is your fault?"

"I . . . what?"

She dropped her hand. "You've been trying to find a cliff to throw yourself off of since Connor died. I won't pretend I've been cool with it, but I remember dying so many times—I remember being the one mourned for and the one in mourning so many times—that I've been willing to let it slide. I figured you'd find your way back to yourself. Only now you've finally found a cliff that might actually stand a chance of killing you, and you're going to take us right over the edge with you. Why didn't you call? Why didn't you warn us?" She took a heavy breath, let it out, and asked, "Are you mad at us for surviving when he didn't?"

Fetches are created when a night-haunt drinks the blood of a living person. It's Oberon's way of keeping the night-haunts from getting out of control and killing everyone they meet. One of the first things I did when I came back from my fourteen-year absence was go up against my former mentor, a man named Devin. He'd replaced me with two new kids, Manuel and Dare. Dare said I was her hero. I got her killed. But somehow, that didn't change her mind, and when the night-haunt with her memories had the opportunity to help me, she took it. In the process, she got herself called as a Fetch. *My* Fetch.

She'd already died for me once. If she thought I was mad at her for not dying for me a second time, I was doing something unforgivably wrong.

My silence had lasted too long. Something hardened in May's eyes, and she started to turn away from me. "Yeah. I thought so."

"May, wait." I grabbed her shoulder, stopping her. She didn't look back at me. That was okay. She could hear me whether she was facing me or not. "I didn't call because I didn't think of it. That was stupid, and I'm sorry. I honestly didn't think Samson would come here."

"Are you going to try telling me you haven't been attempting suicide every day since Connor died?" She looked over her shoulder without turning around, so that only a half-crescent of her face was visible. It was enough to let me see her eyes. They were the foggy no-color gray that had been in my mirror for most of my life, but the look in them wasn't mine. It was the look I saw once in the brilliantly green eyes of a teenage girl who died because I couldn't save her.

"No," I said quietly. "I think you're right. You're all right. Tybalt accused me of the same thing, and I couldn't even get mad, because you're all right. But I'm done now. I'm done throwing myself off cliffs and hoping I won't be there after I hit the bottom. I'm sorry. I shouldn't have done that to you. I'm sorry."

The corner of May's mouth pulled into a smile. "You just said you were sorry like three times."

"It bears repeating. I have a lot to be sorry about."

"Yeah. You do." She finally turned to face me. "You're sure you're done being an idiot?"

"Well. I'm sure I'm done being more of an idiot than I normally am."

"That's a start." May removed my hand from her arm. Then she stepped closer and hugged me, hard.

I've never been much of a hugger. There have always been people that didn't apply to. I wrapped my arms around her, returning her embrace. Her skin smelled like cotton candy and ashes, the remnants of the magic she'd called up during the fight with Samson. Even fae who don't have access to combat charms will tend to call their magic under that kind of duress. It's instinctive, a way of grabbing the thinnest straws of hope the world has to offer. Since none of our races began knowing what they were capable of, it makes sense; one day, you might call your power and learn that you were capable of something you never guessed you could do.

May sighed against my shoulder, and said, "This is all fucked up."

"Yeah, it is. But it's going to get better." I pushed her away. "We'll call Danny and get him to come pick you up. Jazz will be safe at Goldengreen. Samson won't be able to get past Dean's wards, even if he's dumb enough to try—which I doubt. You weren't his target."

"And what are you going to do?" May asked.

I managed a smile. "I'm going to eat a box of Pop-Tarts and drink all the milk in the fridge, because if I don't give my body something else to work with, I'm going to collapse. Then I'm going to put on different clothes. What I'm wearing right now isn't going to inspire much confidence in the people around me."

"Those jeans are trashed," said May. "There isn't enough hydrogen peroxide in the world to deal with that much blood."

"I know," I said dolefully. "I'd just managed to get them broken in, too."

"The true tragedy of the day is at last revealed," said Tybalt from the doorway. "Not the assassination attempts, the injuries, or the betrayals. The loss of a pair of denim trousers."

"Hey, man, I worked *hard* to make these jeans fit exactly how I liked them," I said, turning. Tybalt was holding the kitchen door open. Jazz was standing behind him, still clutching her injured arm. "What's going on?"

"We grew concerned when your disappearance was not followed by the sound of screaming, and I wanted to be sure our Lady Fetch had not elected to bury one of the kitchen knives in your eye." Tybalt offered a bow toward May. "I appreciate your failure to stab her. I doubt she has any blood left to lose."

"I took some of that Canadian Tylenol Quentin keeps in the medicine cabinet," said Jazz. "It's helping a little, but I'd still really like to get to Goldengreen."

That was a hint if I'd ever heard one. May and I exchanged a look before I nodded and started toward the kitchen phone. "I'm on it."

I dialed and handed the phone to May, not waiting for Danny to pick up. She was the one who needed the ride, and if I tried to explain what was going on, he'd want the whole story. We didn't have time for that. Technically, I'd been wasting time by stopping to talk to May in the first place, but that part hadn't been optional. It was my fault she got hurt. It was my fault Jazz got hurt. If she wanted me to explain myself, I owed her that.

May was still talking when I grabbed a pack of Pop-Tarts from the box and left the kitchen, heading for the stairs.

Tybalt followed me out of the kitchen. "Where are you going?"

"To my room," I said. "I need to change my clothes. I would wash the blood out of my hair, but then it would freeze solid when we went back to Tamed Lightning. I'll have to be a redhead for a little longer."

"Charming."

"Hey. I work with what I've got." My stomach rumbled. I opened the Pop-Tarts, looking back at him as I climbed. "You probably need fresh clothes, too."

He raised an eyebrow. "Are you about to tell me you have a pair of sweatpants in just my size sitting in a drawer somewhere? Because I think I would prefer to be naked."

We still had all of Connor's things in a box in the attic, but he and Tybalt weren't the same height; Connor had actually been a few inches taller than Tybalt, probably because he was born more recently, and people are taller now than they were three or four centuries ago. I'm not sure why the human-form purebloods have continued getting taller along with the human population of the world; maybe it's an automatic thing, one more form of subtle camouflage. Regardless, Tybalt would have looked like an idiot in Connor's pants.

Even as I had the thought, I realized that it didn't

hurt. I was thinking about Connor, and it didn't hurt. Maybe I was getting better after all.

"No, but if you want to run back to the Court of Cats, I can wait for you here."

A shadow flickered across his face, there and gone in an instant. "Would that I could, October, but that door is not open to me at the present."

I stopped as I reached the landing. "What do you mean? You're the King."

"Yes, I am. And if I return to the Court, I will need to begin the process of resolving the dissent Samson has so industriously sown." Tybalt paused, rubbing his hand across his face before he added, "I don't know when I'd be able to come back, Toby. I'd be leaving you when you need me the most—and while I wouldn't normally put your welfare above that of my Court without true agony, this time, the two are the same. Whatever Samson has against me, he has against you as well. I will not leave you vulnerable to him."

He sounded so tired and so earnest. I worried my lip between my teeth before asking, "Does this have anything to do with what you told me before?"

Tybalt blinked. Then he snorted a brief laugh, and asked, "October, in the years since your return . . . has anything *not* been in some way related to what I told you before? You handed me a hope chest in a dark alley. You took my heart as collateral, and you've never returned it."

Things always get messed up when I think about them too much. So this time, I didn't let myself think. I took a few quick steps down, closing the distance between us, and planted a kiss on Tybalt's mouth. His eyes widened in surprise. Just as he was recovering enough to kiss me back, I stepped away, and said, "I'm going to get changed. Go make sure May and Jazz go off with Danny, okay? I'll be down as soon as I can."

"Yes," said Tybalt, sounding slightly dazed—and then he turned and went.

It wasn't until I was in my room with the door securely closed between us that I realized that this was the first time *I* had kissed *him*. He'd kissed me, sometimes for show, sometimes because he truly meant it . . . but I'd never kissed him before. Things between us really were changing. With that thought weighing heavy on my mind, and the fate of Faerie potentially hanging in the balance, I went to get changed.

TWENTY

IT TOOK ME LESS THAN TEN MINUTES to strip off my shredded, bloody clothes and replace them with a clean black tank top and jeans. I wiped the worst of the blood off my face and hands with some wet wipes I'd snagged from KFC the last time I took Quentin out for junk food. By the time I was done, I looked, if not respectable, at least marginally less like I'd just survived one of May's trashy horror movies. For a finishing touch, I brushed most of the blood out of my hair and skimmed it into a ponytail. Any Daoine Sidhe who got within ten feet of me would smell it, but most other people would assume it was a weird dye job and move on.

At some point during the process, I ate the first Pop-Tart and most of the second. It says something about how low my blood sugar was that I neither noticed nor cared what flavor they were. I shrugged my leather jacket back on, stuck the last piece of Pop-Tart in my mouth, and opened the bedroom door.

Tybalt was downstairs, leaning against the wall and looking at Cagney and Lacey, who were sitting by his feet with oddly dejected looks on their furry faces. All three of them turned toward me as I stopped on the bottom step.

"What's going on?" I asked.

"Your resident felines were explaining how they could allow Samson to burst in without sounding the alarm," said Tybalt. Catching my expression, he added, "There was nothing they could have done. I am reassuring them, not scolding them."

"You know, every time I think my life can't get weirder, it ups the ante." I started walking again, heading for the kitchen. Tybalt paced me. I gave him a sidelong look. "Did May and Jazz leave?"

"Yes. Danny said hello and that he would have stuck around to talk to you himself, but he was sure you already had enough to worry about, and besides, the Barghests were almost certainly working on eating the backseat." Tybalt's pupils narrowed to amused slits as he spoke. "He seemed oddly . . . unsurprised . . . to hear that you were unable to greet him because you were upstairs changing into something less bloodstained."

"I have my friends well-trained." I opened the fridge, beginning to gather the makings for a ham sandwich. "Let me just get a little more food in me, and then we can get back to Tamed Lightning." I paused. "Do you want a sandwich? You haven't eaten anything all day, and you lost a lot of blood, too."

"I would love a sandwich," said Tybalt, with enough gravity to make it sound like a formal proclamation. Resolved: that we will have ham and cheese sandwiches.

"Just get the bread out of the cupboard, and I—"

The doorbell rang before I could finish my sentence. I frowned, bumping the refrigerator door closed with my hip before dropping the ham, cheese, and condiments on the counter.

"None of the people who want to kill us right now would use the doorbell," I said. "It's probably neighborhood kids selling something."

Tybalt snorted. "Your range of options is very specialized."

"Yeah, well. Welcome to my world." I shook my head, grabbing a handful of air. The smell of cut grass and copper rose around me, mingling with the smell of the blood in my hair, as I wove a quick human disguise. "Wait here. I'm going to go get rid of whoever it is."

"Certainly," said Tybalt. He was opening the cheese when I left the kitchen. I closed the door behind me—no point in explaining the pointy-eared man making sandwiches if I didn't have to—and made my way to the front door.

When I opened it, Officer Thornton of the San Francisco Police Department was standing on my porch. I blinked at him, briefly too surprised to speak. He blinked back, looking almost as surprised to see me as I was to see him. Then he cleared his throat.

"Good evening, Ms. Daye," he said. "Do you have a moment?"

"I—" When dealing with the mortal authorities, there is no answer to that question that doesn't begin with "yes." When dealing with the mortal authorities who had *followed me to Fremont*, all the answers I wanted to give began with slamming the door in his face.

If I did that, I might as well start packing my things, because I would be moving to the Summerlands full time shortly afterward. I swallowed my panic and stepped to the side, holding the door open wider. "Of course, Officer. Would you like to come in?"

"Yes, thank you." Officer Thornton looked around with unabashed curiosity as he stepped into the foyer. Fortunately, there was nothing really incriminating in view. We're an inhuman household, but the detritus that builds up around the edges of our lives is reassuringly normal. It's the lives themselves that tend to be a little weird.

My stomach sank. Tybalt was in the kitchen without a human disguise on, and the living room was totally destroyed. Unless I could convince Officer Thornton that he wanted to go upstairs with me, I was screwed—and I didn't even know how to open that conversation without sounding like I was coming on to him.

"Um, Officer, what can I do for you? I thought that there were no charges against me?"

"This is an unofficial visit, Ms. Daye. I'm still in uniform because my shift just ended."

"Oh." And probably because he wanted me to remember that he was an officer of the law, but that was one of those things that did perfectly well when left unspoken. "So, unofficially, what can I do for you?"

"Have you lived here long, Ms. Daye?"

"Um, no. We just moved in a few months ago."

"'We' being?"

"Me, my sister, May, and our nephew, Quentin." Legally, May was my sister, and calling Quentin a nephew was easier than any of the other available explanations. I'm old enough to be his mother, but I'm never going to look it by mortal standards. "He's from Canada," I added, in case Officer Thornton decided to follow up with a question about where Quentin's parents were. "I don't know, I've never met them" was unlikely to score me any points.

"It's a lovely home," he said instead, still looking around the hall.

You won't think that for long if you see the living room, I thought. He didn't need to ask the next logical question: I've lived in San Francisco for most of my life, and I knew what it was going to be. "Yeah, we got really lucky," I said. "Our Uncle Sylvester inherited this place from his parents, and it was just sitting empty until we needed somewhere to live. He lets us stay here for utilities and maintenance costs." And would gladly sign the deed over to me if I asked. That was another thing I didn't need to tell the nice officer.

"You sound like you're close to your family." Officer Thornton turned to face me. There was something in his expression—a certain calculation—that I didn't like. Then again, I didn't like the fact that he'd been following me. "Family is important, don't you agree?"

"Yes, Officer, I do. If I can ask, what is this all about?"

"Ms. Daye, what were you doing in Fremont earlier today?" The calculation in Officer Thornton's face became suddenly coherent, resolving into suspicion. "I ask because an associate of mine from the Berkeley Police Department informed me that she had encountered you at the site of a recent disappearance, and as you had been brought into my station the night before . . ."

I blinked. "I'm a private detective. I specialize in kidnappings and divorce cases. Bridget called me."

"But you didn't tell the officers on the scene that. You allowed them to think you were a friend of the family. Was there any particular reason?"

"The police have a lot on their plates. I didn't want to risk deprioritizing Chelsea's disappearance because Bridget was worried enough to bring in outside help." I didn't let myself glance away or break eye contact. "I understand how this works."

"Ms. Daye, you haven't answered my question. What were you doing in Fremont?"

"She was collecting me from the train station." I turned to see Tybalt standing in the kitchen doorway, an amiable smile on his suddenly human face. "I don't drive, and she wanted me home in time for dinner for a change."

"And you would be . . . ?"

"I'm the boyfriend. Rand Stratford." Tybalt stepped forward, offering his hand to Officer Thornton, who took it, seemingly on autopilot. "It's a pleasure to meet you, sir. We didn't have time for introductions when I was meeting October at the station last night."

"Ah." Comprehension washed away Officer Thornton's suspicion as he placed Tybalt into a context he could understand. "We appreciate your coming to escort her home. The streets are no place for a lady alone that late at night."

"I'm probably safer in her company than I am out of it," said Tybalt as he reclaimed his hand. He pushed the kitchen door a bit farther open, in invitation. "Would you like a cup of coffee? I just started a fresh pot, and the living room is, well . . ." He wrinkled his nose before saying, conspiratorially, "It's a bit of a mess. We weren't expecting company."

The offer seemed to answer some question Officer Thornton hadn't been voicing. His frown deepened for a moment before smoothing into neutrality. "Well, I won't take up any more of your time. You two have a nice evening. And Ms. Daye, while I respect that your profession makes your involvement with Ms. Ames an understandable thing, I have to ask that you not interfere with the police. We're going to bring this girl home."

"I wouldn't dream of interfering," I said, with as much sincerity as I could muster. "Thank you for dropping by, Officer."

"It's my pleasure, Ms. Daye," said Officer Thornton. Then he turned, letting himself out. The front door closed behind him with a click, and for a moment, everything was silence.

That silence held for several seconds, until I heard the distant sound of a car door slamming shut. I opened my mouth, and Tybalt motioned for me to be quiet. I stopped, blinking at him. A few more seconds slipped by, and he dropped his hand.

"I was waiting for the sound of his actually driving away," he said, half-apologetically. "There was always the chance he would have slammed the car door before attempting to return to the porch and listen to our conversation."

"I get that," I said wearily. "I have two questions before I decide what happens next."

"Ask away." Tybalt tilted his head to the side, regarding me calmly with his bizarrely human eyes. The Tybalt I know has eyes the color of malachite, with all the deep, banded shades of green the comparison implies. This Tybalt's eyes were simply green. I would have found them attractive on a human man. On him, they were just *wrong*.

"Is there really coffee?"

"I assure you, October, while I might tease about many things, I value my life too much to hang my jests on coffee when you are involved."

"You know, a simple 'yes' would have sufficed."

Even the human disguise couldn't dull his feline grin. "Yes. There's coffee."

"Okay. And the second question . . . Rand?"

Tybalt's grin dulled, but didn't die. "It was my name, once. It seemed less likely to inspire human curiosity than 'Tybalt.'"

"This is San Francisco. I wouldn't be so sure." I stepped past him, through the open kitchen door. The kitchen itself smelled like fresh coffee and, more faintly, the mingled scents of pennyroyal and musk. The remains of the spell Tybalt had used to cloak himself. "I didn't expect the save. You have good timing."

"I was listening from the moment you left." He stepped through the door behind me, releasing his human disguise at the same time. The smell of pennyroyal and musk intensified, and my shoulders unknotted a little. Seeing Tybalt as a human was just bizarre. "Had things gone badly . . ."

"Then they would have gotten really bad, because you can't knock over a police officer and snatch me away to the Court of Cats. Not with Bridget involved." I walked over to the coffee maker, grabbing a Thermos from the counter on the way. I was going to need more coffee than I could reasonably stand here and drink. "One way or another, the mortal authorities are going to stay on this one."

Tybalt sighed. "You say the most charming things."

"I'm a realist."

"Of all the labels I would think to hang on you, that has never come anywhere near the top of my list." Tybalt picked up a plastic bag from the kitchen table, holding it up for me to see. Ham sandwiches. "I have food."

· My stomach rumbled, reminding me of the calories I *hadn't* consumed before the police showed up. "Gimme," I said. Tybalt raised an eyebrow. "Please," I amended.

He handed me the bag.

I was midway through the first sandwich, barely tasting the ham, cheese, and odd mixture of condiments—who uses steak sauce and strawberry jam on a sandwich? — in my haste to get something into my stomach before Tybalt spoke again.

"If you can focus, would you release your illusions?" he asked. "I'd rather avoid the masks when possible."

I swallowed the bite I'd been chewing and waved my hand through the air, snapping the thin web of magic that held my human disguise in place. It wisped away into the smell of cut grass and copper, leaving us both exposed as we really were, bloodstains and all. I kept eating, too anxious for food to stop and ask him why he'd wanted me to do that.

Besides, if he felt anything like I'd felt when I saw him in a human mask, I already knew why he'd wanted me to do that. I still wasn't sure what I thought about this new development — half of me wanted to jump up and down and punch the air, while the other half counseled caution, reminding me of dead loves and the dangers of the world I lived in. There would be time to think about that later. I hoped.

The second sandwich was gone before my stomach stopped growling. I straightened, and realized that the spinning had finally stopped: my body was done ordering me to keep still. "Are you ready to move?" I asked.

"I am." Tybalt looked at me gravely. "October, before . . . "

"I kissed you," I said, cutting him off. "I figured it was my turn, you know? And I know there's a conversation that we need to have, but we need to have it at a time that isn't now. After Chelsea's back. After Samson isn't trying to kill you — and me — anymore. Okay?"

Tybalt stepped toward me and planted a kiss on my forehead. "I've waited long enough to have you realize I was waiting. I can wait a short time more."

"Good." I stepped back, filling my Thermos with coffee before capping it firmly and offering him my hand. "Can we get back to Tamed Lightning?"

"You only ever needed to ask," he said, and he took my hand in his and pulled me into the shadows. There was time for me to take a deep breath before the darkness closed around us, but barely; he'd had time to recover, too, and the Shadow Roads were responding quickly to his call.

Tybalt swung me up into his arms as soon as we were in the shadows. I didn't resist. There are times to insist on carrying your own weight and times to let yourself be carried. Running the Shadow Roads from San Francisco to Fremont was definitely the latter. I closed my eyes, letting my lashes ice together rather than trying to fight it, and relaxed into his embrace.

Tybalt ran like he'd never been injured, never been tired, never been anything but what he was: a King of Cats at the height of his powers, running down the length of his domain.

We emerged into the brightly lit cafeteria at ALH Computing, where Raj, Quentin, Li Qin, and Elliot were seated around one of the white plastic tables. All four of them looked up at the sound of Tybalt's footsteps and watched as he put me down carefully.

It was Elliot who spoke first: "Why is it that every time you come to visit, I come to work and find the cafeteria positively *swimming* with blood?"

"I just want to help. I mean, I figure they're not working you hard enough." I paused to wipe the ice from my eyelashes and eyebrows before asking, as innocently as I could manage, "Don't you appreciate the challenge?"

"Not really," said Elliot . . . but he was grinning, displaying a white crescent of sharply pointed teeth.

The mess in the cafeteria was gone as though it had never existed. That wasn't surprising. In addition to being April's Seneschal, Elliot was a Bannick, a type of Russian fae, and couldn't abide messes. He'd probably cleaned the whole place within five minutes of coming in. "Well, if you're that opposed to challenges, I guess I won't ask you about these bullet holes . . ."

Elliot laughed. "Take a deep breath and close your eyes."

"Yes, sir." I did as I was told, almost laughing when I heard Tybalt step away. Then a hot wave of lye-scented water seemed to burst around me: Elliot's hearth craft at work. When it receded, my hair was clean and dry, and a quick feel of my jacket confirmed that the bullet holes were gone. I opened my eyes and smiled. "You're awesome."

"I try."

I looked around. "Where's Etienne? And where's Jin?"

"Jin has gone for a nap in one of the break rooms, since healing is tiring, and Etienne is with April," said Li Qin. "They're going over her list of security incursions over the last twenty-four hours. I think the idea is that if Chelsea has been crossing our lands, April might not have known what was causing the blips, but Etienne would be able to identify them as traces of Tuatha magic."

"It's worth a try," I said, and turned back to Elliot. "Did they bring you up to speed?"

"Missing half-Tuatha changeling with the potential to destroy Faerie by mistake, possible involvement on the part of Duchess Riordan—because her becoming involved with things is excellent for my blood pressure—and an angry mortal folklore professor who wants her daughter back," said Elliot. "Oh, and you went to Annwn and nearly died."

"In that order, even," I said, with a nod. Raj was watching me with anxious eyes, like he knew that whatever I said next, it wasn't going to make him happy. I took a breath. "We need to get moving. Chelsea's just going to keep doing more damage the longer we let her run around loose. But there are a few more things you need to know . . ."

Tybalt didn't say anything as I filled the room in on what had happened since we left, but he did move to stand behind Raj, putting his hand on the younger Cait Sidhe's shoulder in a silent show of solidarity that said more than any words. Samson's crimes were not the crimes of his son. Raj would not be punished for what his father did. That, more than anything else, told me that I was right to be harboring the thoughts about Tybalt that were starting to gather more and more heavily at the back of my mind.

The room was silent when I finished, except for the low buzz of the fluorescent lights and the thrumming of the motors in the vending machines. Then came the question from behind me, asked in an innocently quizzical tone: "Why do we not remove the mortals from the equation? If they were pulled into the Summerlands, they would no longer present any difficulties."

"Because, April, people tend to ask questions when policemen disappear, and even if I'm not all that thrilled about having Officer Thornton tailing me, I'm not going to banish him to another world for doing his job." I paused, reaching for a word that she would understand, before turning to her and adding, "It would be rude."

"Ah." April nodded, accepting this as a valid reason not to kidnap a police officer. Sometimes I think it must be refreshing to be quite that removed from the rest of the world. "Etienne and I have finished reviewing my security reports. It was an enlightening process. We found seven distinct traces that may indicate Chelsea's passage through my lands. I have adjusted my security systems accordingly, and will know immediately if she returns."

"Good." I paused, frowning. "April ... where's Etienne?"

She blinked at me. "He has departed for Dreamer's Glass. All seven traces indicate a trajectory that would terminate with Chelsea inside the demesne of Duchess Treasa Riordan."

"Oberon preserve us from fools and heroes," I muttered. Louder, I asked, "Did he stop to think that maybe he should take some backup with him?"

"He said that he was sure you would be amenable to this course of action." April paused, eyes widening, before she said indignantly, "I believe he may have lied to me!"

"It happens to the best of us." I turned to the others. They were watching me like spectators at a tennis match. "We need to get to Dreamer's Glass."

"I'm going with you," said Quentin, and "I'm staying here," said Li Qin, at the same time. The two paused, turning to blink at each other.

Then Li Qin laughed. "I'm staying here," she repeated. "I stand the best chance of bailing you out if Riordan catches you in her lands without an invitation, and it's easier for me to bend your luck if I'm not standing in the middle of a battlefield while I'm trying to do it. I can't keep anything truly bad away, but I may be able to at least skew the odds slightly in your favor."

"We'd appreciate that," I said. I paused, a thought occurring to me. "You're being awfully nice."

"I am," she agreed. "I want something. I'm more likely to get it if you survive."

"What is it that you want?"

She smiled. "That would be telling." Before I could get mad, she added, "I'll explain everything when this is done, and I swear, I expect nothing. I simply want you to be well-inclined toward us when the time comes for me to ask the things that need asking."

I blinked, glancing toward the others to see if their expressions would give me any idea. Elliot ducked his head and looked away, refusing to meet my eyes. Quentin and Raj looked as confused as I felt. That was reassuring. At least I wasn't the only one who'd managed to miss the memo. "Fine," I said, finally. "But you'd better be ready to tell me what's going on when we're no longer in mortal peril."

Elliot laughed. "So in about ten years, then?"

"Something like that." Now for the harder one. I turned to Raj. "You're staying."

His eyes went wide and wounded. "What? You can't mean that."

"I can, and I do. Your father tried to kill me earlier today. I don't want to put you in the line of fire if he comes after me again." I hesitated before adding, "What he did isn't your fault, and I'm not rejecting you. I just want you to be safe."

"I'm a Prince of Cats!"

"And as my only heir, I need you to remain here," said Tybalt. Raj transferred his wounded look to his uncle. Tybalt smiled. "Glare all you like, kitten. You'll still stay behind."

"You can't tell me what to do forever," said Raj.

"Yes," agreed Tybalt. "I'm counting on that."

There was a subtext I wasn't getting in their conversation. Cait Sidhe successions are generally fatal. I couldn't imagine Tybalt was looking forward to that. I decided it wasn't important for the moment, and straightened, saying, "We need to go. Quentin, come on."

"Okay," he said, and rose, coming to stand beside me. "What's the plan?"

"We go in, we find Etienne, we find Chelsea if we can, and we do our best to get out without starting a diplomatic incident too big to stop." I turned to Tybalt. "You can handle us both?"

"So nice of you to ask me, but yes. I can handle your transport, and that of your stripling, at the same time. More than that may become a strain if it has to be maintained for terribly long, but . . ." Tybalt shrugged. "That is a bridge to be crossed when we come to it, I suppose."

"Good." I offered him my hand, gesturing for Quentin to do the same. "If Chelsea comes back here, try to stop her from leaving, and call me."

"Someone will contact you," said April.

"Good. Then let's—" I stopped myself mid-sentence as a thought struck me. Dropping Tybalt's hand, I said, briskly, "Come on," and started at a fast walk toward the cafeteria door.

"She still does that?" asked Elliot.

Tybalt just laughed as he and Quentin followed me out into the hall. I kept walking, heading for the car as quickly as I reasonably could. When I got there, I dug the keys out of my pocket, barely pausing to check the backseat for intruders—long story—before unlocking the passenger side door and grabbing Walther's cooler from the foot well.

"Oh!" said Quentin, sudden comprehension in his

tone. "She's getting the power dampener Walther brewed for us."

"Thank you, Captain Exposition," I said. The leather of my jacket was thick enough to keep the stuff from getting on me even if the glass broke. I paused before digging around in the glove compartment. I didn't know what the Luidaeg kept there, but ... "Well, I'll be damned," I said. "She has Baggies." I wasn't sure which was weirder, that the Luidaeg had them, or that I'd thought to check. Either way, they were getting put to use. I put a dose of dampener in one and a dose of counteragent in another, before tucking them into my jacket pockets. Then I paused, looking at my thermos, and sighed. "If Etienne ever doubts my devotion to doing the right thing, I will kill him," I said.

"What?" asked Quentin.

"Nothing." I uncapped the thermos, pouring half its contents down my throat and the other half out on the concrete. The smell of spilled coffee filled the air as I slammed the edge of the thermos against the top of the car, knocking it again and again until the interior seal came loose and I was able to yank the entire center piece free. I threw it into the car, grabbed another dose each of dampener and counteragent, and slid them carefully into the place where the center piece had been. As I'd expected, they fit perfectly.

I sighed again. "At least my thermos didn't die for nothing." Putting the lid back on, I twisted it as tight as it would go and tossed the whole thing over to Tybalt.

He caught it, frowning at the brightly colored plastic cylinder. "What, precisely, is this?"

"Well, the orange stuff on top is an alchemical concoction designed to block the powers of anyone it gets spilled on for a year and a day. Walther specifically said not to get it on any shapeshifters, since he has no idea what that would do; let's try to do what the alchemist says."

Tybalt blanched. "Yes," he murmured. "Let's. October, please don't think I'm inclined to reject any gifts you choose to give me, but why, pray tell, have you chosen to give me *this*?"

"If you see Chelsea, you need to dump it on her. I would have done it before, if I'd been carrying the stuff." And if dampening her powers then and there wouldn't have stranded us in Annwn, possibly forever. That was the sort of detail that couldn't always be accounted for.

That didn't seem to make Tybalt feel better. He eyed the thermos the way I would eye a venomous snake and asked, "What happens if I spill it?"

"There's a jar of green stuff underneath the jar of orange stuff. It's a counteragent. If you apply it within twenty minutes, you can cancel the effects of the power dampener. Or at least Walther thinks you can. This is all theory at this point." I jabbed a finger toward the cooler. "Quentin. Gear up."

"How come he gets the thermos?" grumbled Quentin, as he moved to retrieve jars of variously colored goo from inside the cooler.

"Because he's the one whose side effects are completely unknown if he gets doused, whereas you get to wear baseball caps for a year, and I get to spend a lot more time sitting on the couch watching late-night television while enjoying a brief respite from being forced to leave the house. In this particular instance, we're both better risks than Tybalt is."

"I'm not sure whether I should be flattered or appalled," said Tybalt.

"Neither am I," said Quentin.

I smiled. It wasn't a happy smile, but it was a genuine one. "You know, if I have to march off to certain doom, I can't think of many people I'd rather be marching with."

"You can think of any?" asked Quentin, sealing his own jars of glowing goo in Ziploc Baggies.

"Anybody who owns a tank is at the top of the list. But you're right underneath them." I tossed the box of Baggies back into the car and closed the door, locking it before tucking the keys back into my pocket. There was a thick patch of shadows underneath the eucalyptus trees separating the campus from the street. I gestured toward them. "Shall we?"

Tybalt nodded. "I suppose we shall."

The three of us walked into the shadow of the trees, our pockets heavy with the promise of magic's end. And then Quentin took Tybalt's hand while I took hold of his elbow, and he pulled us backward into the darkness, and the world fell away again. It was time to end this. One way or another, it was time for us to find Chelsea, and bring her home.

TWENTY-ONE

WE EMERGED IN A SMALL, familiar antechamber inside Riordan's knowe. Quentin stumbled, shivering and trying not to cough. I managed to keep my feet, barely, and only because I knew we needed to do as little knocking about as possible. We were in enemy territory now, and if we were found, things weren't going to go well for us.

Tybalt was leaning against the wall opposite from Quentin, his own eyes closed. The effort of carrying two of us immediately after he'd been injured appeared to have exhausted him. I bent forward, bracing my hands on my knees, and forced myself to take deep, slow breaths.

"It's so much easier when we take the Tuatha Express," I mumbled.

"The cost of travel should be high," said Tybalt. He straightened and paced toward the entrance to the antechamber. "It's what keeps us from roving frivolously."

"Etienne seems to think it's pretty hard, at least when he's going more than a few miles," I said. "He doesn't usually teleport casually. But Chelsea isn't playing by the usual rules."

"Yes. I know." Tybalt shook his head. "The shadows are starting to push back against us. They only do that when their destination is unclear, or when they have no-where to end. The tethers between the Shadow Roads and the Summerlands are beginning to fray—as are the tethers between the Shadow Roads and the mortal world. If this continues too long, we may find ourselves with nowhere to run."

I thought about that for a second, then put the thought aside. It was too big a problem for me to fix; it was some-thing I couldn't hit. All I could do was get Chelsea to stop ripping holes and let the people who *could* fix things get to work.

Of course, that meant we couldn't stay huddled in this tiny antechamber forever. "Riordan's guards are mostly Folletti," I said. "I can tell when they're nearby, but only if I'm looking for them. Most of the time, they're going to be effectively invisible."

"Charming," said Tybalt.

"Yeah. Can you scout the hall? Just make sure we're alone before we leave here."

"It would be my pleasure," said Tybalt. The smell of musk and pennyroyal swirled around him and he was gone, replaced by a large tabby tomcat. He walked over to me, rubbed himself against my ankles, and turned to slink out of the antechamber, vanishing behind the tap-estry that covered the entrance.

Quentin had his breathing back under control. He came to stand next to me, and we stayed where we were, waiting for whatever was going to come next. I kept one hand on my knife and the other on Quentin's shoulder, ready to shove him behind me if something attacked us. I could take the damage. He couldn't.

The minutes ticked by. I was on the verge of becoming genuinely worried when the fabric of the tapestry stirred, and Tybalt slunk back into the room, ears pressed flat and tail carried low to the ground.

I let out a relieved breath. "Took you long enough," I said.

The smell of pennyroyal and musk rose around him. He straightened on two legs, a troubled expression on his face. "Going unseen is an art as much as a skill," he said. "I can smell the Folletti when I go in feline form. That doesn't make it wise for me to risk discovery by exposing myself where they might see."

"What did you find?"

"These chambers are scattered all along this hall, and the ones to either side. It seems our Duchess Riordan is quite fond of the spy's art, providing she can control the placement of the spies. I doubt she would be pleased to know we were using her clever hidey-holes against her."

"If you don't want people using your secret little rooms for nefarious purposes, you shouldn't make them this easy to find," I said. Then I paused. "Or maybe they're not just here for spying on guests. Quentin, remember when you showed me how to navigate the servants' passages at Shadowed Hills?"

Quentin blinked as understanding dawned. "Give me a second," he said, and moved to the back of the antechamber.

Tybalt watched him go before turning his frown on me, clearly puzzled. "Would you care to explain?"

"Most knowes—ones that don't belong to the Court of Cats—are built to suit the nobles who own them. Even the good nobles want their servants to be invisible, although most don't take it as literally as Riordan here. Service is supposed to be quiet, efficient, and only noticed when something goes wrong. So they hide little passages and back routes through the knowes, to make it possible for their servants to stay out of sight."

"Ah." Tybalt frowned. "The Divided Courts are sometimes more alien to me than I like to admit."

"If it helps at all, I think they tend to feel the same way about the Court of Cats."

Tybalt shook his head, still frowning. "I am not sure it helps anything to know that we are all strangers to one another."

"Got it!" Quentin's triumphant whisper stopped me before I could say anything I'd regret later. I turned to see him standing in front of a narrow open rectangle in what had seemed to be a solid wall only moments before. He was grinning, visibly pleased with himself—as well he should be. "She uses a pressure code to keep the doors closed. It's pretty clever, but it's also pretty common. I've seen it in a bunch of knowes."

"My little cat burglar," I said dryly. "How proud your parents must be."

His grin, if anything, brightened. "I'd bet you a dollar that you're right."

"As long as it's not a Canadian dollar, you're on." I started toward the opening. "Let's see what's behind door number one."

"Is the answer ever 'unending pain and a suffering beyond imagination'?" asked Tybalt. He still followed me. Either his sense of self-preservation was weakening, or he was confident that whatever might be lurking up ahead would eat the rest of us first.

"Sometimes," said Quentin. "Other times, it's a pantry."

I smothered my laughter behind my hand as I stepped through the door Quentin had managed to open in the wall, gesturing for the others to wait. They did, Quentin calmly, and Tybalt with obvious annoyance. At least he was listening to me. That was going to be essential if we were going to get out of this with everyone still breathing.

The floor on the other side of the wall was as plain as the antechamber behind me. I still stepped carefully, testing the wood with my toes before moving forward. If there were any booby-traps, they were the kind that needed more than a little weight to trigger them.

The servant's hall was dark, lacking the glowing spheres that dotted the hallway outside. I paused, then dug the Luidaeg's Chelsea-chaser out of my pocket. Its glow brightened as I brought it into the open, chasing back the worst of the shadows. It was in its neutral state, glowing like a handful of captive starlight . . . but it hadn't been this bright since it was first activated. I wasn't sure what that meant. I had to hope it was a sign that

Chelsea had been here at least once, and might be here again.

Finally, I closed my eyes, let my mouth drop open, and breathed in. Nothing. The only magic I smelled was my own, cut grass and copper, underscored with the whisper of frozen wind across lonely moors. The Luidaeg's charm was making its presence known. Beyond that, we were alone. "Come on," I said, opening my eyes. "The coast is clear."

Tybalt and Quentin stepped through the wall, Quentin pausing to slide the panel back into place and tap his fingers against the "hinge" in a rapid, elaborate pattern of strokes and beats. When he pulled his hands away, the panel remained set firmly into the wall.

"Nice trick," I said.

Quentin nodded as he turned to face me. "Like I said: clever but common. If you don't know the right pattern, you can try for hours and never get through."

I raised an eyebrow. "So how did you . . . ?"

"There are only ten right patterns. I learned them when I was a kid." It was said with simple matter-of-factness. I decided to let it drop. We had bigger things to worry about than why Quentin knew how to break into any knowe that used a "clever but common" lock system for its service passages. Being fostered definitely seemed to come with some unusual skill sets.

"Duchess Riordan's receiving room was this way," I said, turning. "We might as well start our search in familiar territory. If Chelsea's not there, we can go looking for the dungeons."

"Which will doubtless be in the opposite direction," said Tybalt.

"Yeah, but there's going to be a connection between them," said Quentin. "That way, she can send servants to check on anybody she has locked up, and she won't have to wait long to hear back. When you've got somebody in your dungeon, you're not usually feeling very patient."

"You are just a wealth of unexpected information today," I said. "We start with the receiving room. Tybalt . . . ?"

"I'll scout ahead." The smell of musk and pennyroyal had barely settled when he was racing on four legs into the darkness, ears flat against his head and tail held straight out behind him. I could see his coat for a few seconds, bands of brown moving through the shadows. Then he was gone, not even leaving footprints behind.

"Stay close," I said, gesturing for Quentin to move in next to me. "Get out your own charm. A little extra light could be a good thing in here—and it's not going to make us any easier to spot. We're already the only light in the place."

Quentin nodded, digging the sphere from his pocket as he moved into the position I'd indicated. Together, the two charms were enough to make every detail of the walls visible. Not that there was much to see. If there were other doors around us, they were well fitted enough to be invisible, leaving nothing but blank wall both ahead of and behind us. I drew my knife with my free hand. Quentin did the same, producing a short sword I'd never seen before from his belt. I raised an eyebrow. He shrugged, saying sheepishly, "I asked April if she had anything I could borrow when you didn't come back for so long. I figured it was better if I was prepared to defend myself."

"It was a smart move," I said, and started walking. Quentin paced me. "There's just one thing I want to know."

"What's that?"

"Why the hell did April have a sword? I don't think there's anyone in that County who was traditionally trained."

"She didn't say."

"Right."

We exchanged strained smiles—just two more idiots whistling past the graveyard—and walked on in silence. Quentin let me take the lead, although only by a few steps. It was reassuring to know that he was at my back.

I wasn't walking into yet another brutally stupid situation alone. I needed people. Losing Connor had made me lose sight of that for a little while. Even that little while had been too damn long. I had too much to live for to sit around letting myself be lost in mourning.

The light from our charms reflected off a pair of green eyes ahead of us. Quentin stiffened. I smiled and held out my arm to stop him from doing anything we'd all regret. "What did you find?" I asked.

The green eyes rose, going from floor level to the height of a normal man, and Tybalt stepped out of the dark. "You were right; the receiving hall is ahead. But there's something strange about this passage."

"What's that?"

"It used to be used frequently. I can smell the tracks of dozens of people, all of them hurrying about their business."

I didn't ask how he knew they were hurrying. If I can tease a person's family history from a drop of blood, I'm perfectly willing to believe a King of Cats can tell whether they were in a rush by smelling the tracks they left behind them. "And?"

"And no one has been here in days. These passages have been deserted."

"That fits with what April said about Riordan withdrawing her forces. If she's moved her army somewhere, she probably moved most of her household staff to the same place. Otherwise, you wind up with a hungry army sacking the nearest McDonalds, and that's not good for anybody."

Quentin frowned. "But where are they all *going?*"

"That's the twenty-million-dollar question. Come on." This time, Tybalt walked with us, a silent, reassuring presence that paced slightly ahead as we made our way down the hall. I let him take the lead. He knew where we were going, after all, while I just had a vague sense that we were heading in the right direction.

The hall eventually started presenting us with turns. We had made the second when the charm in my hand flared to a brilliant, blazing red. Quentin's charm did the same half a heartbeat later. The light painted the hallway the color of blood, dancing and wavering like candlelight, flickering like a star.

"Root and branch, she's here!" I said, and took off running before I realized what I was going to do. At least I didn't need Tybalt to direct me anymore; the charm knew which way to go, and I was just the vehicle it was using to get there. It yanked on my hand like a living thing, urging me to greater speeds. Tybalt paced me, each of his long strides equaling two of mine, while Quentin lagged behind—but he was still running, all of us racing toward something we knew nothing about.

Well. We did know one thing. We knew that whatever we were racing toward, Chelsea was there.

The hall ended in another blank wall. I nearly slammed into it, the charm pulling me on faster than my feet could process what was happening. I managed to skid to a stop, putting out my arm to force Quentin to do the same. He made a soft "oof" noise as he collided with my elbow. Then he ducked under my arm, shoving the short sword into his belt before beginning to tap a rapid pattern against the wood with his now-free hand. The charm kept trying to jerk me forward, not seeming concerned by the fact that I can't walk through walls. That was my problem. It just wanted to get me to Chelsea, and if it had to break my skull to make that happen, it really didn't care.

"Almost there," said Quentin through gritted teeth. The strain in his voice told me just how hard his charm was yanking on him.

"Breathe," I advised.

He shot me a grateful look and kept tapping. A few more seconds passed, and the section of wall slid smoothly open. There was fabric on the other side; another of those damn tapestries Riordan was so fond of. I signaled the others to silence—maybe unnecessarily, but I was definitely more interested in being safe than sorry—and moved past Quentin, stepping through the opening.

The tapestry was actually hanging about two feet away from the wall, creating an artificial corridor for servants to use when entering the reception room. That made sense; if the tapestry had been flush with the wall, it would have been hard to get the illusion of invisible service to work the way that it was supposed to. I inched carefully along until I reached the end of the tapestry, and peeked out into the receiving room.

It was empty, unless you wanted to count the enormous hole cut out of the air behind the throne. It was unguarded, and through it I could see the bracken-choked Annwn moors stretching off toward the distant shadow of a high-walled castle. I stopped where I was, staring, even as the Luidaeg's charm tried to pull me toward the hole.

Tybalt and Quentin stepped up behind me and joined me in silent contemplation of the portal. We were safely hidden by the tapestry, and we needed a moment to regroup. It was a little reassuring that I wasn't the only one completely floored by what I was seeing.

Finally, Quentin asked, "What *is* it?"

"Annwn," said Tybalt. "One of the deeper realms."

"Chelsea," I said, and started walking. Tybalt and Quentin followed close behind me, all of us moving as fast as we could.

"What is it *doing* there?" asked Quentin.

"Well, sugar, it's standing open, waiting for me," said Riordan. I stiffened, coming to a stop. Tybalt hissed, a soft, almost smothered sound. Slowly, the three of us turned to see the Duchess of Dreamer's Glass stepping out from behind a tapestry on the other side of the room, back in her jeans and black T-shirt, with a faint smile on her classically beautiful face.

"Where's Chelsea?" I asked.

Riordan shook her head. The light from our charms glittered off the ruby at her throat. "That's what I don't

like about you, Sir Daye. You're always right to business,
no pleasantries, no playing nice. It makes a body want to
play rough, just to show you that you ought to have some
manners."

"I assure you, her manners are among the best in this
room," said Tybalt, tone frosty.

"I have no trouble believing that." Riordan turned
her attention on Tybalt, smile growing wider. "It was awfully nice of you to come with her. Saves me the trouble
of having someone go find you."

I stared at her, a sudden, horrible realization growing
in the pit of my stomach. Duchess Riordan was paranoid.
Everyone knew that. It was what made her such a dangerous neighbor to have. Why would someone with that
well-earned a reputation for paranoia leave a hole in
their defenses as large as the one Tybalt had exploited to
bring us to her knowe?

Answer: she wouldn't.

"Tybalt, get us a doorway to the Shadow Roads," I
murmured, hoping that Riordan was too far away to
hear me. "Get us a doorway to the Shadow Roads *now*."

He gave me a sideways look, but he didn't argue. His
fingers twitched, moving toward the shadows to our
left. Then they stilled, his pupils narrowing to startled
slits.

"I . . . I can't," he said. "They aren't there."

Riordan was still smiling. "If you were just going for
your back door, sorry, sugars, but I had it locked down as
soon as you were through my wards. You're going to be
the recipients of my hospitality whether you like it or
not."

"I'm voting not," I said, loudly enough for her to hear.
"Where's Chelsea? I'm not going to ask you again."

"You shouldn't lie when you don't have to. Makes it
difficult to believe a word you say. You're going to ask
me again and again, and keep on asking, probably right
up until the point where we get tired of it and have you
gagged." Riordan's smile subsided into a look of weary
irritation. "You know, my life would be a lot easier if

people like you would just learn your place and not bother with things like this."

"She's a little girl."

"She's a changeling. She's got no place in this world and no place in the world she comes from. But because she's a useful tool, maybe she can find herself a place." Riordan indicated the hole with a sweep of her hand. "Maybe it's waiting for her out there."

"The worse you scare her, the more she undermines Faerie!" said Quentin. "This is treason."

"Against whom, little boy? The mad Queen in her castle by the sea? Or maybe the High King and Queen, off in their ice palace in Toronto? By the time anyone thinks to tell them I've been naughty, I'll be long gone. And you talk like this has never happened before. The Summerlands have always survived. That's the thing about tools. They may do a lot of damage while they're working, but, inevitably, they break."

Her voice was calm and reasonable throughout. The sinking in my stomach got worse. I've dealt with madmen and zealots, people who were so far down their personal rabbit holes that they genuinely thought that whatever they were doing was the right thing. Duchess Riordan didn't fall into that category.

Duchess Riordan was perfectly, dangerously sane. And that was something I could see being a major problem if we wanted to get out of this alive.

"I'm going to give you one more chance," I said, as calmly as I could. "Give Chelsea to us, and we'll leave your lands, and we won't come back. You haven't done any permanent damage. You haven't committed any crimes." Even after everything she'd done, she hadn't done a single thing most purebloods would acknowledge as "wrong." Stealing a changeling who'd never been given her Choice would practically be viewed as community service in some circles. The Queen might even give her a public commendation, if it weren't for the part where Chelsea was undermining the fabric of Faerie.

"No," said Riordan.

Folletti appeared around us, seeming to materialize out of thin air. And a figure stepped out of the portal connecting the throne room to Annwn.

"Hello, Sire," said Samson. He was smiling poisonously. "I told you your association with these ... people ... would be the death of you. Better to keep to your own kind."

"Sadly, a skill I have never possessed," said Tybalt wearily.

"Lay down your arms, all of you, or I'll tell my guards to dispose of you," said Riordan.

"You'd break Oberon's Law?" asked Quentin. He sounded wounded, like he couldn't believe that an otherwise reasonable member of the Daoine Sidhe—his own race—would break the law so cavalierly. I guess dealing with so many crazy people really upped his standards for the sane ones.

"Oberon's Law applies only to the places that Oberon is watching," said Riordan. "Tell me, kiddo, what part of this room is Oberon watching? What part of *anywhere* is Oberon watching? We'd never have been able to open this door," she indicated the portal to Annwn with a sweep of her hand, "if he'd been paying attention. Oberon's gone. He's not coming back for us. All you people still playing by his rules are backing the wrong horse. It's the ones who realize the rules have changed who'll win the race."

"Not to be rude or anything, but you're sort of mixing your metaphors," I said, as mildly as I could with a dozen semi-visible swords being pointed at my vital organs. I'd survive being stabbed ... probably. Quentin and Tybalt wouldn't.

"Why do people always say 'not to be rude' when they're about to be rude?" asked Riordan. "Now, are you going to lay down your arms, or are my men going to punch some nice new holes in you?"

My knife clattered against the receiving room floor. A few seconds later, Quentin's sword did the same. Tybalt had no weapons to discard, but he raised his hands, showing that his claws were securely sheathed.

Riordan smiled. "Good," she said. As quickly it had come, the smile faded, replaced by a look of cold dismissiveness. "Boys, take them."

The Folletti closed in. Tybalt snarled. And something hard hit me on the back of the head, and everything went black.

TWENTY-TWO

I WOKE WITH MY HANDS TIED behind my back and my ankles tied together, lying on my side in a tangled bed of fresh-cut bracken. That, and the sweet, clean smell of the air coming through the window in the stone wall behind me, told me plainly that we were no longer in Riordan's knowe. We were no longer anywhere in the Summerlands at all. There was no light in the room.

"Tybalt?" I whispered. I didn't move while I waited for my eyes to adjust. "Quentin?"

Silence. I squirmed in the bracken until I could lever myself into a sitting position, making as little noise as I could in the process. Once I was upright, I opened my mouth enough to "taste" the air, breathing deep and searching for signs of the Folletti. There were none. There were no signs of Cait Sidhe or Daoine Sidhe, either. For the moment at least, I was alone. The room was small and round, making me suspect that it was some sort of tower. The walls were made of rough, unfinished stone.

"Fairy tale cliché anyone?" I muttered, and looked down at myself, taking stock. I had my shoes, which was nice. Actually, I had all my clothes, including my leather jacket. At least I wasn't going to freeze while I was tied up in Riordan's stupid tower. I tugged my wrists apart, testing the cord that bound them. It was rough and scratchy against my skin, like twine. It wasn't quite tight enough to cut off the circulation, but it came close. I could work with that.

If anyone had been watching what came next, I'm sure they wouldn't have been able to observe what followed without laughing so hard they gave themselves away. I half-scooted, half-tumbled my way across the room, nearly landing on my face several times before I managed to reach the wall. Once I was there I twisted until my shoulders were pressed flat, with my hands pinned between my back and the stone. And then, gritting my teeth against the pain I knew was coming, I began scraping my wrists up and down the wall.

The thing about tying someone with rope or twine is that it's an innately fragile sort of bondage. Rope can be cut. Twine can be frayed. But if you do it right, most people, won't be able to achieve these things without hurting themselves—and most people aren't interested in hurting themselves when they don't have to. I'm not a fan of hurting myself. I've just learned that sometimes it's the only way.

My skin started giving way before the rope did, the smell of my blood seeping into the air to mingle with the scent of the bracken. I hate the sight of blood, but the smell of it strengthens me, even when it's my own. It's just one more annoying side effect of my increasingly inhuman biology. Still gritting my teeth—against actual pain now, not the promise of pain that might be coming—I pressed my back into the stone and sawed harder. The hardest part was forcing myself to keep sawing when the stone finished wearing through the skin at the base of my wrists. I could feel my flesh shredding. I could also feel the twine shredding. I kept going.

The first strand of twine snapped just when I was starting to think I'd have to stop and throw up from the pain. I tugged experimentally, and the remaining twine drew tight, giving me something new to saw against. I took a shaky breath, bit my lip, and went back to work.

The fact that I can bounce back from almost any injury that doesn't kill me is usually an asset. At times like this, when I would have once needed to worry about permanently damaging my hands, it's a godsend. There's just one problem: I heal supernaturally fast, but pain still hurts. Normally, if you hurt yourself enough, and keep hurting yourself, your nerves will give you up as a lost cause, and you'll stop hurting. Not optimal, but better than the alternative.

I, on the other hand, was already starting to heal. There was an itching underneath the agony that meant the cuts I'd made were beginning to knit themselves closed, flesh and muscle regenerating. And I was still sawing, which meant I was reopening those wounds faster than they could close, and the pain never got any duller. Blacking out was starting to sound like a great idea when the twine finally snapped.

I yanked my hands apart, ignoring the way the remains of the twine dug into my wounds, and bent forward to brace my palms against the floor, lean to the side, and puke. I stayed in that position for a while, dry-heaving and waiting for the pain to subside enough to let me sit up.

Eventually, my head cleared, and I pushed myself upright. The worst of the damage to my wrists was gone, although my hands were sticky with blood. I peeled away the last loops of twine with shaking fingers, wadding it up and throwing it into the bracken. The room was dark enough that the blood on my hands was just blackness, like spilled ink.

It's just ink, I told myself firmly and wiped my fingers on what was soon to be yet another ruined pair of jeans.

It says something about Faerie's sense of humor that the daughter of the best blood-worker in Faerie can't stand the sight of her own blood. At least the effort of wiping the blood off distracted me from the vague itch of my wrists healing themselves.

Once the pain was gone and my hands weren't quite

so sticky, I bent forward and untied the twine around my ankles. The knots were tight, but not so tight I couldn't unpick them with my fingers. Carefully avoiding the puddle of puke to my side, I braced one hand against the blood-dampened wall, and stood. My head spun one last time as I adjusted to being upright. Then everything settled, and I was loose, relatively uninjured . . . and entirely unarmed.

"Crap," I said, and scrubbed at my eyes with the back of my hands. The movement caused my jacket to shift, and something in my pocket went "clink."

I dropped my hands.

When Duchess Riordan's guards knocked me out and took me away, they'd confiscated my knife, but they hadn't searched my pockets for less obvious dangers. I still had the Luidaeg's Chelsea-chaser, which was currently glowing neutral starlight pale. And I had both the power dampener and its counteragent tucked into their respective pockets. Which meant that Quentin and Tybalt, wherever they were, probably also had theirs. Things were looking up.

Speaking of looking up . . . I crossed to the window, leaning onto my toes as I looked out on the moonwashed moor. I was definitely in Annwn, and I just as definitely wasn't looking *up*: the waves of heather and broom that stretched out around the tower where I was imprisoned were way, way *down*. Far enough down, in fact, that I couldn't even consider jumping a viable means of escape. If it had been only fifty feet, I would probably have broken the bones in both my legs, but I would have recovered. This was more like two hundred feet, and no matter how quickly I heal, a drop like that would kill me.

When all else fails, try the direct route. I dropped back to the floor and walked to the door, a heavy oak monstrosity barred with magic-dampening rowan wood. This must be the humane dungeon. They didn't want prisoners using magic to open the door, but they hadn't resorted to barring it with iron. Thank Oberon for that. The last thing I needed to add to my day was a bad case of iron poisoning.

The door was locked. That was no surprise; I would have been more surprised, and substantially more concerned, if it hadn't been. I bent to peer through the keyhole, making sure there was nothing unexpected in there. Then I went back to the pile of bracken, selected a particularly green piece of woody stem, and set to work.

My old mentor, Devin, fancied himself a cross between Fagin and Peter Pan—a thief and con man with an army of eternal children to do his bidding. Most of the lessons I learned while I was with him were the sort of things I've spent the years since then trying to forget. Some of them, on the other hand, have proved to be surprisingly useful. Like how to pick a lock with improvised tools when I couldn't use magic to make the process any easier.

It probably says something about my life that I've been in a position to use this particular lesson more than once. And I bet not even Devin imagined I'd one day be using his techniques to pick a tower lock in Annwn. That's me. Always doing my best to surpass expectations.

Something inside the lock clicked. I twisted my bit of bracken hard upward, and was rewarded with a second, louder click. Moving cautiously, in case there was some sort of secondary lock spell on the door that I hadn't noticed before, I tried the latch.

The door opened smoothly. The hinges didn't even creak—probably, I realized as I straightened up, because they were made of hand-carved oak. This was a realm where humans had never been common. Given a choice between metal and wood, humans almost always choose metal, and fae almost always choose wood. That probably says something deep and profound about our two species. At the moment, I was just relieved to know I wasn't going to need an oilcan if I wanted to move quietly through the building.

I opened the door a little wider and peered into the

hall. I didn't see anyone. That didn't necessarily mean anything; not with Riordan using Folletti for bodyguards. I breathed in, searching the air for signs of other fae. All I found was the smell of blood, and the unmistakable traces of Dóchas Sidhe. I already knew I was there. That meant that, for the moment, I was alone.

Stepping back from the door, I gathered my magic—something that was easier than I expected, thanks to all the blood in the room—and spun a don't-look-here over myself. It wouldn't keep me safe forever, but it might be enough to keep me safe until I could find myself some backup. I shook the last clinging bits of magic off my hand before grabbing a few more pieces of bracken and tucking them behind my ear. There's no telling what might turn out to be useful, and I was probably going to be picking a few more locks before I was finished.

There was nothing else in the tower room for me. I wiped my hands on my jeans one last time, trying to get off a little bit more of the blood, and stepped out into the hall.

I didn't have any way of relocking my door, so I just pulled it as tightly closed as I could and hoped no one would come to check on me until I was safely away. Pulling the Chelsea-chaser out of my pocket, I held it close to my body to keep the light from possibly shining outside the boundaries of my spell, and started making my way cautiously down the hall.

The irony of the situation was that nothing about it was new to me. I'd been a captive in Blind Michael's lands, and while they weren't as deep as Annwn—nothing we can access normally is as deep as Annwn—they were still disconnected from Earth and the Summerlands. And while I was there, I used the light of a magic candle created by the Luidaeg to find the children that he'd stolen.

Back then, I'd been trying to deny I was a hero. These days, no matter how unhappy I may sometimes be about it, I know I'm a hero. Oddly, knowing that made it easier to walk down the hall, keeping my back to the stone wall and watching for Folletti. There was none of the old urge to run and tell them to get someone else to deal with things; this was mine to deal with. My friends were somewhere in this hall. I was going to find them, and together, we were going to find a lost little girl who deserved better from Faerie than she'd ever gotten.

The Luidaeg's charm flickered when I was halfway down the hall. Then it flared, turning not its customary red, but a dark, almost puzzled-seeming shade of purple. I paused. There was only one door nearby. It was plain oak, with no convenient little window to let me see what was on the other side. Hollywood castles always get the little windows.

"Stupid Hollywood castles," I muttered, tucking the charm back into my pocket. I pulled a piece of bracken from my hair and knelt, getting to work on the lock. This one was easier, maybe because I was getting warmed up, and maybe because I'd had a little more time for the feeling to come back into my hands. The lock clicked open, and I cautiously opened the door.

This room was the mirror of the one where I'd been held: the same round stone walls, the same heap of fresh-cut broom and heather on the floor. Etienne was propped against the wall under the window, a blindfold tied across his eyes. I stepped into the room, tugging the door shut behind me.

His chin came up. "Who's there?" he demanded. "If you can't fight me fairly, at least stop creeping around like cowards in the dark."

"Shh," I said, crossing the distance between us before releasing my don't-look-here. It wisped away into the smell of cut grass and copper. "Etienne, it's me. Keep your voice down. I don't know where Riordan's Folletti are, and I'd rather not find out the painful way."

"October?" he said, lowering his voice to something just above a whisper. "Is that you?"

"I just said it was, didn't I?" I reached behind his head, untying his blindfold. He blinked at me as it fell away. I offered a small smile, adding wryly, "I don't know whether to be relieved or insulted that they felt the need to blindfold you when they didn't bother with me."

"They didn't want me to see where I was being taken."

"I guess that's more of an issue with a teleporter, huh?" I was trying to keep my voice light. It wasn't the easiest thing I'd ever done. Etienne had clearly been beaten. One of his eyes was swollen, and there was a heavy bruise on the right side of his jaw. He'd arrived at Dreamer's Glass on his own. Tybalt and Quentin . . .

I set the thought aside. I would find them. For the moment, I needed to get Etienne loose. Having a teleporter with me would be more use than any amount of brooding.

"I cannot travel if I cannot see," he said.

"Well, at least we've fixed that," I said. "Hang on. I'm going to get you untied."

His wrists and ankles were tied the same way mine had been. Etienne had struggled against his bonds, but had stopped before he could really hurt himself. That made him smarter than me. It took several minutes before I could pick the knots holding his wrists loose. Etienne hissed with pain as the twine fell away. Livid red marks ringed his wrists where it had been.

"These are friendly people," I said, bending to begin work on his ankles. "Remind me to hit them a lot if I get the chance."

"I assure you, I am unlikely to forget." Etienne rubbed his wrist with one hand, watching me work. Finally, awkwardly, he said, "October . . ."

"We all got caught, Etienne. Not just you."

"I was the one foolish enough to go by myself. Perhaps if I had waited . . ."

"Hindsight is always twenty-twenty." I worked a thumbnail into the knot holding the twine in place. "Let's just find Tybalt and Quentin. Then we can find Chelsea, kick Riordan's arrogant ass all the way back to the Summerlands, and get the hell out of here. How does that sound?"

"Excellent, if improbable."

"Improbable is sort of my specialty." I peeled the twine away, sitting back on my knees. "All done. You're free to go. Do you think you can stand?"

"My daughter is in danger. I think I can do whatever is required of me." Bold words aside, Etienne stumbled when he pulled himself up to his feet. I moved to catch him, and he waved me off, grimacing as he leaned against the wall. "I can walk unassisted."

"Are you sure about that?" I asked, standing.

Etienne lowered his chin, dark eyes blazing. "Somewhere in this place that we should not be, my daughter is being held by a woman who is using her to no good ends. Yes, I am sure. I would be sure if doing it meant my death. This will not stand."

"Okay. Just trying to make sure you're all right." I pulled the Luidaeg's charm out of my pocket. It was still glowing purple. The color intensified when I moved it closer to Etienne. "You're Chelsea's father, so this thing is picking up on your presence. We need to fix that if we want to use it to find *her*."

"How—"

"Hang on." I'd attuned the first charm by touching it to a place where Chelsea's magic had been used, and I attuned the second charm by touching it to the first. Feeling only slightly foolish, I leaned forward and tapped the charm against Etienne's shoulder.

The purple flared, and turned back to the familiar neutral shade of frozen starlight.

"It knows who you are now," I said. "That means we can keep using it to look for Chelsea and not worry about you throwing it off."

Etienne eyed the charm. "Do you understand how it works?"

"Nope," I said, with more cheer than necessary. "I usually don't know how magic works. I use it anyway. Are you feeling up to casting a don't-look-here over the both of us? I lost a lot of blood getting out of my room, and I'm not sure how many of those I can cast."

That wasn't strictly true: losing the blood slowed me

down for a few minutes, but it didn't seem to be doing anything to slow me down now. At the same time, if I was going to be the one picking every lock we came to, I couldn't also be the one putting up and taking down the don't-look-here spells. I would exhaust myself before we accomplished anything useful, and then I wouldn't be able to do anything for anyone. Not Chelsea, not Quentin, and not Tybalt.

Assuming Tybalt was even alive. Samson could never be King. He could still kill the man who held the throne.

Etienne paused, apparently seeing the change in my expression. "October? Are you all right?"

No. "I'm just worried about the others. Can you cast the spell or not?"

"I believe so." Etienne took a breath before raising his hand and sketching a quick series of motions in the air. The smell of limes and cedar smoke rose, and the spell settled down on my shoulders like a veil. Etienne lowered his hand. "That should hold."

"Good. Come on." I turned to head back toward the door. Etienne followed, and I did my best to match my pace to his. Don't-look-here spells are a form of illusion. This one would work best if we stayed close to one another. Besides, I didn't trust him yet not to fall.

His clothing hid most of the evidence of the beating he'd received at the hands of Riordan's guards, but I could see the signs of it in the stiffness when he moved and the way he was favoring his left leg. I was just glad they'd satisfied themselves with blindfolding him, rather than putting his eyes out entirely. That probably meant Riordan thought he might be useful later and wanted him intact when later came. Maybe that was an upside to dealing with sane people. They'd kill you just as dead, but they understood how to conserve their resources until they didn't need them anymore.

Etienne's pace was slow enough that we moved through the rest of the floor at about half-speed. The Luidaeg's charm continued to glow a neutral white the whole time. Eventually, we came to a flight of stairs, spiraling both upward and downward from where we stood.

I paused at the doorway to the stairs, and then motioned for Etienne to remain where he was. He nodded, stepping back. I went six steps up toward the next floor, breathed in, and retreated. I did the same with the floor beneath us. Then I returned to Etienne, stepping close as I murmured, "Definitely Folletti on the floor below us. None I can spot on the floor above, although that doesn't mean they're not there."

"Then we go up," he murmured back. I nodded, and together, we began making our way up the stairs.

Nothing stopped us as we climbed to the next landing, where another floor like the one we'd been kept on was waiting. Again, I motioned for Etienne to remain where he was while I stepped forward and checked for Folletti; again, if they were present, they weren't close enough for me to detect them. I waved Etienne forward, and together, we made our way down the hall, looking for doors.

What we found was an empty room above the one where I'd been kept, and a locked one above where Etienne had been. I pulled a piece of bracken from my hair and dropped to my knees, getting to work. This lock went even faster than the prior two. Practice was definitely making perfect. I tucked the half-bent piece of bracken back behind my ear, and pushed the door open gingerly.

Then I yelped, only remembering to swallow the sound at the last moment, and ran to where Tybalt lay motionless on his side in the heaped-up brush. He'd been beaten as badly as Etienne, if not worse; he was stripped to his trousers, barefoot and shirtless, as if to guarantee that he had no hidden weapons. His wrists and ankles were bound. Our captors must have seen him as more of a risk, because unlike us, they hadn't used twine.

Tybalt's wrists and ankles were bound with iron.

I dropped to my knees next to him, the bracken barely cushioning my fall, and grabbed his shoulder, trying to ignore the way the heat off the iron baked into my skin. "Tybalt? Tybalt, can you hear me?"

He didn't respond. That didn't strike me as a good sign.

Iron isn't just a way of hurting the fae: it's a way of torturing us, distorting reality and cutting off access to the magic that normally permeates our days. The stink of it rose from him, iron death and poisoned blood. I shuddered, pulling away enough to shove my hands into the bracken and search for something sturdier than my little makeshift lock picks. I didn't even hear Etienne's approach until he spoke from behind me, saying, "We shouldn't linger. The iron—"

"Go without me if you can't handle it," I said, yanking a piece of broom from the pile. I stripped the leaves and smaller twigs from it with quick, businesslike motions, forcing my hands to stay steady. "I can't leave him here."

"October—"

"*I can't!*" We both froze as we realized I'd yelled. I turned to look over my shoulder at Etienne, who was staring at me, wide-eyed and stunned.

Then he nodded stiffly. "I understand," he said, and turned away. My heart sank a little, even though I'd been half expecting it. He was looking for his daughter, after all, and Tybalt, while an ally, had never been a friend of his.

Etienne closed the door, sealing us inside the room with Tybalt, and the iron.

"Work quickly, if you would be so kind," he said. "I don't know how long it will remain safe for us to be here."

"Watch the door," I said. Gritting my teeth against what was about to come, I bent over Tybalt, grasping his wrist just below the iron cuff, and touched the twig of broom to the lock.

Most of the dangers in Faerie are worse for changelings than they are for purebloods. Changelings are the ones with less magic, less physical resilience, and less to protect them from whatever's decided to eat them for lunch. The one time this really falls down is when iron gets involved. Iron doesn't hurt humans, and so the more

human a changeling is, the less it hurts them. There was
a time when I could handle iron with relative ease, even
going so far as to carry an iron knife on a regular basis.
That time has passed. I'm a lot less human than I used to
be.

When my fingers brushed the cuff around Tybalt's
wrist, the metal burned and froze at the same time, an
impossible contradiction of sensations that my nerves
had no way of processing. Since they couldn't translate it
into anything else, they turned it into searing pain, bad
enough that I bit down on my lip until I tasted blood.

That helped steady me, and I forced my hands to keep
moving despite the pain, twisting the sprig of broom inside the lock. I was about to let go and step back to recover when something deep in the mechanism clicked
over, and the first cuff snapped open. I repeated the process with the second. When the lock released I yelped,
more out of shock than anything else, and jerked away,
letting the cuffs fall to the floor. They landed in the
bracken with a soft thump, and lay there, gleaming dully
in the thin light. My temporary lock pick stuck out of the
open keyhole. I left it there.

"October . . ."

"I'm almost there, Etienne." My fingertips were
charred, and it was harder to bend my fingers than it
should have been. I shook my hands, trying to get some
of the feeling back, before I started digging through the
bracken again, looking for a fresh lock pick.

Tybalt groaned. I froze.

"Tybalt?"

The sound wasn't repeated. I swallowed, hard, and
dug down into the brush until I found a sprig of broom
that suited my needs. Then I scooted down, bending to
begin fiddling with the locks holding his ankles together.

Some pains get better with exposure, familiarity
breeding a sort of physical contempt. The pain of flesh
touching iron isn't one of them. You'll eventually go
numb from all the poison being pumped into your system, but that isn't the same thing. Gripping the cuffs on

Tybalt's ankles was just as bad as gripping the cuffs on his wrists had been. At least this time I knew that I'd eventually be able to get the locks open. I bit my lip harder still, and somehow got the first of the ankle cuffs unlocked. I kept working.

"Almost . . . there . . ." The last lock let go. The cuffs fell away. I scooted back in the bracken, clutching my burned fingers to my chest and trying to figure out what I was supposed to do now.

And Tybalt opened his eyes.

Cait Sidhe can see through don't-look-here spells. I don't know why; maybe it's something to do with that whole "a cat can look at a King" thing. "Tybalt?" The question was half-whisper, half-plea, as if I didn't know whether I wanted to hear the answer. I bit my lip, scooting a little closer, careful to avoid the fallen cuffs. "Are you okay?"

He didn't answer. Instead, he sat up slowly, touching the burned places on his wrists with shaking hands before raising his head and looking at me. His pupils were so wide they all but devoured his irises, making his eyes inhuman and strange.

I could hear Etienne moving in the room behind me, but that didn't matter. What mattered was Tybalt, looking at me like he didn't know me at all. "Tybalt, it's me, October . . ."

Tybalt moved almost too fast for my eyes to follow, closing the distance between us in less than a second. His hands caught my shoulders as he crushed his lips against mine, tasting of sweat and crushed broom as well as the more customary pennyroyal and musk. I returned the kiss without thought or hesitation, molding myself into him, trying to express my relief without words. We didn't need any words. Not anymore.

His teeth cut my lip. I welcomed the taste of my own blood, letting myself draw strength from it. The wound had healed by the time he pulled away from me, and the burning sensation in my fingers was fading, replaced by a numbness I knew couldn't last. My body could recover from almost anything. Iron poisoning isn't "almost anything." The pain would come soon.

And that didn't matter, because Tybalt was looking at me, eyes returning to normal as his breathing evened out. "October," he whispered, and the sound of his voice was the sweetest thing I'd ever heard. "I was afraid . . ."

"So was I." I put my hand against his cheek. "Don't *scare* me like that."

"I assure you, it wasn't my intent." He looked past me, pupils narrowing, and offered a small nod. "Sir Etienne."

"Tybalt." There was a scuff of boots against the floor as Etienne stepped up behind me. "Loath as I am to disrupt this reunion—almost as loath as I am to ask any questions about it—we must move. Chelsea is somewhere in this place, and we need to find her."

"Yeah, we do," I said, and pulled my hand away from Tybalt's cheek. "Can you stand?"

"For you, little fish, I would do anything." Tybalt paused before adding, regretfully, "But desire does not mean ability. I'm not sure I can walk right now."

"Can you change shapes?"

Tybalt blinked. Then he nodded. "I believe so."

"Try," I said, and leaned forward to press another kiss against his forehead.

A smile tugged at the corners of Tybalt's lips. Then the smell of pennyroyal and musk rose in the air between us, and he was gone, replaced by a striped tabby. The beating he had received was more evident in this form, without clothing to hide his wounds; the fur above his paws was worn away, and there were several gouges in his side. His breathing was labored—something I hadn't noticed when he'd been in human form, but I hadn't been looking for it, either. I'd been too relieved to see him awake.

Looking up at me, Tybalt meowed.

"We need to get out of here." I stood, scooping him into my arms. He settled against my chest, offering a single rusty purr before going perfectly silent, perfectly still. I zipped my jacket to hold him there and turned to Etienne. "Now we just need to find Chelsea and Quentin."

"Assuming they're being held in this same location," he said grimly.

"Let's at least try to look on the bright side, okay?" I walked toward him. "So far, we're not too hurt to keep moving, and that's more than I was hoping for. Now let's go find our kids."

"I was waiting for you," said Etienne, and opened the door.

His don't-look-here spell was still holding, hanging around the three of us like a shroud as we stepped back out into the hall. I paused to breathe in, testing the air. Then I froze, the smell of Folletti hitting me like an ice-pick to the temple. There was nowhere for us to run, and no time to explain. I yanked the door shut and clapped a hand over Etienne's mouth, hoping he'd get the message.

Years of training served us both well. Etienne's eyes briefly widened before he offered me a short, sharp nod, acknowledging my unspoken request. Together, we waited in silence for what was coming next.

We didn't wait long. Three Folletti came drifting down the hall, their semi-transparent bodies gliding about two feet above the floor. All of them had their swords drawn, and were looking around suspiciously. I didn't need to see their faces to know they were on edge.

My experience with the Cloud Kingdoms—and hence the Folletti—is limited enough to verge on nonexistent. Since they were made of air, and illusions are technically bent air and light, they might see right through Etienne's don't-look-here. On the other hand, being made of air might make the illusion work even better on them. It was a gamble. As their searching eyes found our side of the hall, I tensed, ready to throw myself at them in order to buy Etienne time to open us a portal.

The Folletti looked right through us and drifted on their way. I kept my hand over Etienne's mouth and began slowly, silently counting, refusing to let either of us move until I was certain we were alone. When I had reached a hundred without the Folletti returning I pulled

my hand away, jerking my chin toward the end of the
hall. Etienne nodded. Still holding Tybalt to my chest, I
pushed away from the wall and started walking toward
the doorway to the stairs.

If Riordan thought we were safely confined in our in-
dividual rooms, she wasn't likely to have multiple squads
of Folletti checking up on us. That would be a waste of
resources, and whatever she was planning was big
enough that I didn't expect her to have resources to
waste. Holding that thought in mind, I put my free hand
on the bannister and began descending the stairs. Etienne was close behind me.

That's what saved us. When the second group of Folletti floated up through the open central column of the
spiral stairway, Etienne yanked me backward against
him, covering my mouth the way I'd covered his only a
few minutes before. The Folletti drifted by without noticing us. Once they were past, Etienne let me go, and we
resumed our downward trek.

With the Folletti above us now, we were able to continue down past the floor where Etienne and I had been
held. There was another floor below it, identical to the
two above. I stopped at the landing, pulling the Luidaeg's
Chelsea-chaser out of my pocket. It was still glowing the
color of pale starlight. Chelsea wasn't here. But that
didn't mean Quentin wasn't.

Bringing my mouth close to Tybalt's ear, I whispered,
"Are you feeling strong enough to check the hall for
prisoners? I don't need you to get into their rooms. Just
find out if there's anyone here for us to save."

Tybalt opened his mouth in a silent meow—the secret
weapon of cats everywhere—and squirmed to tell me
that I should put him down. I bent to set him gingerly on
the cold stone floor, and watched uneasily as he slunk
out of sight down the hall.

Etienne put his hand on my shoulder. I looked back
to him, forcing myself to smile. He glanced down the hall
after Tybalt before raising an eyebrow in silent question.
I hesitated, considering my answer . . . and then, finally, I

nodded. Yes. I was worried about Tybalt, and yes, I was worried for reasons beyond simple friendship. Oak and ash. If I was going to fall in love with the man, couldn't I have picked a more reasonable time to do it?

Then again, when do I get a reasonable time to do anything anymore? There's always something going wrong. If I put my life on hold until everything was calm, I'd be waiting forever for the chance to start living.

Tybalt came slinking back along the hall and wound himself around my ankles in a complicated figure-eight pattern before starting back the way he'd come. I followed, catching his intent, and Etienne followed me. The three of us made an odd procession as we continued along the hallway to another of those damn locked doors. I dropped to my knees, pulling a sprig of bracken from my hair. By the time this night was over—if nights in Annwn ever really ended—I was going to be well practiced in the arts of breaking and entering.

Tybalt sat next to me and Etienne stood guard as I picked the lock. If it was Quentin on the other side, we'd be back together; we could hunt for Chelsea in earnest. I wouldn't need to worry that my squire was in Riordan's boudoir, waiting for her to come along and make him an offer he'd really want to refuse. If it was Quentin . . . the lock let go. I pushed the door open.

It wasn't Quentin.

Officer Thornton of the San Francisco Police was lying bound in a heap of bracken like the ones we'd found in each of the other rooms. Like Etienne, he was blindfolded; like both Etienne and Tybalt, he'd clearly been beaten. Unlike either of them, he was human. I stood slowly, too startled to know what to say.

Much to my surprise, it was Etienne who found the words I couldn't: "Oh, Oberon's honor," he said.

"Yeah," I agreed. "That."

Riordan was kidnapping humans. That wasn't technically against any fae laws—Faerie has always had a generous definition of "acceptable" when it comes to messing with the human world. As long as you don't get caught or leave witnesses, no one cares. But she had a mortal life, too, and that meant that Officer Thornton's presence signaled one very big, very bad thing.

She wasn't planning to go back to a world where she might be in trouble for kidnapping a police officer.

If we didn't find Chelsea soon, we were going to be stuck in Annwn.

TWENTY-THREE

THERE WAS BLOOD ON OFFICER THORNTON'S forehead and caked under his nose, but he was alive, and he was awake. He turned toward the open door, snarling, "You are interfering with an officer of the law. Take off this blindfold, take off those stupid masks, and release me at once."

I only had a moment to make a decision. Close this door and leave him behind, or try to get him to see reason and work with us. I wanted to close the door. Faerie was in danger, Chelsea was in danger, and a human police officer was one more distraction we didn't need. That's why I stepped into the room.

My humanity has always been a tenuous thing, and I'd been able to feel it slipping since Amandine shifted the balance of my blood. If I was sawing through my hands without hesitation and letting myself be ripped open because it was the most logical route, that meant I was losing my grip on what it meant to be human. A human—a good one, the kind I'd always tried to be—wouldn't leave another human behind. Until I was certain I wanted to lose that part of myself, I couldn't leave another human behind, either.

"Officer Thornton?" I kept my voice level as I walked toward him, the bracken muffling my footsteps. I motioned for Etienne to release the don't-look-here. The smell of cedar smoke and limes washed through the room, almost obscuring the pennyroyal and musk smell of Tybalt resuming his human form. "Are you all right?"

The officer's brow furrowed above his blindfold, matching the frown creasing his lips. Finally, he said, "Ms. Daye? Is that you?"

"Yeah." Pointed ears and all. "Are you all right?"

"Are you aware that abducting an officer of the law is a felony, Ms. Daye?"

"I am, but I'm not particularly worried about it, since my friends and I didn't abduct you." I knelt next to him, reaching for his wrists. My fingers brushed his skin. He jerked away. "Hey. I'm trying to help."

"I was trying to find you when this happened."

"Maybe you should have given up on that a little sooner." Luckily for me, Riordan's people hadn't viewed Officer Thornton as enough of a risk to break out the iron; he was bound with twine. I started picking at the knots on his wrists. "Why were you after me, anyway? It doesn't make sense."

"I don't . . . I don't know." Officer Thornton looked briefly, utterly lost. Then his expression hardened, and he said, "There's a teenage girl missing, and you have a history of being around missing teenage girls."

Tybalt took his meaning before I did; I heard the quiet growl from behind me, like the sound a cat makes when confronted with a dog on its territory. I paused, my hands going still. "Are you implying what I think you're implying?" I asked, in a soft voice.

Officer Thornton was smart enough to realize that maybe he didn't want to continue down this road. He was also clearly strait-laced enough to feel that he had to. "You must admit, there has been a high incidence of crossover."

"I'm a private detective. It's what I *do*. And you followed me to Fremont."

"I felt I had to," said Officer Thornton. The confusion was back in his voice.

"Chelsea Ames is my daughter," added Etienne, not to be left out of what was becoming an increasingly awkward conversation. "I retained Si—Ms. Daye to find her."

Etienne's hastily swallowed "sir" didn't slip by Officer Thornton, whose frown deepened. "Who *are* you people?" he demanded. "Are you involved with some kind of a cult?"

"Something like that." I went back to untying the twine around his wrists, being less careful about pulling it tight against his skin. "We're the good guys here, believe it or not. As exhibit A, I want to present the fact that we're not the ones who kidnapped and drugged you."

"Drugged me?" said Officer Thornton, a note of suspicion creeping into his voice.

When all else fails, lie. That's practically the first rule of life in Faerie. "Hallucinogens in the air supply. I was seeing flying pigs when I woke up. We're in a warehouse somewhere—I suspect San Jose, but I'm not sure—and it's hard to tell up from down. So the first thing I need to ask you to do is not to freak out when I take your blindfold away."

I glanced over my shoulder to see whether Etienne and Tybalt could see where I was going with this. Etienne frowned. Tybalt smirked, curling one lip up to show the inhumanly sharp points of his incisors. Hallucinations could never be this vivid. It was still the best shot we had at convincing Officer Thornton that he hadn't completely lost his mind.

"Ma'am—"

"My daughter's life is in danger," said Etienne. His voice was calm, reasonable, and without compassion. "If you cannot promise to remain in control of your faculties, you will be no use to us, and may endanger her further. I'm very sorry, and I'm sure you're a very nice man in your own element, but I will not have Chelsea harmed for the sake of your pride. Do I make myself clear?"

Officer Thornton's frown, which had been starting to fade, returned in force. "I don't believe I caught your name."

"That would be because I did not release it." Etienne turned to look at me. "October. I understand why you feel the need to free this man. I ask you, as a friend and as a father, are you sure this is the right course of action?"

"I'm not leaving him here for Riordan's goons to beat on when they realize we're gone. Besides, it's too late to change my mind. He's loose." I peeled the last of the twine away from Thornton's wrists and scooted down to start working on his ankles. "You can remove the blindfold now, Officer. It's pretty dark in here."

True to form, Officer Thornton ripped his blindfold off, glaring into the darkness. "Pretty dark?" he said. "This is pitch black! How am I supposed to see my hand in front of my face without some lights?"

Etienne and I exchanged a startled glance, and I bit back a gust of relieved, semi-hysterical laughter. Human eyes were made for a daylight world. Fae eyes weren't, and even changelings see in the dark better than any mortal. Etienne and Tybalt were purebloods, and I was fae enough that I hadn't really realized how little light was coming in the room's single window. It was even darker in the hall, with just the arrow slits in the walls letting moonlight in. We might actually be able to pull this off without needing to ask the Luidaeg to melt the mind of a San Francisco policeman.

"Your eyes will adjust," said Tybalt, with almost believable sincerity.

"In the meanwhile, we need to get moving." I pulled the twine off Thornton's ankles. "Are you hurt?"

"I've felt better," said Officer Thornton, and levered himself to his feet. He was moving slowly, but he wasn't visibly favoring either leg. Maybe they'd been gentler with him, assuming that since he was only human, he wouldn't be much of a threat. He touched his belt and scowled. "My weapon is missing."

"Our captors weren't dumb enough to leave us armed." I offered my elbow. "Here, hold onto me. We're going to need to be really, really quiet while we make our way down to ground level. Can you keep your mouth shut?" With a human in our party, asking Etienne for another don't-look-here was out of the question. He could cast it, sure. We'd never be able to make Officer Thornton understand why he had to walk the way we told him to walk—not without a lot of explanations that we really didn't have the time for.

The look Officer Thornton shot in my direction was withering. Pity it was directed at the wall to the left of my head. "If it gets me out of here, I can be as quiet as you need me to be. But I'm going to be very interested in your statements—all of you. Don't think that you're absolved of involvement just because you're helping me escape."

"You're not the only one who's here against his will, and my...nephew...is missing somewhere in this place," I said. Looking chagrined, Officer Thornton took hold of my arm. "Good. Now come on."

We crept out of the room and into the dark, Folletti-free hallway. I paused long enough to taste the air, finding no traces of Daoine Sidhe nearby, and waved the others toward the stairs. Officer Thornton clung to me the whole while, staring into the shadows with blind, intent eyes, as if he could somehow force the world to become bright enough to let him see.

Considering the fact that we were creeping along in a medieval hallway with windows that looked out on a night that was nothing like Earth, it was probably for the best that he couldn't see a damn thing, even if it did make descending the stairs a little more dangerous. Tybalt stayed in human form all the way down, leaning heavily on the rail. I shot him a grateful look. Explaining his disappearance—or where the cat had come from—would just be one more thing to tax Officer Thornton's grasp on the situation. Although, at the moment, what Officer Thornton was grasping was mostly the banister.

Etienne and I took the lead as we moved downward. Etienne stepped in close enough to murmur in my ear, saying, "This is a terrible idea, Sir Daye."

"Maybe," I agreed. "But there was no way I was going to leave him there. Even if I was sure the Folletti weren't going to come back, I don't know how many shots we're going to have at the exit. We're not supposed to be in here."

What I could see of Etienne's face through the blackness of the stairwell was grim. "Yes," he said. "I know."

The stairwell grew lighter as we approached the end of the stairs, and we stepped out into a wide hall filled with more of those globes of floating witchlight from Duchess Riordan's knowe. "She's really moving in," I murmured. There was no one in sight, but I couldn't count on that situation lasting. I glanced around, finally spotting a dark recess in the wall across from us, and beckoned for the others to follow me.

It might have worked . . . but Officer Thornton didn't move. Instead, he stopped where he was, staring out the nearest window. Unlike the windows upstairs, these were wide and high, giving an excellent view of the star-speckled sky and the wide, unearthly moor stretching outward to the sea. "What *is* this place?" he asked.

"Hey! Hush!" I rushed back over to him, gesturing for him to keep his voice down. "It's a bad place, okay? It's a place we're going to get you out of as fast as we can. But you have to keep quiet, or else—"

"You might find yourself in a bit of a pickle." Samson's voice was self-assured enough to make my teeth crawl. He stepped out of the shadows in front of me, a smile on his face that showed the points of all his teeth. To add insult to injury, he had my knife tucked into his belt. "Then again, you might find yourself in a bit of a pickle no matter what your human pet chooses to do. Really, *Sire*?" He looked past me to Tybalt. "This is the woman you would betray your people for? The sort of sentimental fool who can't even make an escape without saddling herself with invalids and idiots? I thought better of you, once."

"My first mistake was in letting you stand beside your

son, Samson," said Tybalt. His voice betrayed nothing of his injuries. "Run, and I may let you live."

"That gift is no longer yours to give." Cait Sidhe can move almost impossibly fast when they want to. I didn't see Samson preparing to lunge; I barely saw him moving. Officer Thornton fell to the side, shouting in dismay, and then Samson was behind me, my hair knotted in one hand, the claws of the other hand pressed against my throat. "It seems to me, *Sire*, that the right to dispense life lies elsewhere."

I swallowed, feeling the points of Samson's claws prickling against my skin. "Uh . . ."

"Got something to say, slattern? Wishing you hadn't interfered with the Court of Cats?" Samson leaned close, his breath hot against my cheek as he murmured, "I've seen the way you heal. I may have to dig all the way to your spine before you stop breathing. It should be one of the more interesting deaths I've granted in years."

"Samson . . ." There was a warning in Tybalt's voice that would have made my blood run cold if it had been directed at me. "Release her."

"Surrender," Samson countered. "Give me your word as both cat and King that you will put your throat into my son's hands, and then, perhaps, I'll let your little bitch walk free."

The smell of cedar smoke and limes drifted through the air. I stiffened. Samson, oddly, didn't. Maybe he didn't know the smell of Etienne's magic, or maybe he just thought there was nothing anyone could do to interfere with his plans—not at this stage, not when he had me in his hands. Whatever the reason, he didn't slacken his grip until he went stiff, claws digging into my skin. I yelped, feeling blood start to run down my neck toward my collarbone. Then Samson's hand fell, and I ducked away from him before he could get any more bright ideas.

Samson wasn't getting any ideas about anything. He was just standing there. I turned to look back at him and saw him staring down at his own side in amazement. Etienne was right behind him, his hand grasping the hilt of my knife. The dark stain spreading through Samson's shirt told me the rest of the story.

Tybalt's hand closed on my shoulder, stopping me from stumbling any further backward. I leaned into it, clamping my own hands over the punctures in my throat. Etienne pulled the knife out and stabbed Samson again, and again.

And Samson raised his head, pupils narrowing to hairline slits. "This isn't over," he spat, and pulled away from Etienne, moving shakily, but still moving. He grabbed something from his pocket, throwing it into the shadows, and dove after it. The smell of apples and snowdrops rose, overlaying the more distant smell of Chelsea's magic, and he was gone.

"Oh, goody," I said faintly. "This is the *best* day."

"Sir Daye, you're wounded." Etienne vanished, reappearing next to me in another wafting gust of smoke and limes. "Let me see."

"It's nothing. Really. It's already starting to heal." I didn't actually know that, but recent experience told me the odds were on my side. I kept my hands where they were, feeling them turning sticky with blood. "Did you get my knife?"

"I did." Etienne held it out to me, hilt first. "I am afraid you may need to clean it."

I took a hand away from my neck and reached for the knife, relaxing as the weight of it settled into my hands. Then the weight of Etienne's words hit me. Clean it. I needed to clean it.

The knife was covered in Samson's blood, a thick coating of the stuff that looked almost black in the moonlight. Samson was working with Riordan. Samson knew enough to know where we'd be, and to be the one who had my knife. The thought was enough to turn my stomach. That didn't mean I could just ignore it.

"What—what *are* you people?"

The panicked note in Officer Thornton's voice was enough to make me set all other thoughts aside as I raised my head and looked at him. He was backed up against the wall next to the window, staring at us with wide, terrified eyes. The blood had drained from his face, leaving him as pale as the moonlight washing over him.

"This isn't a cult," he said. "This isn't hallucinogenic drugs. You're not human." Then he turned and ran, heading for the end of the hall.

I groaned. "Etienne—"

"Of course." The smell of cedar smoke and limes rose again, and Etienne was gone. He would intercept Officer Thornton, and if he couldn't calm him down, he could knock him out. That might be enough to buy us the time we needed. I hoped.

Tybalt's hand tightened on my shoulder. "You don't have to do this."

"Got a better idea?" He didn't say anything. I sighed. "Didn't think so. Come on." I pulled away from him, heading for the dark alcove that had been my initial destination on this floor. With Samson running wounded, presumably for Riordan, and the Folletti somewhere in the hall with us, we didn't have much time.

Tybalt walked with me, frowning. "October—"

"Just watch my back, okay?" I raised my knife before he could say anything else, and ran my tongue along the flat of the blade.

Samson's memories slammed into me, a thick cloud of resentment, jealousy, and unresolved hatreds. They were a tangled mass of images, hard to sort through or comprehend. I staggered, trying to figure out why it was hitting me so hard, and felt Tybalt's hands catch me. Then the world dropped away, taking reassuring hands and the Annwn night with it, and everything was the red haze, and the weight of Samson's bitter memory.

Bastard. He gets everything he wants—he always has, Prince of Londinium, King of San Francisco, and how much of it has he worked for? How much of it has he earned? Not a bit, and yet there he sits, and here I stand, hoping he'll exploit my son enough to grant me the power to pull us away from this cursed place, these cursed people who walk and talk and call themselves our equals.

I'd always known that Samson was a cruel, resentful man, but I'd never understood how angry he was until that moment. Angry about his place in Cait Sidhe society, angry at the accident of birth that made Tybalt a King and him a subject, angry at the fact that his only living child would eventually have that same level of power and privilege. He resented Raj, even as he viewed his son as the one opportunity he'd ever have to achieve the status he thought he deserved.

I was dimly aware that I was on my knees on the cold stone floor of the hall; I could feel a hand gripping my shoulder, fingers clutching hard enough that I could feel them despite the leather of my jacket and the distance imposed by the heavy veil of blood between us. I clung to that sensation—to the knowledge of *self*, and the even better knowledge that there was someone ready and waiting to call me back—as I forced myself deeper into the spell.

"So you can get me the girl?"

"I can." I do not brag—cats do not brag—but I still speak the truth. Riordan came to me with rumors, and I proved them to be reality. An untrained, unwatched Tuatha changeling. She could have amounted to nothing. Instead, she came to be so much more.

"How?"

"She walks the same route every day. I can take her into the shadows and bring her to you before she musters her senses enough to run."

"If you fail me . . ." She does not complete the sentence. She doesn't need to. I know the price of failure better than she does, because I understand what this is. She thinks it's an escape from the eyes on her borders. I know it for something more.

This is a coup.

"I will not fail."

Riordan says nothing. She simply nods, and I think again that power is the one thing the Divided Courts got right. They understand that power should belong to the strongest—if you can take a thing and hold it, it should be yours. She would have made a fine cat. A pity, then, that she must belong to the lesser Courts. Unlike some, I will never dirty myself.

But still, she's lovely in the moonlight.

Seen through Samson's assessing eyes, Duchess Riordan was a beautiful tool, as clueless and malleable as the rest of the Divided Courts but with a strength of character that he found himself compelled to admire. The taste of his admiration was alien in my mind, so cold and calculating that I would have mistaken it for another flavor of hatred if I hadn't been wound so deeply in his memories.

Too deeply; I was seeing Riordan in her own territory, and not in the moonlight of Annwn. I forced myself to move forward through Samson's memory, clawing my way through the blood-soaked veils of recollection until the red shattered and re-formed into something more familiar. The cliff at the edge of the moor, overlooking the sea.

The mongrel girl is flagging. I thought she would collapse long before this, but fear, it seems, is a grand motivator; a few threats to the mother she loves and the father she's never known, and she was so much more willing to work with us. Still, holding a portal this size open for so long is doubtless . . . draining. I doubt she will live. Through his eyes, I watched Chelsea struggling to keep a passageway large enough to drive a car through open. I could see Riordan's garage on the other side—and they *were* driving a car through, of a sort. A footman in Riordan's livery was steering a cart through the opening, drawn by fae steeds and laden with farming equipment. From the tracks crushed into the bracken, it wasn't the first, either.

"How much longer?"

Riordan turns her back on the supply train as she looks toward me. Behind her, that mongrel bitch's spoiled little squire is bound and gagged in a wicker chair, watching helplessly as the wagons roll through. "Why in such a hurry, my friend?" she asks. "We're both getting what we want. Shouldn't you savor your victory?"

"I'll savor it when that door is closed, and I never need to see your face again," I snap. "How much longer?"

She sighs, looking disappointed. "You never did have a sense of humor, Sammy. Most of the supplies and live-stock are through, and all my people. Why don't you make yourself useful? Go check on our prisoners. Make sure they're not getting into any mischief."

Her laughter follows me out as I use her blood charm to access the Shadow Roads that would otherwise be locked to me in this place, the cold and the dark numbing the sting of being mocked by a member of her debauched Court. And then the light, and sweet Titania, what a gift— they're here, and this time, no one will stop me from doing what needs to be done—

I jerked myself free of the blood when my/Samson's eyes fixed on the four of us standing in the darkened hall. There was nothing he could tell me after that, except for maybe what it felt like to get stabbed with my own knife. It probably wasn't going to be that different from getting stabbed with anything else, and none of those stabbings were much fun. Pass.

"That's why she was willing to kidnap a police offi-cer," I muttered, half-gasping. "I knew she wasn't plan-ning on going back, but this . . . this . . ."

"October?" Tybalt's hand tightened on my shoulder.

"We need to get back to the cliff." I spat on the floor, trying to get the taste of Samson's blood—of Samson's *life*—out of my mouth. "Riordan's there, she's got some sort of supply train going. This was never just a kidnap-ping."

"What is it, then?"

I managed to lift my head, twisting around to look at him. "It's a colonization," I said. "Riordan is recolonizing Annwn, and she's using Chelsea to do it."

TWENTY-FOUR

ETIENNE DIDN'T COME BACK as the minutes ticked by, until we couldn't wait any longer. Riordan's wards couldn't shut off the Shadow Roads completely—not here—but Tybalt hadn't been in Annwn long enough to anchor them, and we didn't have Luna's favor to open the Rose Road for us. I was grateful not to be alone as Tybalt and I crept out of the hall and onto the moon-drenched moor together.

The bracken was so thick that don't-look-here spells were useless; even if I were invisible, I'd be leaving a trail that would point our pursuers directly to us if I did anything but follow Tybalt's lead through the brush. The way he blended into the landscape was unreal. Anyone following us would find him as hard to track as a tiger in the jungle, while I felt like a giant neon sign blundering across the field. "Hero incoming, look over here." Even hunching over didn't do me any good. Boughs of broom and heather disturbed by Tybalt's passage kept slapping me in the face, and being hit with swinging greenery didn't precisely help my attempts at stealth.

At least following his trail meant that I'd be a little harder to track. I could tell from the way our path twisted and curved that he was choosing the easiest terrain for both of us, while still moving us the way we needed to go. I wanted to break into a run. I wanted to order him into cat form and just *go*, stealing every bit of speed my fear could offer. I didn't. Instead, I kept my eyes on the sky, watching for distortions in the starlight overhead. If the Folletti came for us, that might be all the warning we got.

I was so busy looking up that I ran straight into Tybalt's outstretched arm, bringing myself to an abrupt halt. I managed not to yelp, biting down hard on my lip to smother the urge. Tybalt looked over his shoulder at me, pressing a finger to his lips. I nodded. Silence was the way to go. Then I looked past him, and my appreciation for silence died, replaced by the urge to start hurting people and not stop until I was sure there was no one left to hurt.

The scene was basically as Samson's memory had shown it: Chelsea, struggling to hold open a glittering portal in the air; Quentin, bound and tied to a chair; Riordan, watching with smug delight as her wagons rolled through the gateway. What his memory hadn't shown—maybe because he didn't consider it important enough to bother remembering—were the bruises on Chelsea's face, and the blood in Quentin's hair. They'd been beaten, both of them. They were *children*, and she'd had them beaten.

Tybalt's arm stayed extended, keeping me from charging forward. "Is she truly undefended?" he asked.

I took a breath to steady myself, and then took another breath as I tried to focus on the air around us. "No," I whispered. "The Folletti are here. I just can't tell you where 'here' is."

"Charming." Tybalt scowled at the patch of open ground where Riordan stood. "What, then, is our next move?"

"I don't suppose you've got a flamethrower on you, huh?" Tybalt blinked before shaking his head, apparently taking the question seriously. "Didn't think so." I frowned at the portal, and then took a deep breath. "I have an idea," I said. "But you're not going to like it."

Tybalt frowned. "Anything you introduce in that manner is a thing I am absolutely guaranteed to dislike."

Still, he listened as I explained my admittedly idiotic plan, and although he didn't like it, he saw the sense. At least that's what I tried to tell myself as I shoved my hands into my jacket pockets and strode, whistling a jaunty tune, out of the bracken.

Riordan's head whipped around at the first run of off-key notes, her eyes widening as she took in the sight of me. I pulled a hand out of my pocket and offered her a wave as jaunty as my whistle.

"Guards!" she shouted.

I'd been expecting that. It would have been nice to get a little farther into the open—I was only about five yards from the edge of the bracken—but beggars can't be choosers. Her shout was still echoing when the Folletti appeared all around me, their weapons drawn and at the ready. I stopped where I was, putting my hand back into my pocket, and beamed at them.

"Howdy," I said. "So you know, she's not paying you nearly enough for this. Seriously, you guys should have renegotiated your rates the second I walked into Dreamer's Glass."

The Folletti frowned in confusion but didn't lower their swords. I'd been expecting that, too.

"Now, you may be asking yourselves, 'How is she up and wandering around and coming to see what we're up to after the beat-down we gave her earlier'?" I kept beaming. It seemed to be making the Folletti uncomfortable. Cool by me. "You may also be asking yourselves, 'What do we know about her species?' I mean, that's what I'd be doing, if I were you. That, and maybe running like hell."

The Folletti's confusion turned into scowling. "Surrender," commanded one of them, his voice almost vanishing into the wind blowing across the moor.

"No," I replied genially, and pulled my right hand out of my pocket.

This close to Chelsea and one of her gates, the Luidaeg's charm went into instant overdrive. It was red when I pulled it out, but as it hit the air, it turned a shade of incandescent scarlet that was almost bright enough to mistake for white if you tried to look at it from the side. The Folletti, who hadn't known what I was about to do, weren't looking at it from the side. Their eyes had been drawn to the sight of my hand emerging from my pocket, trained soldiers looking for signs of a weapon. I guess they weren't expecting a pocket-sized piece of the sun.

They screamed in eerie unison, like a hurricane trapped inside an echo chamber. Riordan shouted, clapping her hands over her ears. I wanted to do the same. Sadly, that wasn't an option. Instead, I broke into a run, heading for Quentin as fast as my legs could carry me.

I was almost there when Samson appeared in front of me, surrounded by the weirdly mingled scents of Chelsea and Riordan's magic. Blood drenched his shirt, smeared over his face and neck. He snarled, face contorted with an inhuman rage, and drove the claws of his right hand into my stomach, bringing me up short. I felt things inside me rip and tear—things that were never meant to be ripped or torn, things I'm pretty sure you need in working order if you want to stay alive. Pain lanced through me, overwhelming enough to make the screaming of the Folletti seem like an understated counterpoint. Evisceration will really focus a girl's thoughts.

Most of me wanted to black out. The rest of me wanted to live. It was the part that wanted to live that drew the knife from my belt, slamming it into Samson's belly in a parody of what he was doing to me. His eyes widened, the reflection of the light from the Chelsea-chaser making them seem to glow. Then he twisted his fingers inside me, and I screamed.

Please, Tybalt, please, I thought, even as I struggled not to drop to my knees. The Luidaeg's charm fell from my hand, rolling off into the bracken. The world was starting to go fuzzy around the edges. There was a time when this much pain would have been unimaginable; I would have been dead long before it could hit me. *Please stick to the plan. Get everyone else out of here. Please.*

"At least I'll take you with me," hissed Samson, and raised his other hand at an angle that would allow him to bring it down across my throat.

Maybe I could have survived that. Maybe. If I'd been running at full power, and hadn't already used up most of my body's resources healing from my earlier injuries. As it was, when that hand came down, I was going to die. I knew it, and so did Samson. I closed my eyes. Better that than watching the blow descend.

It never came. Samson made a choking noise, his fingers going limp as they released their hold on whatever vital part of my insides they'd been clenching. I opened my eyes to see Etienne behind him, with the iron cuffs that had been used to bind Tybalt's ankles hooked around Samson's throat. The skin of Etienne's hands was visibly blistering. That was nothing compared to what was happening to Samson, who was trying to turn red and go pale at the same time. He settled for splitting the middle and going limp. He wasn't breathing anymore. Etienne still gave the cuffs one last twist before he dropped them, a disgusted expression on his face.

"Are you—?"

"Don't worry about me," I wheezed, shoving my knife back into my belt without bothering to clean it before I clapped my hand over the hole in my stomach. I wasn't sure whether I was trying to hold my insides in place or keep Etienne from seeing the extent of the damage. Maybe a little bit of both. One thing was for sure: I was never going to get into a hand-to-hand fight with a Cait Sidhe again if I had any choice in the matter. I like my internal organs to stay internal. "Get Quentin loose. Tybalt is taking care of Chelsea."

Etienne nodded and disappeared, leaving the scent of smoke and limes behind him. I shakily straightened, looking down at Samson's body for a moment before I started stumbling forward, toward where Quentin was tied down. Ahead, through the black spots clouding my vision, I could see Etienne appear next to my squire and start dealing with the knots.

The Folletti weren't screaming anymore. I had time for that to register, barely, when the first of them struck Etienne from behind. He shouted and disappeared, leaving the Folletti to stumble forward. Quentin ducked as best he could while tied to a chair, missing a sweep of the Folletti's sword, and kicked out at the same time. His feet impacted with the Folletti's ankle, sending him stumbling and sending Quentin's chair over backward. I forced myself to walk faster, every muscle in my body protesting the movement. I could feel the twisted things inside me trying to untangle themselves and my skin trying to knit back together at the same time. It was too much. All of it was too much.

The Folletti got his balance back and raised his sword, the tip aimed at Quentin's chest. I had no more running left in me. It was all I could do to stay upright, still stumbling forward, knowing that I would never get there in time. On my best day, I couldn't have made it there in time. There are races in Faerie who can bend space, sling fire, and freeze their enemies with a glance. All I could do was refuse to fall down and die. And it wasn't enough.

Quentin didn't make a sound. He didn't even move. He just stared up at the Folletti standing over him, his hands balled into fists and still held down by the ropes that bound him.

I was so distracted with the effort of staying upright and moving that I barely heard the gunshot. The Folletti who was standing over Quentin stiffened, his sword dropping from his hands before he pitched forward, landing on Quentin with a thud. There was a second gunshot. I whipped around—too fast, way, way too fast, according to the still-gaping wound in my abdomen—to see Officer Thornton standing at the edge of the clearing, his service weapon held at arm's length. One of the temporarily blinded Folletti must have dropped it. If Officer Thornton had been hiding in the brush, he would have seen his chance when the gun hit the ground.

As to how he wasn't blinded, I guess there are some advantages to having less sensitive eyesight.

"All you ... you ... whatever you people are, drop your weapons!" he shouted. "Drop them *right now!*" Prolonged exposure to Faerie isn't good for human sanity. From the look on Officer Thornton's face, he was finding that out firsthand.

Riordan scowled. "Where the fuck are my guards?" she shouted. With a sound like the wind, screaming, the Folletti finally descended on the officer.

I was injured, and he was the one with the gun. Much as I wanted to worry about him, I couldn't afford to. I turned back toward Quentin, forcing myself to keep going, and finally dropped to my knees next to his chair. Pulling the bloody knife from my belt, I began sawing through the twists of braided bracken that held him.

"Toby!" Quentin's eyes went wide, fixing on my middle. "You're hurt!"

"Understatement of the week," I said, still sawing. "I'll be fine. Can I borrow your shirt? I need something to bind the wound so I can use both my hands." The blackness had receded to the edges of my vision. I honestly didn't know whether that was a good sign or not.

"What happened?"

"Samson. Again. What is it about Cait Sidhe and disemboweling me? Do they need more hobbies?" The last of the bracken holding Quentin in place snapped. I leaned back, only wincing a little as the motion pulled on the skin of my stomach. I was out of resources. This was taking too long to heal.

Quentin rolled out of the chair and scrambled to his feet before pulling his shirt off and offering it to me. That gave me an excellent view of his injuries, which weren't as severe as Tybalt's or Etienne's, being confined to massive bruising of his abdomen, throat, and arms. It was still enough to make bile rise in my throat, barely outpacing the rising tide of rage.

I took the shirt and wound it around my stomach, tying it as firmly as I could with the blood soaking through the fabric. "Help me up," I said, once I was sure the knot would hold. Quentin reached down and took my arm, pulling me to my feet. "Come on."

Officer Thornton was keeping the Folletti occupied on the other side of the clearing. I hadn't been counting gunshots, but the odds were good they hadn't either; most of them probably had no idea how many bullets were in a standard sidearm. The latest of Riordan's wagons had rolled clear of the portal, its drivers looking with confusion and awe at the landscape . . .

And on the other side of the portal I could see Tybalt creeping up behind Chelsea, moving slowly, so as to remain as much a part of the scenery as possible. She seemed oblivious to his approach. That was good. That meant he might actually be able to get hold of her. All he had to do was grab her, get her through the portal, and not stop to think about what that was going to mean for the rest of us.

No Chelsea, no portal to Annwn. No portal to Annwn, no way we were getting out of here. "I hope he can forgive me," I murmured. At least we had farming supplies. We really could take over one of those castles, as I'd been joking with Raj about.

We probably wouldn't paint it pink, though.

Quentin followed my gaze. His eyes widened as he realized what my plan had to be. Then he nodded and offered me his arm. "You look like you're going to fall over."

"That's because I am," I said, taking his arm and leaning on it heavily, grateful for the support. Then I paused, frowning. "Wait. Where's Etienne? He didn't reappear after the Folletti—"

"Behind you!" shouted Etienne.

We whipped around to see one of Riordan's empty wagons bearing down on us with Etienne on the driver's seat. He rode past us and pulled the horses to a stop. "Get in!"

Quentin scrambled to obey, crawling up into the back of the wagon before turning to pull me up after him. I helped as much as I could, finally collapsing onto the rough wood. He put a hand on my shoulder, steadying me. Then he turned and bolted for the front of the wagon, joining Etienne on the driver's seat.

I heard, rather than saw, what came next.

"Take the reins!" shouted Etienne. The smell of cedar smoke and limes drifted back to where I was lying, and the wagon started moving again, rattling across the uneven ground with bone-shaking jerks and bounces. I was in enough pain that I didn't care as much as I might have. I just lay there, watching the sky pass overhead, and wondered what was going to happen.

More gunshots in the distance; more screaming from the Folletti. And then a hand grabbed hold of the foot of the wagon, and Duchess Treasa Riordan yanked herself up into view. Her face was distorted by rage, and there were bits of broom in her red-black hair. She grabbed for me, snarling, "All you had to do was stay out of the way, you stupid little half-blood bitch! I was giving you people what you always wanted! I was getting out of your precious territory!"

I managed to shove myself out of her grasp—barely—before saying, "You shouldn't have started by kidnapping kids if you didn't want me to get involved." I kicked at her hand. She shifted her grip out of my reach, and kept pulling herself up, while Quentin continued to drive us, full-speed, toward the portal.

Riordan reached into her shirt, producing a slender knife. It was a ritual blade, the kind some Daoine Sidhe purebloods use when a spell calls for bloodletting—like the tool you use to hurt yourself can somehow make the act less painful. And it didn't matter, because I was already so hurt that one more injury might well push me over the point of no return. I tried to scramble farther toward the front of the wagon, pushing against the wood with my ankles and elbows.

Light glinted off the ruby around her neck. The ruby . . . in Samson's earliest memories, she'd been wearing a diamond, but after she got hold of Chelsea, the stone changed color. And Riordan made blood charms. Suddenly, I understood how she'd been calling Chelsea back to her over and over again. All it took was a little bit of blood. Any extra would have been used to craft the teleportation charms she'd been giving to Samson.

He was the one who opened the door to the Fire Kingdoms. He killed Tybalt. The realization made me furious and tired at the same time—it was just one thing too many.

And not everything had been dealt with. "Changeling children exist to be disposable," said Riordan, getting to her feet. She straightened, holding the knife in front of her as she effortlessly kept her balance in the jouncing wagon. "Why else would anyone lower themselves to copulating with a *mortal?*"

I kicked at her again. She stepped aside. "Children are *never* disposable!"

"Spoken like someone who should have been drowned before she could grow up to bother her betters." Riordan shook her head. "You're still a changeling. Even if you spoil things for me, no one's going to be able to touch me."

"Quentin's not a changeling," I gasped, levering myself into a half-seated position, with my shoulders braced against the back of the driver's platform. Raising my voice, I shouted, "Quentin! Drive faster!"

"The horses don't go any faster than this!" Quentin shouted back. He sounded strained, but not worried. That could only mean one thing.

He didn't know Riordan was in the wagon.

Riordan herself grinned, clearly coming to the same conclusion, and took a step toward me. I fumbled my own knife from my belt, holding it in front of me. I wasn't going to scream. No matter what, I wasn't going to scream. If there was any chance of Quentin getting out of here—if he could keep his panicked horses under control long enough to get to the portal that Chelsea was still holding open—then I had to make sure he would take it, and that meant not distracting him with my own impending stabbing.

"I really hate you," I muttered, trying to get into a defensible position. It wasn't working. I'd lost too much blood, and my body was giving up on me.

"The feeling's mutual, sugar," said Riordan, and raised her knife.

Tybalt seemed to appear out of nowhere, vaulting over the side of the wagon and grabbing Riordan by the throat. His teeth were too large for his mouth, distorting it until there was no way he could have managed human speech. He didn't need to. The roar he directed into Riordan's face made his message perfectly clear.

"Tybalt!" I shouted. "The charm!"

He grabbed Riordan's ruby with his free hand, yanking it loose and tossing it to me. I caught it, barely. Then he lifted her, struggling, and flung her off the back of the wagon. She screamed as she fell. I didn't see her hit the ground.

"October!" Tybalt rushed over to me, dropping to his knees as he tried to gather me into his arms and check my injuries at the same time. It was an impossible task. He did his best. "Are you all right?"

Manic giggles bubbled from my lips before I could stop them. I pressed my forehead into his shoulder, and said, "No. Not even a little." Then I stiffened. "Tybalt, Chelsea—"

"Etienne has her. He's helping her keep the portal stable long enough for us to get through." Tybalt raised his head, looking past me to where Quentin was steering us, hell-bent, toward the portal. "We're almost there. Can you hold on?"

"I made it this far, didn't I?" I tucked the ruby into my pocket and closed my eyes. Sometimes the hardest part of heroism is admitting that the battle is out of your hands. This wasn't my fight anymore. It was Etienne's, and Chelsea's, and Quentin's race against a changeling girl's endurance. All I could do was let Tybalt hold me and try to pretend that I wasn't still bleeding. At least it was slowing down. Maybe that was a good sign. Or maybe I was just running out of blood.

My wounds weren't closing. The damage was done.

The smell of sycamore smoke and calla lilies grew as we approached the portal. Tybalt snarled, carefully settling me on the wagon floor, before leaping to his feet and swatting something out of the air. One of the surviving Folletti screamed. I sort of wished I could lever my eyes open long enough to watch. Then the smell of smoke and lilies became overwhelming, and the whole wagon shuddered, shaking hard from side to side.

The ground beneath us changed textures, going from uneven earth to the smoothly polished stone of Duchess Riordan's "parking garage." Chelsea wailed, and I heard Etienne answer her. I couldn't make out words, but his tone was soothing. The wagon slid to a halt. Almost immediately, a hot wave of magic washed over us, mingling the scents of smoke, calla lilies, and limes. Etienne was helping his daughter close the portal.

Somewhere behind us, Riordan screamed, the sound cutting off in the middle, as if a plug had been pulled—or a hole had been closed.

"October?" Tybalt's voice was close enough that I knew he had to be right beside me. I just couldn't have said exactly where. "October?!"

There are limits to everybody's endurance. Mine have changed a lot in recent years, but they still exist, and I had reached them. With a sigh, I stopped clinging to consciousness and let myself tumble the rest of the way into the dark.

TWENTY-FIVE

I'M NOT SURE WHICH was more surprising: that I woke up in the white velvet room off Duchess Riordan's entry hall or that I woke up at all. I blinked up at the ceiling, realizing a moment later that the light levels had changed. The globes of floating witchlight were gone, replaced by a portable array of modern-looking fluorescent lights. "What the—?"

"She's awake!" I recognized Jin's voice before she leaned into my field of vision, scowling down at me. "By which I mean, of course, 'She's miraculously not dead, again,' since by all rights, you *should* be. Oberon must really love your dumb ass."

"Jin?" I levered myself into a sitting position, blinking at her. We were alone in the room, but only on a technicality; I could see faces peeking around the edges of the doorframe behind her. Tybalt, Quentin—and May, of all people. "What's going on?"

"You nearly died. *Again.* I put you back together. *Again.* Oh, and you owe Tybalt and May so many favors I can't even put it into words, since he's the one who made sure we both got here, and she's the one who donated three pints of blood to your sorry ass." Jin folded her arms and scowled at me, her wings vibrating into a hazy blur behind her. "Congratulations, you've figured out where your crazy healing powers stop working. You should be dead."

"You already said that." My mouth tasted like road kill. I licked my lips, which tasted like blood—not much of an improvement, all things considered.

"I intend to keep saying it until you start to listen. You. Should. Be. Dead." Jin looked over her shoulder, calling, "She's awake, and there's nothing I can do to make her less stupid. You can come in now."

Tybalt was the first into the room, with Quentin close on his heels. I expected May to be right behind them. I was wrong. Instead, Li Qin sauntered in, an In-and-Out Burger takeout bag dangling from one hand. She held it up while Tybalt and Quentin bent to crush me from either side in an exuberant hug and asked, "Hungry?"

As if on cue, I was suddenly starving. "Yes," I said, sitting up farther and freeing one arm to reach for the bag. "What are you doing here? Where did these lights come from?"

"Ah. You see, the regent of Dreamer's Glass has disappeared under mysterious circumstances, and the nobles she shares a border with were concerned, especially since she left no named heir. So Tamed Lightning decided to occupy her fiefdom. Just in case people get ideas they shouldn't." Li Qin's smile was surprisingly predatory as she gave me the bag. "Naturally, if she fails to return, we'll be claiming the regency. It's only fair, considering we'll be expending resources in her defense."

"And the lights . . . ?" I opened the bag, grabbed the first burger, unwrapped it, and crammed about a quarter of it into my mouth. Calories. Thank Maeve.

"Home Depot, with one of April's Summerlands-compatible batteries powering them." Li Qin's smile died as quickly as it had come. That was good. It had been starting to creep me out. "We have a problem."

I swallowed. "Don't we always? What is it this time?"

"Chelsea," said Tybalt, pulling away from me. His voice was grim. I looked toward him. He met my eyes, shaking his head. "She's still bouncing, and she's speeding up. Etienne is following her, and she's managed to stay out of Annwn so far, but I don't know how long he can keep up—and I don't know what's going to happen when he loses her."

I winced. "Oh, Oberon's eyes. Did you try catching them?"

"In between running for your doctor and your Fetch? Yes." A humorless smile crossed Tybalt's face. "I once thought myself a King of infinite space. It seems a Tuatha in panicked pursuit of his daughter can put a girdle 'round the earth in forty minutes."

"Okay, points for the Shakespeare references, but you lose some for mixing your plays." I pushed Quentin gently away and levered myself to my feet, noting the way my head spun as I stood. That was a combination of vertigo and needing to eat more of the burgers Li Qin had so thoughtfully provided. "We need to find them. We need to stop her before she damages something we can't repair."

"How are you planning to do that?" asked May. "I mean, they were moving pretty fast the last time we saw them. It's not like you'll have time to string a net."

"It's not like we're going to need to." I took another bite of burger, swallowing it without really tasting it before I said, "Chelsea herself said that she kept cycling back to places she'd already been, like she couldn't help opening those doors over and over. Riordan was using blood magic. I have the charm she was using. We can get Chelsea to come here."

"How are you going to stop her?" asked May.

I stuck my free hand into the pocket of my leather jacket—now in need of a serious cleaning—and produced the baggie holding Walther's jar of power-dampening solution. "I'm going to hit her with a guaranteed stop sign. And then I'm going to give her the Changeling's Choice, whether she wants to take it or not."

May's eyes widened. Then her expression softened, with a mixture of sorrow and understanding. "Toby, I'm sorry."

She wasn't sorry because I had to give the Choice to Chelsea. She was sorry because the only other person I'd given the Choice to was my own daughter . . . and Gillian Chose human. I shook my head. "We knew this was coming. I just hope I'm up to it. Tybalt, Quentin, I want you with me in case something goes wrong."

"I'm coming, too," said May. I raised an eyebrow. She shrugged. "I *am* indestructible. You just think you are. I figure I'll jump in front of the next thing that tries to rip your guts out."

"You'll need me to bend the luck," said Li. "Successfully using someone else's blood charm is unlikely under the best of circumstances. Without me, you won't have the best of circumstances."

I gave her a sidelong look. "There's something you aren't telling us about how your magic works. Otherwise, why would anything ever go wrong for the people around you?" *Why would your wife have died?*

Li Qin hesitated before admitting, in a smaller voice, "There may be a reason you've had quite so many life-threatening injuries since we met."

"And here I thought she was finally living up to her potential," said Quentin.

"I have the power to ground you, you know," I said. He grinned at me. I shook my head and focused on Li Qin. "So the luck you bend, you have to take it from somewhere? And that means what, that we wind up with little pockets of bad luck waiting for us?"

"Sometimes the bad hits before the good, but yes, essentially," said Li Qin.

I only had to think about what she was saying for a second. "Works for me," I said. "Come on, all of you. And Li—this is the last time I want you twisting our luck around, okay? We get Chelsea home, and then you let us take our chances with normal probability."

"Absolutely," said Li Qin, looking relieved.

"Great. Let's go."

We walked down the dimly lit halls of Riordan's

knowe in silence, me too busy cramming burgers into my mouth to say anything, and the others holding their peace for reasons of their own. Tybalt paced next to me, eyes fixed forward. I gave him a sidelong glance and reached over to take his hand. He shot me a startled look. I smiled. After a moment, he smiled back.

Riordan's throne room looked like the scene of a war. In a way, I suppose it was. The tapestries had been ripped from the walls by a strong wind, and there were charred spots on the walls. A patch of the marble floor looked like it had been bleached white. I paused, reaching down to touch the stone, and yelped as I lost a layer of skin to the freezing chill.

"She's hitting the Snow Kingdoms, too," I said, straightening up. "On the plus side, we know she's cycling through here."

"Accompanied by lava flow, blizzards, and Maeve knows what else," said Tybalt dryly. "Oh, yes, this is a definite plus."

"I'm taking my good things where I can get them right now," I said, and I stuck my frostbitten hand into the In-and-Out bag to grab the last burger. The spinning feeling in my head was almost gone. "Quentin, May, I want you on the other side of the room. Li, take the floor in front of the throne. Tybalt and I will wait here."

May frowned. "And you're splitting the party Scooby Doo-style exactly why?"

"Because when Chelsea comes through here, we need to be ready to tackle her and pin her down long enough for one of us to douse her in power dampener. Quentin has a dose; so do I. Tybalt can cross the distance to Li Qin if he needs to—"

"—but my luck manipulation means that wherever I'm standing in the room is where Chelsea is *least* likely to appear, which is why I'm by myself," said Li. She glanced at me. "Am I close?"

"Yeah, but you're also standing by yourself because I'm annoyed at you for getting me disemboweled. Twice.

I'd managed to go my whole life without having someone stick their hands inside me, and I was planning to keep it that way."

Li Qin smiled lopsidedly. "You only got hurt because I helped so much."

"That's why I'm annoyed, not homicidally enraged. Does anybody else want to argue with me right now?"

"I always want to argue with you," said May, and grabbed Quentin's arm. "Come on, kiddo. Let's get out of the blast radius." Quentin laughed, letting himself be dragged away. With an amused snort, Li Qin turned and walked to the spot I'd assigned her.

As soon as the last bite of burger was crammed into my mouth and swallowed, I dug Riordan's ruby out of my pocket. I dropped it on the floor and stomped on it. It shattered with a satisfying "crunch." The smell of blood—Chelsea's blood—filled the air. I couldn't use someone else's blood charm, but I could use the blood itself. "Come back," I murmured, fixing the image of Chelsea in my mind. "Come back, and be free."

After that, there was nothing we could do but wait. I was out of burgers, so I started finger-combing my hair, wincing every time I hit a snarl. Tybalt raised an eyebrow. "I thought I was the one who was meant to indulge in self-grooming in public."

"I'm nervous." I sighed, letting my hands drop. "When Chelsea gets here . . ."

"You'll do what must be done."

"No matter what she chooses, she's losing one of her parents. She's only just met Etienne."

"The decision is hers, October." Tybalt placed a hand on my shoulder. "Changelings Choose because they must belong to one world or the other. You can grant her the gift of truly belonging in the world that she chooses. View it as a blessing, not a burden. I've seen too many changelings die for lack of someone like you."

I sighed again, leaning into his hand. "Who gave you permission to know me this well?"

"Believe it or not, little fish . . . you did."

I was mulling that over when the smell of calla lilies and sycamore smoke started to suffuse the room. I stiffened. "Everybody get ready!"

The words were barely out of my mouth when a hole opened in the middle of the ceiling and Chelsea tumbled out, like a lost Alice plummeting into Wonderland. She made a small, wounded sound when she hit the marble, scrambling almost immediately to her feet. Her eyes widened when she saw us.

"Stay back!" she shouted. "You have to stay back! I don't know when I'm going to jump again!"

A second hole opened next to the first, and Etienne dropped through. Unlike his daughter, he landed on his feet. Both were dirty, with scorch marks on their clothing. Etienne was missing a shoe and looked like he was on the verge of collapse. Chelsea looked even worse.

There was no way I could get to them in time. But I didn't need to. Pulling the jar of power dampener out of my pocket, I yanked off the baggie and shouted, "Etienne! Think fast!" He looked up just as I threw it at him as hard as I could. His eyes widened, and he snatched the jar out of the air.

Tybalt grabbed my arm. "The plan—"

"I don't want you touching that stuff. No shapeshifters, remember?"

Across the room, Etienne was struggling with the lid of the jar. Passage through searing cold and magical portals seemed to have done an excellent job of tightening it; he was a trained knight, and the lid wasn't even budging.

"Daddy!" wailed Chelsea. The air around her was starting to glitter again.

Etienne swore loudly enough for me to hear him, and he stepped closer to Chelsea before flinging the jar at the floor. It exploded, showering glass and power-dampening potion in all directions—including on Chelsea and her father. The glitter in the air died as the solution hit Chelsea's skin. She stared at Etienne.

"What did you do? How did you stop me?"

He didn't say anything. He just reached out, gathered her into his arms, and hugged his daughter for the first time.

I waited long enough for them to finish their embrace before starting toward them, stopping well outside the splash radius from the broken jar. "All better?"

Etienne looked up, raw gratitude painting his face. "Yes. Thank you, October. I don't know how I can ever repay you."

"Don't thank me yet," I said, holding up my hand. The gratitude in his expression died, replaced by broken-hearted understanding. "There's still something I have to do."

"I understand." He let go of Chelsea. "Do what must be done."

Chelsea looked up at him, confusion and betrayal in her eyes. "Daddy?"

It was amazing, and a little bit heartbreaking, how fast Etienne had become "Daddy" to her. She must have wondered all her life about the man who'd provided the genes that made her not quite human. I just hoped I wasn't about to take her away from him forever.

"It's all right, Chelsea. You need to go to October. She'll make everything better."

"I'll try, anyway," I said, and forced what I hoped would look like a sincere smile. "Hi, Chelsea. Can you come over here?" I paused before adding, "Wipe your hands really, really dry first, okay? I need to hold them, and it's sort of important we not get any of that goo on me."

"Is the goo why I stopped jumping?" I nodded. She smiled shyly. "Okay." Chelsea started toward me, rubbing her hands against the seat of her pants as she approached. When she reached me, she held them out, showing me that they were dry.

"Good." I took one hand, drawing my knife with the other. Her eyes widened, but she didn't pull away. "I need to ask you a question, and I need you to give me an honest answer. It's important. You have to answer for you, and not for your parents—either one of them. Can you do that here, or do you want to go somewhere private?"

Chelsea glanced back at Etienne, who was watching us with a silent, burning intensity. She turned back to me. "I can answer."

"Okay. Chelsea, when you think about yourself, your place in the world . . . do you think of yourself as human? Or do you think of yourself as fae?"

It seemed like the whole room held its breath, waiting for Chelsea to answer. I know I wasn't breathing. No matter how she answered, what I was going to do to her would hurt. I'd done it to my own daughter, but Gillian was unconscious at the time; she didn't understand the source of the pain. Chelsea would understand. She'd know I was the one doing this horrible thing to her. I didn't know her well enough to know whether she'd be able to forgive me.

Chelsea frowned, looking down toward her feet. A drop of the power dampener was on the toe of her shoe, glistening slickly. "When I was little, all I wanted was to be normal, so Mom wouldn't have to spend all her time worrying about me," she said slowly. "All the other kids got to have sleepovers and do sports, and I had to pretend I wanted to grow up to be Mr. Spock or one of Tolkien's elves."

"I bet you made a great Arwen at Halloween," I said.

"Yeah." She glanced up at me, smiling—a quick, shy thing that died just as fast. "But I'm not human, am I? I've never been human. All the wishing in the world can't make me human."

All the wishing in the world can't, but I can, I thought. Aloud, I said only, "So what are you? Human, or fae?"

"Does it have to be one or the other?" Chelsea looked at me hopefully, eyes searching my face for an answer. My silence must have been answer enough. Chelsea sighed. "I'm fae. I wanted to be human, but I'm not. I wouldn't know how to start. I'm me, and being me means being fae."

"Okay." I took a breath, not sure how to say what needed to be said. Finally, I settled for just coming out with it: "Chelsea, right now, you're dangerous. The way you've been jumping isn't normal for Tuatha de Dannan like you and your father. It's because you're half-human. Usually, being half-human means you're less powerful. Sometimes it means the opposite. Sometimes it means you get all the power in the world and nothing to help you control it."

Chelsea frowned. "So how do we fix that?"

Here it was. "I take the human out of you."

"You can *do* that?" Her eyes widened. "Can you put it back if I change my mind?"

"No. Once it's done, it's done forever, but you won't be dangerous anymore. You'll be able to learn to control your powers. You'll have a normal life." A life that would last for centuries, if not millennia.

Chelsea bit her lip. Then, marginally, she nodded.

I didn't let myself look up. I didn't want to see the look on Etienne's face as I turned her hand so that her palm was facing toward the ceiling and ran the edge of my blade—clean, thanks to someone's efforts while I was asleep, and keen-edged enough to slice through skin without a hitch—across the center of it. Blood welled up immediately, scenting the air with its presence.

I repeated the process with my own hand before sheathing my knife again. Raising my hand to my lips, I got a mouthful of blood. Then I bent, and pressed my mouth against the cut on Chelsea's hand in a parody of a kiss.

My magic rose around us in a heavy cloud, the smell of copper all but overwhelming the smell of fresh-cut grass. There was a momentary pause as Chelsea's body tried to figure out what happening.

Then Chelsea screamed like she was being murdered and tried to jerk her hand away.

Etienne was abruptly there, holding her in place. "No, Chelsea, shh, it's all right, honey, you have to be still. Let October work. It will be over soon. Let her work."

Chelsea screamed again. I did my best to shut her out and focus on what I was doing: reaching for the tangled threads of humanity that wound through her and pulling them free, one by one. I patched the holes with Tuatha de Dannan, expanding the other part of her heritage until it was all she had. She was still screaming, her voice growing hoarse, and I was getting lost in the dark tangles of her self, the places where human and fae collided and made her something unique in all of Faerie.

Somewhere in her was the answer to what made some changelings too powerful to live; the key to that strange, unavoidable quirk of biology. But I didn't know what to look for, and so I wiped it away, along with everything else that made her human. I wiped it all away.

When I straightened up, Chelsea was slumped against her father, unconscious. I hadn't even noticed when she stopped screaming. The world around me spun. What I'd done with Gillian hadn't taken half as much power. She'd been less than a quarter fae. Chelsea, on the other hand, was the real deal, half and half. I felt like something had been ripped out of me in the process of changing her.

"Thank you," whispered Etienne.

"Any . . . time . . ." I said, through numb lips. Then I fell backward and was only distantly aware of Tybalt's arms coming up to catch me as the darkness closed in again.

I woke up back in the white velvet room. Li Qin was gone, as were Quentin and May. In their place were Etienne, kneeling next to the couch where Chelsea was sprawled, and Sylvester, standing off to one side and watching the scene with an unreadable expression on his face. Only Tybalt remained the same. His leg was the pillow my head was resting on.

Sylvester smiled a little when my eyes opened. "Welcome back to the land of the living, my dear. In more ways than one."

"Annwn is not a good tourist destination. Just an FYI." I struggled to sit up. Tybalt put a hand under my back, supporting me. "When did you get here?"

"About an hour ago. Your King of Cats thought I might want to be here and came to fetch me." Sylvester seemed amused by this.

I considered telling him Tybalt wasn't *my* King of Cats but decided it wasn't worth the fight—and besides, that might not be true anymore. Instead, I focused on the important question. "How's Chelsea?"

"Asleep while she recovers. Jin has been in and out since you both blacked out. It's impressive, the language she uses when she feels that you've been risking your life needlessly." Sylvester's smile died. "Why didn't you call?"

"Etienne asked me not to."

"Since when does he command you? You could have died."

"I didn't."

"Don't split hairs with me, October."

"I gave him my word. He was worried about his daughter. He didn't mean to get me hurt." I bit my lip. "Please don't be mad."

"I can't help being angry and disappointed. And yet . . ." Sylvester looked toward Etienne. To his credit, Etienne raised his head and met his liege's eyes without flinching. "I suppose I would have done the same in his position, and he's been more than suitably chastened. Still, I will miss his talents for the next year or so."

"The next—oh, oak and ash." I grimaced. "The power dampener."

"In the chaos, no one thought to use the antidote," said Etienne. His voice was calm. "What is a year, compared to a daughter? A price gladly paid."

"I'm sorry."

"Don't be." Etienne reached over and brushed a lock of Chelsea's hair away from her face. Her cheekbones were more pronounced than they'd been before, and her ears were more pointed. The color of her hair hadn't changed, but I was willing to bet she wouldn't be able to hide her eyes behind tinted glasses anymore. "I've gained more than I could have dreamed."

"About that . . ." I took a breath. "Bridget still knows about Faerie. You're going to have to deal with her. And the fact that she really did lose her daughter when you came back into her life. There's no way Chelsea's going back to the mortal world now."

"I know." Etienne looked up. "Will you come with me? She knows you."

"If by 'knows' you mean 'tried to hit me with a frying pan,' sure." I leaned back into the couch, closing my eyes. "But I am going to need a *lot* of coffee before you can convince me to go anywhere."

TWENTY-SIX

THERE WAS SOMETHING WEIRD about having Etienne in the car, rather than having him teleport us all to our destination. The fact that I was maintaining his illusions was even stranger. Quentin was in the back with Chelsea, keeping up the illusion that made her look human. Between the two of us, we were almost up to the challenge.

When this was over, I was going to spend a week sitting on the couch, watching television, and not using any damn magic at all.

I pulled up in front of Bridget's house, turning to look at Etienne. He looked back at me, edges slightly blurred by my hasty human disguise. "Are you sure you're up for this?"

"This is something I should have done sixteen years ago," he replied. "Chelsea?"

Chelsea sighed. "I don't think it's going to get any easier if we put it off."

"If it were done . . ." I muttered. More loudly, I said, "You're right. Okay, everybody. Let's go."

Etienne and Chelsea were the first out of the car. I lagged behind, and Quentin did the same, waiting until the passenger-side doors were closed before he asked, "Do you think Bridget's going to go after us with her frying pan?"

"Just be ready to run," I advised as I opened my door. It was a little ironic; here we were, escorting the most powerful teleporter in the last few hundred years to her mother's house, and we didn't have a means of making a quick escape if we needed one. Tybalt had gone to check on Raj as soon as Chelsea was ready to make the trip to her mother's house. We'd stopped at Tamed Lightning long enough for Elliot to work a little Bannick magic on everyone's skin and hair, while April produced fresh clothes from an undisclosed location. I just hoped she hadn't robbed an Old Navy or something.

Oh, well. Not my problem if she did.

Bridget must have been watching the street. She was out her front door by the time I was out of the car, and she intercepted Etienne and their daughter midway down the front walk. I saw the frying pan in her hand a split second before she flung its contents over both of them, resulting in Chelsea and Etienne being doused again with Walther's power-dampening solution.

Etienne blinked. Chelsea blinked. Bridget dropped the frying pan, threw her arms around her daughter, and burst into tears.

Quentin gave me a sidelong look. "Did you hold back because you knew that was going to happen?"

"I suspected it might. It was either going to be something like that, or it was going to be water balloons." I gestured for him to follow as I started up the walk. Bridget was still hugging Chelsea. Possibly a little too tightly—I wasn't sure the girl could breathe. "Hi, Bridget. Nice use of aim, there. I'm glad I didn't go first."

"The bastard deserves it." Bridget lifted her head, glaring daggers at Etienne, who looked uncomfortable. "He can learn how it feels to live like the rest of us mortals."

Etienne's look of discomfort deepened. "Bridget, please. Can we take this indoors?"

"Why?"

"Mom," said Chelsea. She sounded more tired than any girl her age should be capable of being. "We need to go inside."

Bridget looked at Chelsea, the animation draining from her face. Finally, she nodded. "All right, sweetheart. We'll go inside. All of us."

"Can we get some towels?" asked Chelsea.

Bridget didn't answer her. She didn't even smile. She just walked a little faster, reaching the door ahead of the rest of us, and she held it open while Etienne and Chelsea walked past. For a moment, I thought she was going to slam the door on me and Quentin, but she relented before she did more than twitch in that direction. "Come in if you're coming," she said.

"We're coming," I replied, and walked past her into the house.

Silence fell once the door was shut, all of us standing there like strangers, no one quite sure where to begin. Finally, Etienne said, "October. The masks, if you would be so kind."

"Right." I gave Quentin a nod, and together, we released the illusions that made us look human. There was a pause as Bridget got her first look at Etienne without a mask between them. She'd never really seen the father of her child before. There was something incredibly sad about that.

Then she saw Chelsea. The details that seemed subtle to me must have been glaring to her mother's eyes. Bridget's face went so pale I was afraid she might pass out. "Chelsea?" she whispered, in a voice that seemed as faint as wind in the trees.

"She had to, Mom," said Chelsea. "It was the only way to make me stop jumping. I was going to get a lot of people hurt if I didn't stop. This was to save me." She shrugged, smiling a little as she added the bravest lie I had ever heard: "It didn't hurt."

"What did you do?" Bridget wheeled on me, clearly seizing on the word "she" as proof of my guilt. "You fairy-tale bitch, *what* did you do to my daughter?!"

"I saved her life," I said, as calmly as I could. "She's not human anymore. Not even half. But she's still your little girl, and she's still here. That's better than it could have gone."

Bridget stared at me. Then, bitterly, she turned to Etienne. "So you've won. You've stolen her after all."

"No, Bess," said Etienne. His tone was gentle. "I don't want to steal her. I *never* wanted to steal her. Had you told me about her sixteen years ago, I wouldn't have stolen her then. Things might have gone differently over these last few days . . . but I wouldn't have stolen her from you."

"Then . . ." Bridget stopped, taking a breath before she continued, "Then can she stay with me? Can everything be like it was? Will you leave us alone?"

"No, Bess," said Etienne again, even more gently. "I can't do that. Faerie has rules. You know that as well as anyone."

"Ah." She straightened. "Then you're to kill me, are you?"

"What?" squeaked Chelsea, eyes going wide.

"I'd rather not," said Etienne. "You can't stay here, knowing what you know. And Chelsea can't stay with you—she's Chosen Faerie, and that means she has certain obligations to it, even as I have obligations to her. But there is another way."

I stiffened. Beside me, Quentin did the same. This wasn't something Etienne had mentioned on the ride over here, and oak and ash, I was afraid to hear what he might say next.

Bridget paused, expression cycling from misery to disbelief to thoughtful canniness. She looked at Etienne and asked, "You're offering to take me into Faerie, aren't you?"

He nodded. "I am. There is precedent."

"How recent?"

Now Etienne cracked a smile. "Not for a very, very long time. But if you'd come, Bess, if you'd live with me beneath the hill, swear to keep our secrets, and let me claim you as my responsibility, you could stay with your daughter, and you and I . . ." He paused, and shrugged, and said, "We could try again. We have reason to, now. It's not like you'll ever be quit of me."

"No," said Bridget. "I don't suppose I will."

"How would this work?" I asked. "I don't mean to sound, I don't know, pessimistic, but no one's taken a human into Faerie in a long time."

"There are rules," said Etienne, in a tone that implied he knew exactly what every one of them was, how to use them, and how to bend them without breaking them. "If my liege agrees, I may claim her as my own."

"He's right," said Quentin.

"It's your funeral," I said. I glanced to Bridget, and added, "No offense."

Her smile was faint, but it was there. "None taken." She focused back on Etienne. "I'll not quit my job, you know."

"Nor would I ask you to," he said. "With the proper geas, you can come and go as you like, and no one will ever need fear that you would reveal us."

Bridget frowned. "I'll want to see the wording. I do have classes to teach."

Etienne laughed. Chelsea smiled. And for the first time in a while, I started feeling like maybe things would be all right.

TWENTY-SEVEN

TWO NIGHTS SLIPPED BY in a haze of questions, phone calls, and cleaning the house. The damage Samson had done was so extensive that it took longer to clean up than it took for our wounds to fade, since we had magical healing but didn't have a magical cleaning service. Several times, I considered going to Tamed Lightning and begging to borrow Elliot. Every time, I put the thought aside. Cleaning the house was something we could all do together, and that was important. We needed to feel like a family again. We had gone too long without really being one. *I* had gone too long without really being part of the family we made.

At the end of the second night, I went out into the backyard and sat down with a cup of coffee in one hand, watching the sky get lighter. Dawn was approaching fast. Inside, May and Jazz were sound asleep, the one at the end of her day, the other getting ready for hers to begin. Quentin was at Shadowed Hills, helping Chelsea get acclimated. He'd be back after he got a good morning's sleep. I wasn't all that worried.

Li Qin was holding Dreamer's Glass for the moment, while the Queen of the Mists looked into the "mysterious disappearance" of Duchess Treasa Riordan. Somehow, I didn't think she was going to find much. Li Qin would hold the Duchy until everyone politely forgot she wasn't supposed to be there, and then she would officially take over. With most of Riordan's subjects stranded in Annwn with her, it was unlikely that anyone would object.

Riordan and her subjects weren't the only ones stranded in Annwn. Officer Michael Thornton of the San Francisco Police Department was also among the missing, and with Oberon as my witness, I had absolutely no idea how we were supposed to get him back again, or if he was even still alive. At least the SFPD didn't seem to have connected me to his disappearance. I hadn't noticed them looking for him at all. One last bit of Li Qin's luck, working in our favor. Hopefully, any bad luck rebound would fall on her. Two disembowelments were about my limit.

Getting Officer Thornton back was something for the Luidaeg to worry about. When I called her, she yelled at me for leaving her charm in Annwn, told me to bring her a box of donuts on Sunday, and hung up on me. Sometimes it's nice to have a few predictable things in life. It was almost dawn, and Chelsea was with her parents, and I finally had room to breathe.

Room to breathe—and time to wait. I'd been waiting for two days. I gave the sky another look, frowning a little at how light it was getting. I'd need to go inside soon. "I can give him another minute," I muttered to myself, and took a sip of coffee.

"I'd like more than just a minute, if I may," said Tybalt. I looked to my left. He was there, watching me with a guarded anxiousness in his eyes. "I assume you were waiting for me?"

"You assume right. What took you so long?"

"I had affairs to settle. Raj was, understandably, upset. He sends his regrets and promises to return here soon. As for the rest of the Court . . ." Tybalt clucked his tongue. "I doubt any of those who remain will mirror Samson's folly any time soon. Those who were loyal to him have left my lands—and no, I didn't kill them. I simply made them understand that it was time to seek residence elsewhere."

"That's reassuring." I took another sip of coffee, studying Tybalt. He was casually dressed, in jeans and a dark T-shirt that matched the stripes in his hair. He could have been anyone.

He was the only person I wanted to see.

He saw me looking and said, "I didn't feel the need to dress up for you." He sounded slightly abashed, as though this was the wrong answer.

It was the best answer I'd ever heard. "I'm not exactly dressed for the ball, here," I said, waving a hand to indicate my attire. "The best I can do is tell you that I've taken a shower since the last time you saw me. Several, actually."

"Decadent," he said, with a small, uncertain smile.

I took a deep breath, putting my coffee down on the step. It was now or never, and I was definitely not in the mood for "never." Standing, I took a step toward Tybalt and offered my hands. He hesitated for only a second before he took them.

"You said you loved me," I said. "Did you mean it?"

"With all my heart. October—"

"Do you know how long I've been telling myself you hated me? Or how hard it's been to keep believing it? You'd do things, these amazing, insane things, like stealing me back from Blind Michael or breaking me out of jail, and I'd say, 'Oh, he just wants to pay his debts,' or, 'Oh, who knows what a cat is thinking?'" My voice broke a little on the last word. Dammit.

Tybalt's eyes widened, hope kindling in their depths. "What are you saying?"

"I'm saying—oak and ash, Tybalt, I'm saying I'm in love with you, I've been in love with you for a while, and the only way I was dealing with it was by not dealing with it, ever." I shook my head. "I knew I'd never have you, so I told myself I didn't want you, and if you don't really want *me*, if you want some idea of me, or just want to chase and not catch, I'll understand, but this has been a hard week, Tybalt, this has been such a hard week. I've been waiting for you to come here, because I need you to tell me. Okay? Just tell me what you want."

"Oh, October. Toby. *My* Toby." He pulled one hand from mine, reaching up to tuck my hair behind my ear. His fingers were shaking. That was what I focused on, more than anything else. His fingers were shaking. "Do you think I'm cruel enough to do that to you?"

I sniffled. "No," I admitted.

"Thank Oberon," he said, and pulled me close, and kissed me.

We were still standing there when the sun rose, our bodies pressed so close together that we might as well have been one person. Dawn ripped the air out of the world, but I already wasn't breathing. Tybalt kissed me through the sunrise. It wasn't until I smelled the ashy remains of dying magic that I realized we had no illusions on. I broke the kiss, pulling away.

Tybalt blinked, looking faintly bewildered. I tapped the tip of one pointed ear. "Ah," he said, nodding his understanding. He couldn't keep the regret from his voice as he asked, "Will I see you tonight?"

"No."

"What?" His earlier bewilderment had nothing on the look he gave me now.

I smiled, taking his hands and pulling him onto the front step as I opened the front door. "You'll see me right now."

Tybalt's laughter as he followed me inside was one of the sweetest sounds I'd ever heard. I shut the door on the morning, leaving my long-cooled cup of coffee outside as I led the King of Cats through my silent house. Nothing stays the same for long, not in Faerie, not in the human world, not anywhere, but some things are worth starting, just like some things are worth fighting for. Li Qin would have Dreamer's Glass. Chelsea would have her parents and a chance at a relatively normal life, under the circumstances. Maybe that was all Tybalt and I would have—a chance—but as he put his hands around my waist and pulled me closer, I found I didn't care.

Sometimes a chance is more than enough. Sometimes that's all you need to have everything.

Sherwood Smith

CORONETS AND STEEL
978-0-7564-0685-1

BLOOD SPIRITS
978-0-7564-0698-1

"A lively heroine, mysterious ghosts, and a complex and intricate plot always get the action going..."
—*Publishers Weekly*

"Highly recommended for all fantasy and general-fiction collections, from urban-fantasy readers looking for something lighter but still complex to young women who grew up reading the Princess Diaries series." —*Booklist*

"A rousing adventure of doubles, political intrigue, and doomed romance. It's a delightful romp, with just enough loose ends to leave some hope that the doomed romance might not be so doomed at all."   —*Locus*

And now available in hardcover:

REVENANT EVE
978-0-7564-0744-5

To Order Call: 1-800-788-6262
www.dawbooks.com

Diana Rowland

The Kara Gillian Novels

"Rowland's hot streak continues as she gives her fans another big helping of urban fantasy goodness! The plot twists are plentiful and the action is hard-edged. Another great entry in this compelling series." —*RT Book Review*

"This is an excellent police procedural urban fantasy that like its two previous arcane forensic investigations stars a terrific lead protagonist... Kara is fabulous as the focus of the case and of relationships with the Fed and with the demon as the Bayou heats up with another magical mystery tour that will take readers away from the mundane to the enjoyable world of Diana Rowland."
—*Midwest Book Reviews*

Secrets of the Demon
978-0-7564-0652-3

Sins of the Demon
978-0-7564-0705-6

To Order Call: 1-800-788-6262
www.dawbooks.com

DAW 176

Tanya Huff

"The Gales are an amazing family, the aunts will strike fear into your heart, and the characters Allie meets are both charming and terrifying."
—#1 *New York Times* bestselling author
Charlaine Harris

The Enchantment Emporium

Alysha Gale is a member of a family capable of changing the world with the charms they cast. She is happy to escape to Calgary when when she inherits her grandmother's junk shop, but when Alysha learns just how much trouble is brewing, even calling in the family to help may not be enough to save the day.

978-0-7564-0605-9

The Wild Ways

Charlotte Gale is a Wild Power who allies herself with a family of Selkies in a fight against offshore oil drilling. The oil company has hired another of the Gale family's Wild Powers, the fearsome Auntie Catherine, to steal the Selkies' sealskins. To defeat her, Charlotte will have to learn what born to be Wild really means in the Gale family...

978-0-7564-0763-6

To Order Call: 1-800-788-6262
www.dawbooks.com